高等学校专业英语系列教材
园 林 专 业

蔡 君　张文英　编著
李　雄　审校

中国建筑工业出版社

图书在版编目（CIP）数据

园林专业/蔡君，张文英编著．—北京：中国建筑工业出版社，2005
（高等学校专业英语系列教材）
ISBN 978-7-112-06642-1

Ⅰ．园… Ⅱ．①蔡…②张… Ⅲ．园林设计—英语—高等学校—教材 Ⅳ．H31

中国版本图书馆 CIP 数据核字（2004）第 137374 号

全书内容分为五部分，第一部分：园林的概述；第二部分：园林历史；第三部分：园林设计要素及方法；第四部分：不同环境条件下的场址规划和景观设计；第五部分：20 世纪园林实践。具体内容包括 18 课，每课一篇课文，配 1~2 篇阅读材料等内容。

本书可作为高校园林专业及相近专业的专业英语教材，也可供相关设计人员参考。

责任编辑：齐庆梅 何 楠
责任设计：郑秋菊
责任校对：王金珠

高等学校专业英语系列教材
园 林 专 业
蔡 君 张文英 编著
李 雄 审校

*

中国建筑工业出版社出版、发行（北京西郊百万庄）
各地新华书店、建筑书店经销
北京同文印刷有限责任公司印刷

*

开本：787×1092 毫米 1/16 印张：18¾ 字数：466 千字
2005 年 2 月第一版 2016 年 8 月第六次印刷
定价：26.00 元
ISBN 978-7-112-06642-1
（12596）

版权所有 翻印必究
如有印装质量问题，可寄本社退换
（邮政编码 100037）

前言

随着我国高等院校双语化教学趋势的发展,为园林专业师生提供一本语言规范、题材广泛、覆盖园林专业课程的主要内容、语言难易程度切合学生实际水平的专业英语教材,已经成为一种需要。

本教材主要选材于美国相关大学园林专业本科课程——园林概论(Introduction to Landscape Architecture)所列主要教材和参考书目。作者选择了一部分20世纪60~80年代美国经典园林教材的内容,同时也注意选录一些90年代以后比较有影响的园林专业著述的部分章节,以延长时效,增加教材的时代感和新鲜活力。基于认识逻辑以及便利教学的考虑,本书按照园林概述、园林历史、园林设计要素及方法、20世纪园林实践的顺序来编排。在语言的难易程度上,课文语言更规范,更易理解,而阅读材料(Rading Material)主要收入一些与课文相关的文章,有些更具个人观点,是课程的拓展部分,以加深学生对一些专业理论、观点的全面理解。

本教材旨在帮助读者提高园林专业英语文献的阅读理解能力,同时改善专业英语的翻译(英—汉,汉—英)、写作、交流能力。另外,通过对本教材的学习和阅读,也能够提高园林专业人员理解及鉴赏不同文化背景之下园林发展的历史脉络,同时将这种理解转化为有效的交流和互动,从而增强园林规划及设计能力。

本教材可作为园林、城市规划及其相关专业本科生和研究生的专业英语教材,也可供上述相关专业的教师、科研人员和设计人员参考。

本教材的框架和素材搜集主要由蔡君完成,并且具体负责第1课、第3课至第9课以及第14课的课文及阅读材料、第18课阅读材料的编辑整理工作;张文英主要负责第10课、第11课以及第13课阅读材料的选材工作,并具体负责第2课、第10课至第13课、第15课至第18课的课文及阅读材料的编辑整理工作。

感谢北京林业大学园林学院李雄教授在百忙之中对本书进行了认真审校,并提出了中肯的建议。

鉴于作者视野和学术能力的局限,在文章选材和编排等方面存在的不足之处,恳请读者和使用者批评指正。

Contents

Part I   Landscape Architecture Interpretation 1

LESSON 1   THE PRACTICE AND PROFESSION OF
                   LANDSCAPE ARCHITECTURE 3
Reading Material   The Three Stakes 9
LESSON 2   LANDSCAPE MEANINGS 15
Reading Material   Landscape Interpretation 22

Part II   History of Landscape Architecture 35

LESSON 3   PARADISE ON EARTH: THE
                   ISLAMIC GARDEN 37
Reading Material   Islamic Gardens of Spain 42
LESSON 4   GARDENS OF SIXTEENTH -
                   CENTURY ITALY 48
Reading Material   Axial Planning on an Urban Scale: The
                              Development of Renaissance Rome 55
LESSON 5   FRANCE LANDSCAPE DESIGN: SIXTEENTH
                   AND SEVENTEENTH CENTURIES 61
Reading Material   Power and Glory: The Genius of Le Nôtre
                              and The Grandeur of The Baroque 69
LESSON 6   THE LANDSCAPE GARDEN IN
                   ENGLAND 76
Reading Material   The Landscape Garden in The
                              United States 83
LESSON 7   LANDSCAPE DESIGN IN THE EAST:
                   CHINA 86
Reading Material   The Influence of Chinese culture on
                              Japanese Garden (Part one) 96
LESSON 8   LANDSCAPE DESIGN IN THE EAST:
                   JAPAN 99
Reading Material   The Influence of Chinese culture on

      Japanese Garden (Part two) ·········· 106
LESSON 9 CONSERVING NATURE: LANDSCAPE DESIGN AS ENVIRONMENTAL SCIENCE AND ART ··· 111
Reading Material Landscape Design as Environment Art ··· 118

Part Ⅲ Design Elements and Methods ·············· 123

LESSON 10 DESIGN AND PLANING METHODS ········ 125
Reading Material Design Thinking ························ 134
LESSON 11 THE PATTERNS OF DESIGN ELEMENTS ·· 140
Reading Material Planting Design ························ 151

Part Ⅳ Site Planning and Landscape Design in Different Contexts ·································· 155

LESSON 12 SITE - STRUCTURE UNITY ··············· 157
Reading Material Is Sustainable Attainable? ············ 164
LESSON 13 PARK AND BOUNDLESS SPACE ·········· 170
Reading Material Spatial Development ···················· 179
LESSON 14 LANDSCAPE DESIGN IN THE URBAN ENVIRONMENT ································· 193
Reading Material Eco - City Plans ··································· 200
LESSON 15 LANDSCAPE DESIGN IN THE RURAL ENVIRONMENT ································· 210
Reading Material Axioms for Reading the Landscape Some Guides to the American Scene (Part one) ·· 217
LESSON 16 LANDSCAPE DESIGN IN THE PRIMEVAL ENVIRONMENT ································· 220
Reading Material Axioms for Reading the Landscape Some Guides to the American Scene (Part two) ·· 228

Part Ⅴ 20th Century Landscape Architecture Practice ·········· 239

LESSON 17 AN ECOLOGY OF DESIGN ················ 241
Reading Material Forstering Living Landscape ·········· 256
LESSON 18 TOWARDS A NEW LANDSCAPE PRACTICE ·· 267

Reading Material A Parks, Botanical gardens, Festival gardens: Germany 280
Reading Material B Barcelona and the Resurgence of Spain 285
APPENDIX A PROFESSIONAL ORGANIZATIONS AND INTERNET SITES 290
APPENDIX B PROFESSIONAL INTERNET SITES 291

Part I

Landscape Architecture Interpretation

LESSON 1

THE PRACTICE AND PROFESSION OF LANDSCAPE ARCHITECTURE

THE PRACTICE OF LANDSCAPE ARCHITECTURE

Over the years and especially since World War II, the realm of landscape architecture has diversified and classified its activities in response to the needs of a changing world. There now appear to be four clearly definable and related types of practice.

First, there is landscape evaluation and planning. It is concerned with the systematic study of large areas of land and has a strong ecological and natural science base in addition to a concern for visual quality. The history of human use and current demands represents a third subject area for analysis. In addition to the landscape architect, the process usually involves a team of specialists such as soil scientists, geologists, and economists. The result is a land use plan or policy recommending the distribution and type of development, for example, housing, industry, agriculture, highway alignment, and recreation within a framework of resource and amenity conservation. The study area ideally coincides with a natural physiographic region, such as the watershed of a major river or some other logical unit of land, but unfortunately these seldom coincide with county and state boundaries. In other cases, the planning function may be less comprehensive and focus on the impact on the environment of single major proposals. The identification of land suitable for one major use, such as recreation, is another function of landscape evaluation and planning.

The second activity of landscape architects is site planning. This represents the more conventional kind of landscape architecture and within this realm lies landscape design. Site planning is the process in which the characteristics of the site and the requirements of the program for its use are brought together in creative synthesis. Elements and facilities are locate on the land in functional and aesthetic relationships and in a manner fully responsive to program, site, and regional context.

Third, there is detailed landscape design. This is the process through which specific quality is given to the diagrammatic spaces and areas of the site plan. It involves the selection of components, materials, and plants and their combination in three dimensions as solutions to limited and well-defined problems such as entrance, terrace, amphitheater, parking area, and so on.

选自 Laurie Michael An Introduction to Landscape Architecture 2nd ed. New Youk, NY: Elsevier

Part I Landscape Architecture Interpretation

The fourth form of landscape architecture is urban design. Although this may seem a recent activity on account of well publicized postwar urban renewal and the construction of new towns, it was, in fact, a central portion of the practices of Olmsted[1], Cleveland, and other pioneers of the profession. Urban design defies precise definition. Two things are sure, however; the setting is the city and several properties are involved. An agency of government may be responsible for assembling the parcels and organizing the program. The location, not the design, of buildings and the organization of the space between them for circulation and public use are major concerns. Typically, but not always, hard surfaces predominate. Streets and malls, river front developments, government and commercial centers, rehabilitation of neighborhoods, and recycling of groups of industrial buildings may be classed as urban design projects. Complicated as they are, with multiple ownership, political, legal, and economic considerations, such projects are rarely in the hands of one planner or designer. They are team efforts sponsored by a major developer or government agency. Planners are involved with the project's viability and infrastructure, architects with buildings. But it is the organization and design of the space between buildings(site planning and landscape design) that is central to its overall success. It is essential to have an understanding of microclimate, sun and shadow patterns, proportion and scale, human needs and behavior, and the potential of space division and differences in level to facilitate and enhance them. In addition, urban horticulture is a specialization that recognizes the extreme and often difficult growing conditions created by glare, drafts, and limited root area for trees. Together, open space design and urban horticulture, although not the most costly elements of a comprehensive urban design project, are critical to its unity.

There is clearly an interrelationship among these four types of landscape architecture: landscape planning, site planning, urban design, and detailed landscape design. The wider landscape, urban or rural, is the context for the site, which in turn is the framework within which lies the details. But just as it is reasonable to expect that small scale projects, such as a garden or a park, should be influenced by and respond to the larger environment, so it is true that criteria for certain large scale land planning decisions or urban design depend on an understanding of the details of design and technology in siting buildings, roads, and facilities. Landscape architects have to understand both scales to do the projects with responsibility and sensitivity.

THE PROFESSION OF LANDSCAPE ARCHITECTURE

Before proceeding further with this theoretical framework it is perhaps useful to discuss earlier and other interpretations of the term landscape architecture. It is a difficult title, for the words seem to contradict one another: landscape and architecture, the one dynamic and ever changing, the other static and finite. Professionals frequently find it frustrating that their role in society has been consistently misunderstood. Landscape gar-

LESSON 1

dening is the usual interpretation, but the terms site planning, urban design, and environmental planning are frequently added to the names of landscape architectural firms as a means of expressing their broader concerns and capabilities.

Frederick Law Olmsted[1], designer of New York City's Central Park, coined the term *landscape architect* in 1858. And in case any of us think it is a difficult name to live with we should know that he apparently chose it in preference to his alternative, "rural embellisher." Olmsted was a prolific man and in addition to city parks he also planned complete urban open space systems, city and traffic patterns, subdivisions, university campuses, and private estates. In addition, he was active in the conservation movement and in 1865 was largely responsible for the first area of scenic landscape, Yosemite Valley in California, being set aside for public use and enjoyment. All this he called "landscape architecture," so it is not surprising that there has been some confusion about what landscape architects do. Olmsted had no training in the profession which he established at the age of 40. His previous experience in farming and engineering, his ability in writing and management, and his romantic disposition fitted him for the role he adopted. Others, such as Horace Cleveland and Charles Eliot, followed in his footsteps and in 1901 the first complete program in landscape architecture was established at Harvard University. The American Society of Landscape Architects was founded in 1899 by five practitioners, four men and one woman.

After these auspicious beginnings, the prestige of the profession waxed and waned. Landscape architects found themselves in competition with other environmentalists of the nineteenth century: architects, engineers, surveyors, foresters, park superintendents, and city planners. In fact, the city planning profession emerged out of landscape architecture in 1907.

Thus from being responsible for some very large and important work in the nineteenth century, the landscape profession entered a somewhat less ambitious phase in the early 1900s with greater emphasis on large estates, gardens, and small scale site planning. However, during the depression years of the 1930s, landscape architects became involved again in larger scale projects, playing a significant role in the various public works programs, particularly those of the U. S. National Parks Service. Since World War II, the work of landscape architects, often operating as members of a team, has changed to include the restoration of derelict land, regional landscape analysis and planning, urban design and site planning for housing, schools, and large scale industrial plants. These now form a major portion of the landscape architecture carried on in public agencies and private practice. In spite of this, the contribution of the landscape architect to the overall development and maintenance of a stimulating, agreeable, and viable environment may not appear to be very great. People of landscape sensitivity and expertise do not occupy all the positions from which decisions affecting landscape are made.

Much of the environment is ill-planned, inefficient, unattractive, and poorly man-

Part I Landscape Architecture Interpretation

aged. The landscape profession is small and perhaps overly protective of the field. With notable exceptions, few practitioners have aggressively entered the political arena where projects are often defined and professionals selected. However, changes in professional strategy and successful demonstration of the economic and social benefits of sound landscape design, may in the years ahead result in a more central role for Landscape Architecture.

It should also be remembered that landscape work, unlike architecture, does not always have an immediately perceptible impact and the effectiveness of planting and land use decisions or policies may not be appreciable for twenty to thirty years[2]. For example, the landscape of the first new towns in England is just beginning to achieve the effect and visual qualities that were in the minds of the designers twenty-five years ago, and war housing built in the United States has often been demolished, leaving mature trees for a replacement project. This fourth dimension, time, is an important aspect of land scape architecture. Olmsted understood it when he talked of the farreaching conception that the designer must have in developing "a picture so great that nature shall be employed upon it for generations, before the work he has arranged for her shall realize his intentions".

WORDS AND EXPRESSIONS

realm [relm]	n.	王国；国土领域；范围
distribution [ˌdistriˈbjuːʃən]	n.	分配；分布
alignment [əˈlainmənt]	n.	队列，一直线
amenity [əˈmiːniti]	n.	（环境，气候的）舒服
coincide [ˌkəuinˈsaid]	vi.	（在空间，时间方面）一致；符合
physiographic [ˌfizrəˈræfik]	n.	地文学，自然地理学 adj. 地文学的；地形学的
watershed [ˈwɔːtəʃed]	n.	流域 分水岭；分界线
county [ˈkaunti]	n.	（英国的）郡，（美国的）县，（中国等国的）县
evaluation [iˌvæljuˈeiʃən]	n.	估价，评价
aesthetic [iːsˈθetik]	adj.	美学的；审美的
diagrammatic [ˌdaiəgrəˈmætik]	adj.	图解的，图表的
parcel [ˈpɑːsl]	n.	（土地的）一块
sponsor [ˈspɔnsə]	n.	发起者；主办者 倡仪者
viability [ˌvaiəˈbiliti]	n.	生存性，生活力
infrastructure [ˈinfrəˈstrʌktʃə]	n.	基础；（社会国家的）基础结构
facilitate [fəˈsiliteit]	vt.	使容易；使便利
draft [drɑːft]	n.	通风，气流；草稿，草图
horticulture [ˈhɔːtikʌltʃə]	n.	园艺
criteria [kraiˈtiriə]	n.	标准，准则
interpretation [inˌtəːpriˈteiʃən]	n.	解释；阐明
dynamic [daiˈnæmik]	adj.	动态的动力，动态

LESSON 1

coin [kɔin]　　　　　　　　v. 创造，杜撰（新闻，新语等）
embellish [im'beliʃ]　　　　vt. 修饰，装饰
prolific [prə'lifik]　　　　　adj. 多产的；富于创造力的
disposition [dispə'ziʃən]　　n. 气质，性情
auspicious [ɔ:s'piʃəs]　　　a. 吉利的，吉祥的；繁荣昌盛的
wax and wane　　　　　　　（喻）盛衰
appreciable [ə'pri:ʃiəbl]　　a. 可估计的，可看到或可感觉到的
demolish [di'mɔliʃ]　　　　vt. 拆毁（建筑物）

KEY CONCEPTS

Landscape architecture
Landscape planning
Landscape evaluation
Site planning
Landscape design
Urban design
Human behavior
Conservation Movement
Scenic Landscape
Landscape Profession
Restoration of derelict land
Regional landscape analysis and planning
Visual quality

NOTES

1. Frederick Law Olmsted
　　奥姆斯特德(1822～1903)美国现代园林先驱，与 C. Vaux 合作，设计纽约中央公园，后又设计波士顿、布鲁克林等地公园。
2. It should also be remembered that landscape work, unlike architecture, does not always have an immediately perceptible impact and the effectiveness of planting and land use decisions or policies may not be appreciable for twenty to thirty years.
　　我们也应当切记，园林工作，与建筑不同，种植和土地利用决策或政策并不能够立刻感觉到其效果和成效，或许在二、三十年后才能够被感知。

QUESTIONS FOR REVIEW AND DISCUSSION

1. What is Landscape architecture?

Part I *Landscape Architecture Interpretation*

2. Identify and describe the four types of practice in landscape architecture field.
3. What do Landscape architects do in their professional practice?
4. Name at least five types of projects that landscape architects work on.
5. What does a landscape architecture student need to learn in term of knowledge, skills and abilities to be successful in a professional?
6. Discuss the landscape as expressions of social and cultural values; landscape architecture as a means of creative mediation between people and environment.
7. As a career in landscape architecture, what position appeals to you at present?

Reading Material

The Three Stakes

A first stake was driven into the throbbing heart of landscape theory by changes in the Neoplatonic axiom that 'art should imitate nature'. So long as 'nature' had meant the world of ideas, the axiom worked satisfactorily. By the end of the eighteenth century, when 'nature' came to mean 'the natural world', as it usually does today, it became ridiculous to make gardens that imitated nature. To have done so would have meant filling gardens with weeds, rocks, broken branches and wild animals. The French Neoplatonist, Quatremére de Quincy, declared that if the objective of landscape gardening was to imitate wild nature herself, then landscape design could not be admitted to 'the circle of the fine arts' (Quatremère de Quincy, 1837). The great ship of Neoplatonism had run aground in a garden of rocks. The practical men had no theory. For landscape designers, this was the immediate and practical cause of the watershed that Hunt identifies. Another possible way out would have been to interpret 'nature' in yet another way, and to have represented the individual's 'inner nature' in gardens. Hunt would like to have seen a 'marvellous flourishing of ad hoc, idiosyncratic, or vernacular gardens' (Hunt, 1992). Some owner-designers, like the Earl of Shrewsbury at Alton Towers and James Bateman at Biddulph Grange, walked down this path. But most professional designers remained lost in the theoretical maze.

A second stake was driven into the weakened heart of landscape theory by Frederick Law Olmsted and Calvert Vaux, when they inadvertently chose landscape architecture as a professional title(Turner, 1990). Their choice would not have mattered, but for the fact that the predominant use of the word 'landscape' was changing, as had the predominant use of 'nature'. In 1860, a landscape was still, more or less, an ideal place. By the twentieth century, it had become any place at all that results from 'shaping processes and agents'. When the picturesque theorists of the 1790s spoke of 'making a landscape', the word represented a Neoplatonic ideal. When the word 'landscape' was adopted by geologists and geographers, it came to mean 'the product of topographic evolution'. If the 'landscape' in 'landscape architecture' is understood in a geographical sense, instead of a Neoplatonic sense, then the profession's title becomes a patent absurdity:

A third stake was driven into the now-rotting cadaver of landscape theory by the advance of scientific functionalism during the twentieth century. Shaking off the historicist styles of the nineteenth century, architects and other designers came to see design as 'a problem-solving activity'. 'Form follows function', they proclaimed. Such slogans are still heard echoing betwixt blank walls and blank faces in the design studios of the world.

选自 Tom Turner. City as Landscape: A Post-Post Modern View of Design and Planning London, E & FN Spon

Part I *Landscape Architecture Interpretation*

Landscape architects were attracted to the new rationalism, but faced two immediate puzzles: What were the problems to be solved? Where were the functions to be followed? This is when the 'desire line' assumed such portentous eminence in landscape teaching and practice. Too often, the 'function' of a space was conceived merely as a route from an origin to a destination. The 'problem', therefore, was to find an alignment that pedestrians might wish to follow. Not too difficult, though many got it wrong.

Having dealt with desire lines, landscape architects began to look for other 'problems' to solve. They discovered needs for 'shelter', 'enclosure' and 'visual screens'. This was no basis for a fine art, an applied art, or any other kind of art. Should anyone believe the approach can produce art, let them look through a book of modern design details. Theodore Walker's ever-popular *Site Design and Construction Detailing* (Walker, 1992) is a good example. The details are functional in the worst sense of the word, though one has no assurance that they actually work any better than the twentieth century buildings that are ridiculed by critics of modernism. Even if they do function, the majority of the details are heartless, soulless, plain, vacant and even downright ugly to the non-professional eye. They are the outdoor equivalent of hotels in the International Style.

The survey-analysis-design(SAD) procedure is an aspect of functionalism that is well known inside the design professions but poorly understood by outsiders(Fig.1). It would be advantageous if experienced planners and designers were to write about it, as Sturt wrote of the wheelwright's craft. Future historians will have to understand this procedure if they are to understand twentieth century cities. The SAD method of planning began with Patrick Geddes. As a scientist, a sociologist and a geographer, he was disenchanted with the engineers' and architects' approaches, which saw city planning as a technical exercise. Take the example of a new street. To the engineer, it was a traffic artery. To the architect, it could also be a visual axis. To Geddes, it should be a vital component of civic structure, affecting regional development, history, culture and everything else. Geddes therefore required a full survey and analysis as a prelude to planmaking. Undoubtedly, he was correct. The problems arose when SAD came to be used by lessenlightened people. Engineers were delighted with the SAD method. Before planning a new street, they surveyed and analysed the existing traffic. If vehicular flow was surveyed at twice the volume of existing street capacity, they doubled the size of the Street. Similarly, architects surveyed the function of a building before producing a plan. This led to the notorious idea of a house as a 'machine for living'.

Lewis Mumford[1], who admired Geddes, recognized Ian McHarg's *Design with Nature*(McHarg, 1971)as a scion of Geddes'*Cities in Evolution* (Geddes, 1915), Mumford praises the empirical foundation of McHarg's ecological method:

He seeks, not arbitrarily to impose design, but to use to the fullest the potentialities -and with them, necessarily, the restrictive conditions-that nature offers.

As the ecological method rested on 'imitating nature', McHarg was led to believe

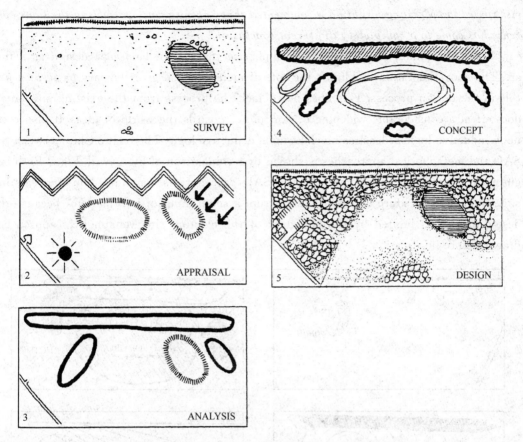

Fig. 1　The modernist landscape architect's SAD method

that 'any man, assembling the same evidence, would come to the same conclusion' (McHarg, 1971). This is naked determinism, red in tooth and claw. Much as I admire Geddes, Mumford and McHarg too, this particular claim appears wholly misleading. The two excellent features of McHarg's method are his single-topic analytical drawings and his Suitability Maps. Conventional Master Plans look to some point in the distant future. They are incomplete for a quarter of a century and cut of date thereafter. McHarg's Suitability Maps are modest by comparison: they imply a desire to guide the future, not to exert control.

　　The deductive aspect of McHarg's ecological method needs to be reconsidered. If landscape design is, to any degree, a fine art, then it simply cannot use a deterministic methodology. Neither ecological determinism nor any other kind of determinism will suffice. Davies and Shakespeare (Davies and Shakespeare, 1993), after working on a project in Paris, declared that:

*　　Landscape design is a form of artistic expression. Designers need freedom to explore the realm of the imagination... We believe the Billancourt project was a triumph for the use of metaphor... By abandoning the SAD method, the groups were able to determine the direction of their schemes very early on. Predictability was broken by taking this high*

risk route. Ian McHarg might have commented that 'every group assembling the same evidence has come to a completely different conclusion'.

Like John Dixon Hunt, they overemphasize the role of landscape design as a fine art. The above quotation highlights the role of metaphor and gives tertiary patterns a key role in the design process. This does not detach the process from the existing site but it does effect a considerable widening of horizons, towards the world of ideas. It also rests upon inductive logic at least as much as upon deductive logic. The relationship between the SAD and metaphorical approaches is shown by a comparison of Fig. 1 with Fig. 2 Both begin with the existing site, but only the SAD procedure is constrained by the existing site. The SAD procedure derives a design from a small input of information, because the design process is limited by the boundary of the existing site. Metaphorical approaches draw in more information.

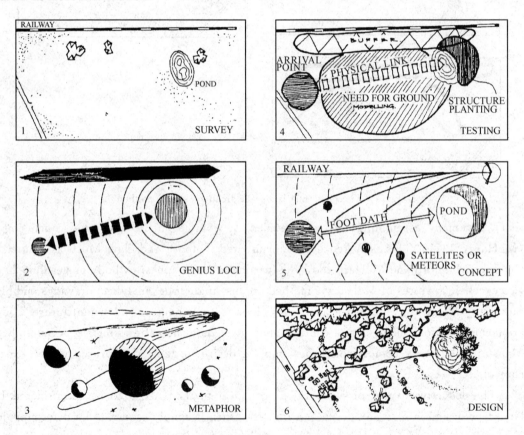

Fig. 2 A metaphorical design procedure (by Rob Shakespeare)

Another problem for the survey-analysis-design method is that it does not accord with our knowledge of how designers actually operate. Schemes often spring into designers' minds at an early stage. After being recorded on the back of an envelope, or a wine-stained table napkin, the scheme is developed over months and years. The process is not linear: it follows different paths. When experienced practitioners recommend the SAD method, it is usually a case of 'Do as I say, not as I do'.

WORDS AND EXPRESSIONS

throbbing [ˈθrɔbiŋ]	adj. 跳动的，颤动的
stake [steik]	n. 桩，标桩
neo-	构词成分：新近的，新式的，新的，现代的
platonic [pləˈtɔnikc]	adj. 柏拉图(哲学)的
axiom [ˈæksiəm]	n. 公理
aground [əˈgraund]	adj. & adv. 搁浅的(地)；触礁的(地)
watershed [ˈwɔːtəʃed]	n. 分水岭；(喻)事情发展中的转折点
dilemma [diˈlemə,dai-]	n. 进退两难的窘境
ad hoc [ˈædˈhɔk]	adj. [拉] 为某特定目的而安排的；特设的
vernacular [vəˈnækjulə]	n. 本国的；本地的，乡土的
idiosyncratic [ˌidiəsinˈkrætik]	adj. 特殊的，异质的
maze [meiz]	n. (事情等的)错综，复杂；困惑
inadvertently [ˌinədˈvəːtentli]	adv. 偶然地；无意地
picturesque [ˌpiktʃəˈresk]	adj. (景色等)似画的；(语言)生动的
topographic [ˌtɔpəˈgræfik]	adj. 地志的，地形学上的
patent [ˈpeitənt,ˈpætənt]	adj. 明显的
absurdity [əbˈsəːditi]	n. 荒唐，荒谬
cadaver [kəˈdeivə,-ˈdæ-]	n. 尸体，死尸
functionalism [ˈfʌŋkʃənlizm]	n. 实用主义
slogan [ˈsləugən]	n. 标语；口号
betwixt [biˈtwikst]	prep. 在…之间
rationalism [ˈræʃənəlizm]	n. 理性主义；唯理主义；唯理论
portentous [pɔːˈtentəs]	adj. 不寻常的；难以置信的
eminence [ˈeminəns]	n. 卓越，显赫；杰出的或卓越的地位
alignment [əˈlainmənt]	n. 排列成行；排成直线；定(准)线
pedestrian [peˈdestriən]	n. 行人
vacant [ˈveikənt]	adj. 空虚的
downright [ˈdaunrait]	adj. (指不喜欢的事物)彻底的，十足的 adv. 完全地；彻底的
disenchanted [ˌdisinˈtʃaːntid]	adj. 不再着迷的
artery [ˈaːtəri]	n. 干线(交通或运输的重要路线)
civic [ˈsivik]	adj. 集镇的；城市的
prelude [ˈpreljuːd]	n. (行动或事件)的序幕，前奏
notorious [nəuˈtɔːriəs]	adj. 声名狼藉的，臭名昭著的
scion [ˈsaiən]	n. 子孙，后代或继承人

13

Part I Landscape Architecture Interpretation

deductive [di'dʌktiv]	adj. 推论的，演绎的，推理的
methodology [meθə'dɔlədʒɪ]	n. 方法论
determinism [di'tə:minizəm]	n. 决定论
suffice [sə'fais]	v. 能满足(某人/某事物)之需要的；足够的
realm [relm]	n. (活动或兴趣的)领域，范围
metaphor ['metəfə]	n. 隐喻
metaphorical [,metə'fɔrikəl]	adj. 隐喻性的，比喻性的
tertiary ['tə:ʃəri]	adj. 第三的；第三等的；第三位的

NOTES

1. Lewis Mumford

   芒福德(1895～1990)，美国社会哲学家、教师、建筑及城市规划评论家，其著作多涉及人与环境的关系，著有《技艺与文明》、《城市文化》、《历史名城》等。

LESSON 2
LANDSCAPE MEANINGS

Landscapes are point-in-time expressions of ecological, technological, and cultural influences. Settings are specific locations, designed or non-designed, generated by these influences, and experienced by people. The individual, for physiological purposes of survival and security, and for psychological ones of community, esteem, and self-actualization, encodes and decodes meaning from settings. Perceptual meanings grow from the perceptual characteristics of settings; associatlonal meanings emerge from the relationship of settings to the observer's direct and indirect experiences. Relationships between designed settings and their context affect meaning. Systemic design integrates these diverse influences, promotes a sense of connectedness, and facilitates individually associated meanings. It integrates with contextual systems that, in turn, become progressively more interactive-Systemically designed settings can be experienced in different ways by different people at different times. Through systemic design intervention, multiple influences are integrated into wholes with enriched experience and intensified meaning, and the landscape becomes richer, and the place(mental construct experienced in the mind's eye of the beholder)more alive.

1 METHOD OF STUDY

In *Peasant, Society and Culture*(1956), Robert Red-field distinguishes between the classic or learned culture and the popular or folk culture in many disciplines(music, religion, and so on)-in House, Form and Culture(1969), Amos Rapoport considers the relationships between the learned and popular culture and physical design. He defines the grand tradition of Architecture as the creation of monuments "built to impress the populace with the power of the patron, or the peer group of designers and cognoscenti with the cleverness of the designer and good taste of the patron." He defines the folk tradition, on the other hand, as "the direct, unselfconscious translation into physical form of a culture, its needs and values, as well as the desires, dreams and passions of a people." He sees the folk tradition as "the world view writ small, the 'ideal' environment of a people expressed in buildings and settlements, with no designer, artist, or architect with an axe to grind."

选自 John L. Motloch., Introduction to Landscape Design, 2nd ed., America, Ball State University, 2001, Page 7~10

Part I *Landscape Architecture Interpretation*

Within the folk tradition, Rapoport distinguishes between primitive and vernacular buildings. *Primitive buildings* (produced by societies identified by anthropologists as primitive based on technological and economic levels) are built by the common person who is a generalist equipped, as part of cultural heritage, with the limited knowledge necessary to build dwellings. *Vernacular buildlngs* (produced in societies with more advanced technologies and economies) are built by tradesmen, but the building type, form, and materials are known by everyone as part of the cultural body of knowledge. The building "type" follows the cultural tradition. Individual buildings subtly adjust the traditional theme to specific conditions (family size, site, microclimate, and so on). Focusing on the vernacular rather than monuments of the grand tradition, *House, Form and Culture* was a seminal study of the built landscape. As Rapoport says.

The physical environment of man, especially the built environment, has not been, and still is not, controlled by the designer. This environment is the result of vernacular [or folk, or popular] architecture, and it has been largely ignored in architectural history and theory... in addition, the high style buildings usually must be seen in relation to, and in the context of, the vernacular matrix, and are in fact incomprehensible outside that context, especially as it existed at the time they were designed and built.

Rapoport's statement exposes a major deficiency of modern architectural education: it has focused on high-styled buildings and on form, to the exclusion of popular architecture, contextual forces, and broader meaning. It has studied architecture as form and object, not as process and integration.

Rapoport was not alone in his concern for these issues. Others of the period, such as Adolph Rudofski (*Architecture Without Architects*, 1964), Robert Venturi (*Learning From Las Vegas*, 1972), Christian Norberg-Schulz (Genus Loci: *Toward a Phenomenology of Architecture*, 1980), and Tom Wolfe (From Bauhaus to Your House, 1981), were struggling with [the lack of relevant meaning in modern, and in the case of the later works, in post-modern architecture. However, the ideas these men promulgated were not widely embraced by the architectural community. The most published designers were not those exploring holistic and cultural meanings, but rather those pursuing design theories, movements, and styles, such as modernism[1] (expression of an industrialized culture), post-modernism (visual topological explorations), and deconstructivism[2] (dismantling conventional mental constructs whereby the populous decode meaning). Integrative building designers, including Buckminster Fuller (1930s to 1970s), Stewart Brand, Pliny Fisk, and Bill McDonough, have been seen by many as "rebels" at the edge, rather than as leaders of mainstream movements. Landscape management, planning, and design have been somewhat more integrative and inclusive-embracing the grand tradition, the vernacular, and design integration with context.

More and more design professionals and laypersons, realizing the need to address the vernacular, are contending that cultural expressions, such as the strip development or

Disneyland, are not inherently bad. They portray the values, dreams, and aspirations of major portions of our heterogeneous culture. However, vernacular expressions that clash with classical notions of design and form, taught in universities, are often discounted by designers. By recognizing the value of common places and the meanings that nondesigners ascribe to landscapes, designers can create locally relvant aesthetics that convey greater meaning to a wider population, resulting in a rich, evocative landscape that functions as an integral part of culture, and that synergizes designed and nondesigned elements for maximum landscape meaning.

2 MEANINGS

With a rudimentary understanding of the forces that influence form and a belief that design should respond to these forces, how does one begin to discover the forces that are in effect at a certain place and time, and to understand the meaning of forms as expressions of these forces? In other words, how do we interpret the landscape? What do we interpret, and how do we make landscape decisions?

In the Introduction to *The Interpretation of ordinary Landscapes* (Meinig, 1979), D. W. Meinig states that "environment sustains us as creatures; landscape displays us as culture" and "landscape is defined by our vision and interpreted by our minds." Landscapes that people inhabit are records of, and transmit meaning about, the culture. According to *Mae Theilgard Watts* (Meinig, 1979), we can "read that landscape" as we might read a book. Any culture can read its autobiography to discover itself.

The largest portion of the landscape consists of the common elements that Rapoport calls the folk tradition. The smaller portion is the preconsciously conceived, professionally designed elements that he calls the "grand tradition." Together, the common and the grand express two sides of "who we are": our innate self and our overt self. They communicate, as Pierce F Lewis ("Axioms for Reading the Landscape") says, "our tastes, our values, our aspirations, and even our fears in tangible, visible form" (Meinig, 1979). The fact that the vast majority of this landscape is unself-conscious, that we seldom think about it, results in a landscape that more honestly reflects the underlying forces to which it responds.

Landscapes are usually quite difficult to read, for two reasons. First, they are confusing, and often contradictory, as they evolve in response to competing, often contrasting influences, and forces that change over time. Second, we have been educated to focus on singular and grand issues, not to perceive the gestalt of landscape, and not to curiously explore the messy and uncontrolled world around us.

3 AXIOMS FOR READING THE LANDSCAPE

To design more responsively in any culture, we can begin by reading that culture's autobiography-its landscape. In so doing, it is helpful to keep in mind Pierce F. Lewis's published "Axioms for Reading the Landscape," which are, as he says, "essential ideas underlying the reading of America's cultural landscape." These axioms, published in The Interpretation of Ordinary Landscapes, (Meinig, 1979), are summarized as follows, with some added comments concerning the implications of the axioms to landscape interpretation, design, and design education.

3.1　Axioms 1: The Axiom of Landscape as Clue to Culture

This axiom asserts that the commonplace elements in the landscape provide insight as to "the kind of people we are." There are several corollaries to this axiom. The corollary of cultural change says that the landscape represents a large investment and that major changes to the landscape occur only in response to major cultural changes. The regional corollary says that if one region looks significantly different from another, the region varies not only ecologically, but culturally as well. The corollary of convergence contends that as landscapes begin to look more similar, their cultures are, in fact, converging. The corollary of diffusion says that landscapes will change through imitation and that the degree of communication affects the rate of diffusion. Finally, the corollary of taste says that different cultures possess different biases as to what they like/dislike, promote/prohibit, and so on.

As we read the cultural landscape, we should keep in mind whether we are looking at an example of the vernacular tradition or the grand one. The first well tell us more about the actual culture and common life; the latter, more about the culture's grand aspirations, as viewed through the eyes of the design intelligentsia.

3.2　Axiom 2: The Axiom of Cultural Unity and Landscape Equality

This axiom says that all items in the human landscape convey meaning and that most convey about the same amount of meaning. According to this axiom, a vernacular building communicates about as much concerning the culture as does an architectural monument of the grand tradition. In areas dominated by vernacular expressions, the primary communication will be that of the common person. In areas dominated by the grand tradition, the main communication will be that of the design intelligentsia.

3.3　Axiom 3: The Axiom of Common Things

This axiom contends that the bulk of landscape design texts and professional journals communicate the grand tradition of design, and that there is a lack of scholarly writing about common elements of the landscape. The corollary is that we can discover the issues that affect decisions made by others than professional designers by observing the wealth of nonacademic literature, such as the writings of Tom Wolfe and Bernard Rudofsky, trade journals, commercial advertisements, travel literature, and books by people studying cultural geography, environmental psychology, or landscape meaning.

3.4　Axiom 4: The Historic Axiom

This axiom addresses the significance of a knowledge of history when reading the landscape. On the one hand, our behavior is conditioned by the past, and understanding past decisions can prevent us from "reinventing the wheel" as we respond to ongoing processes. On the other hand, many artifacts are relics of conditions that have since changed, and a knowledge of history will prevent misinterpreting these as expressions of active forces. A knowledge of history helps us "read" the artifact.

This axiom has two corollaries. The corollary of historic lumpiness asserts that major cultural change occurs in sudden leaps, and that the landscape changes little between these leaps. The mechanical (or technological) corollary asserts tha leaps of cultural change are usually associated with changes in technology or communication, and that a knowledge of the level of technology and communication is essential for one to interpret an element, or the entire landscape.

As we apply the historic axiom to reading the landscape, we should keep in mind that we are reading physical elements not as abstract forms, but as expressions of conditions and influences. We should also be aware that we are currently in a period of unprecedented cultural and technological change; accordingly, our landscapes are changing at an unparalleled rate.

3.5　Axiom 5: The Geographic(or Ecologic)Axiom

To understand the meaning of elements of a cultural landscape, we must study these elements in relation to their geographic or locational context. Our interpretation of the elements should be as must a response to their relation to context, as it is to the physical characteristics of the elements themselves.

Today, this axiom seems to be lost to a great number of practitioners of the grand tradition of architecture. It has been replaced with the notion that the designer's "overriding concept" gives meaning to the design. This trend has progressed to the point that a great number of projects that receive professional acclaim are communicated during the design phases as an "uncompromised" expression of the building, on a plane of green grass that recedes to infinity, where it meets a blue sky. However, once constructed, the building is perceived in its context. While the element in the drawing might be the element that was eventually built, the contextual relationships are dramatically different, as are the perception and interpretation of the element and the designed landscape.

3.6　Axiom 6: The Axiom of
Environmental Control

According to this axiom, cultural landscapes relate intimately to the physical environment, and an understanding of natural systems is essential if one is to read the cultural

Part I Landscape Architecture Interpretation

landscape accurately. Since any landscape is a point-in-time expression of forces, this axiom implies that an understanding of the ecological forces that have created a region is essential to understanding the meaning of that landscape

This axiom speaks for a regional attitude toward landscape design, as well as an appreciation for regionalism in design education. The regionalism suggested here is not, as is often implied in architecture today, the "reference" to an established or relic tradition by some design detail or "abstracted form," but rather a systemic and integrative response to the multiplicity of forces that interact to create a given landscape. This axiom speaks for regional design traditions that evolve from, and integrate with, regional forces.

3.7 Axiom 7 : The Axiom of Landscape Obscurity

While landscapes carry many meanings, they do not convey these messages in a pure and objective manner. Rather, they are somewhat nebulous and schizophrenic. Each statement is subject to many interpretations, and each is communicated in dialogue with a multiplicity of other statements. Discovering appropriate meanings requires that the landscape designer ask the right questions and remain sensitive to the multiplicity of landscape expressions.

The landscape designer should be sensitive to the obscure, dialectic character of the landscape, and to the fact that people prefer "open-ended" landscapes that enable the viewers to complete their message, and that can carry multiple meanings. We should be aware of the human tendency to reduce complex entities to singular statements, and of the reduced landscape meaning and reduced desirability that results from this tendency. We should seek to design open-ended landscapes that communicate multiple meanings as discussed in Christopher Alexander's "A City is Not a Tree."

With the preceding axioms, one has basic tools to interpret the landscape. As one makes these interpretations, it is essential to realize, as Axiom 7 says, that the process is not passive. Landscape elements that convey many meanings through obscure expressions are subject to various interpretations. If the landscape is, as Meinig states, "interpreted by our minds," then the "reader" of the landscape is integral to its meaning. Restated, the same landscape means different things to different people.

WORDS AND EXPRESSIONS

cognoscente [ˌkɔnjəuˈʃenti]　　　　　n. 行家
holistic [həuˈlɪstɪk]　　　　　　　　adj. 整体的，全盘的
heterogeneous [ˌhetərəuˈdʒiːniəs]　　adj. 异类的；不同的
corollary [kəˈrɔləri]　　　　　　　　n. 必然的结果，系，推论
tangible [ˈtændʒəbl]　　　　　　　　adj. 切实的
convergence [kənˈvɜːdʒəns]　　　　　n. 集中，收敛

bias ['baiəs]　　　　　　　　　　　n. 偏见，偏爱，斜线
regionalism ['ri:dʒənəˌlizəm]　　　n. 行政区域划分，地方(分权)主义
overriding [ˌouvə'raidiŋ]　　　　　adj. 最重要的；高于一切的
nebulous ['nebjuləs]　　　　　　　adj. 星云的，云雾状的，模糊的，朦胧的
schizophrenic [ˌskɪdzəʊ'frenɪk, ˌskɪts-]　adj. [心] 精神分裂症的

KEY CONCEPTS

Open-ended landscape
The agrarian landscape
Ordinary landscape
Landscape management

NOTES

1. Modernism is an omnibus term for a number of tendencies in the arts which were prominent in the first half of the 20th century.

现代主义是 20 世纪下半叶各种有影响力的艺术流派的总称。

2. Deconstructivism is a kind of factions of architectural design that was prominent in the last phase of the 19th century.

构成主义是 19 世纪末一个卓有成就的建筑设计流派。

QUESTIONS FOR REVIEW AND DISCUSSION

1. Do you agree that landscape is influenced by ecology, technology and culture? Give some examples.
2. What's your opinion about Rapoport's statement on the deficiency of modem architectural education?
3. Give some examples of the elements of folk tradition and "grand tradition".
4. According the article, it's important for a landscape architect comprehend his culture's autobiography. What are you going to do for this?
5. Do you think that "the same landscape means different things to different people" is an advantage or not to landscape designers?

Part I *Landscape Architecture Interpretation*

Reading Material

Landscape Interpretation

In "The Beholding Eye: Ten Versions of the Same Scene," Meinig (1979) explores "observer bias." He states that "any landscape is composed not only of what lies before our eyes, but also what lies within our heads." He suggests an exercise in which a diverse group of people is taken to a view that includes both city and countryside, and the participants are asked to describe the landscape, and to identify it elements, composition, and meaning. In this seminal article, Meinig then exposes different biases that affect landscape interpretation by discussing ten different perceptions of the viewed landscape. Meinig's ten versions of the same scene present an excellent overview of the range of landscape interpretations that people are prone to perceive. These ten views are listed below, with comments and a visual image for each viewpoint. These images should not be seen as physical settings that express only this meaning, but rather as the tendency of a viewer to perceive this type of image, often with only the slightest cue from the setting, and often in the face of other stronger cues that encourage the observer to see the landscape from different viewpoints.

1 LANDSCAPE AS NATURE

This nostalgic romantic view, that reached its apexduring the Romantic movement of the eighteenth century, holds nature dominant and humans subordinate. Nature is seen as pristine (a wilderness) without the presence of people. This conservationist view holds the natural landscape as an entity that should be preserved at all costs, for its own sake. Proponents prefer decisions that leave the landscape in an unmodified pristine state. They see all human works and human gestures in the landscape as feeble efforts that dim in comparison to the majesty, power, and magnificence of the natural landscape. The purity, power, and magnificence of the natural landscape are the vanguards of this view. Humans are relegated to a secondary, inconsequential position and are considered the negative influence in a natural landscape of perfection.

Proponents of this view are prone to remove people and their visual expressions from the scene. They see the cultural landscape as an aberrant, imposed, and unreal landscape. The undisturbed landscape, even though in many cases a relic no longer expressive of formative influences, is considered the real and appropriate one. This view is held even when, in many cases, the natural landscape envisioned has been physically absent for centuries, and if re-created would not sustain itself in the context of present forces, which themselves can be seen as inappropriate.

选自　JohnL. Motloch., Introduction to Landscape Design, 2nded., America, Ball State University, 2001, Page 10～12

LESSON 2

This viewpoint separates people and nature. It tends, in many cases, to be a reactionary stance that comes to prominence in periods of landscape degradation, in response to human wholesale environmental destruction. Philosophically, it establishes a confrontational relationship between nature and people, with people as aggressors and despoilers of a legitimate, pure, and pristine natural landscape.

Proponents are often politically active at a grass-roots level. They promote legislation that preserves the landscape and limits people's ability to have an impact on the environment. Proponents work actively to create parks and wildlife areas, and to codify ordinances and standards that place constraints on the ability of planners, designers, developers, and others to have an impact on the environment. Environmental impact statements are primary vehicles proponents of this view promote to encourage decisions that will not adversely affect the physical and ecological environment.

Designers who strongly embrace this view perceive their primary societal value to be that of conserving, nurturing, and protecting the environment. Many of these landscape design professionals work in public service for city, state, or federal governments. Others work with grass-roots environmental groups; others, in environmentally oriented private practice offices. Still others teach in landscape architecture or related academic programs.

2 LANDSCAPE AS HABITAT

In this view, the landscape is a home for humankind. People are envisioned as working with and altering land to increase its productivity and redefine it as a resource, and functioning to domesticate the earth. Nature is the benign provider. People interact with nature; accept its basic organization, structure, and behavior; and modify nature so as to convert its materials into resources that sustain and enhance the quality of life. People manipulate the landscape but are motivated by a desire to harmonize, steward, cultivate, and manage the landscape so as to maintain its bounty.

This view, interrelating people and environment, reached its zenith in this country after the American Revolution, when people embraced the traditional structure and spatial arrangement of the agrarian landscape. Wilderness and cityscape were judged against the agrarian landscape and found to be lacking. Landscape as habitat takes its cues from the landscape, with human gesture responsive to condition, and development patterns integrating with natural ones. Landscape as habitat also pursues landscape interventions as physical expressions of ecological roots and seeks to modify nature to enhance its benefit to people. In this view, humankind is one with an environment consciously modified for human benefit. Every landscape is an expression both of nature and of culture.

According to this paradigm, quality of life is seen to be integrally linked to a healthy habitat, decisions that function to maximize the human potential are deemed appropriate, and the maintenance of a quality, healthy environment is promoted. Decisions that degrade the environment are abandoned, and nature heals its wounds.

Part I   Landscape Architecture Interpretation

Perhaps the most well-known proponent of this viewpoint was R. Buckminster Fuller. His *world games* sessions for exploring "spaceship earth's" carrying capacity, and maximizing its ability to sustain cultures, greatly increased our understanding of the landscape as habitat.

This is a synergistic view of people integrating with, and becoming a part of, a managed nature. It tends to be dominant in vernacular approaches and in low-technology, third-world cultures directly dependent on the land for sustenance. These cultures modify the environment to harvest materials as resources but have little ability or desire to change nature in a profound manner. The cultures have a dialectic relationship with the landscape and realize that to use nature, they must obey it. The underlying assumption is that nature is a kind and gentle provider that, if respected and nurtured, will sustain life and provide a healthy, meaningful existence. People who hold this view see their primary societal role as facilitators, helping nature sustain humankind.

In third-world and low-technology cultures, addressing the landscape as habitat is often necessary for survival. This view has also endured in some first-world, high-technology countries. In both cases, the landscapes that have evolved have two positive characteristics. First, they tend to be characterized by a high degree of harmony, with human gestures integrating with ecological expressions and providing a person-environment synergy. The cultural landscapes that evolve under this paradigm are often seen to have a strong sense of place and are preferred by a broad range of people. Many people travel great distances, often at considerable expense, to visit the quaint hamlet, remote village, or unique neighborhood evolved from this world view.

The second benefit is that these landscapes tend to be efficient and self-sustaining. Since human gestures are integrated with ecological ones, natural forces do not set about to destroy these gestures but rather reinforce their condition, function, and maintenance.

3 LANDSCAPE AS ARTIFACT

This anthropomorphic view sees the landscape as an entity created by people. The holder of this view sees human expressions everywhere, and perceives the natural landscape as little more than the stage on which the cultural drama is played and recorded.

From this viewpoint, nature no longer exists. The entirety of the landscape is human-created. The soil, for example, is not seen as a human-modified biologically active medium, but rather as an entity "created" by the complex human activities of clearing, tilling, fertilizing, mulching, planting, irrigating, supplementing, enhancing, and so on. Waterways are not seen as streams and integral parts of a hydrologic system, but rather as engineered infrastructural conduits. The quintessential expression of this view is *made-land*, whereby coastal marshes have been anthropomorphically filled and re-created as major metropolitan areas (for example, most of the land area of Boston, Massachusetts). Another example of this view is the building itself: a human artifact, complete with a human-created climate and atmosphere.

According to the landscape-as-artifact viewpoint, people have conquered nature and reshaped it to their purposes, and use it as an expression of self. They no longer need, or desire, to respond to natural patterns, because they are irrelevant in the presence of an all-dominating technology. Human beings can and should re-create a better landscape, free from the constraints of natural patterns. In this view, humankind is ecologically dominant and superior to nature, and is the quintessential form-giver. The landscape is redefined and reordered in the human image. This anthropomorphic order is not an integrative one, but rather an overt individualistic one.

Like the other views, the landscape-as-artifact viewpoint is a mental construct that has reoccurred at various times in history. However, until recently, because of limited technology, its expression has often been a rather localized phenomenon. For example, people could anthropomorphically re-create nature in the garden, but this restructuring could not be greatly extended in scale. We have recently achieved the ability to apply this view on a much larger scale, due to a rapidly escalating technology. With this increased potential, we have also come to perceive humankind as the technological re-creator of the global condition. This view is driving the engineer to reshape the landscape physically and the biotechnologist to redefine life forms and life processes.

The landscape-as-artifact viewpoint addresses the human desire for self-expression, and when combined with our massive technology, has had profound environmental ramifications. The application of this technology to the wholesale re-creation of the physical condition, without an appreciation for integrating with natural processes, has resulted in widespread pollution and natural-system degradation. This degradation includes problems with groundwater and surface water quality and quantity, loss of topsoil and soil productivity, ozone depletion, and an almost infinite number of other environmental problems. The landscape-as-artifact view is a short-term, ego-driven viewpoint that is unaware of, or insensitive to, the problems created by its implementation.

4 LANDSCAPE AS SYSTEM

In this holistic view the landscape is a system consisting of interdependent subsystems, with elements seen as expressions of and cues for understanding, systems and their underlying processes. This is a relatively new, rapidly expanding and evolving viewpoint. It began as a reaction to a reductive Newtonian science and to a propensity to study things and pieces rather than seeking understanding of complex interrelationships. The landscape-as-system viewpoint has grown rapidly since the emergence (1930s) and growing acceptance of the science of relativity as the view of reality. This new scientific viewpoint is holistic and integrative and sees meaning accruing not primarily from elements, but from interrelationship of elements, with system behavior, and with generative processes. The landscape-as-system view also holds that elements holistically express the various systems of which they are a part.

In this mindset, people and nature are expressions of a systemic oneness. The landscape, as system and subsystems, is the entity understood and managed for environmental and human well-being. Landscape health and wellness are considered essential to ecological and human health and wellness, and human wellness is expressive of a healthy environmental system.

From this viewpoint, elements are not things but integrations of systems. For example, a building is an element within urban experiential, structural, and infrastructural systems. It is an integral part of a spatial system (seen as mass from the outside and as space from the inside) that is experienced temporally as the viewer moves through the landscape. The building is also part of a climatic system and can be designed for optimal water and energy exchange with the landscape (Fig. 1).

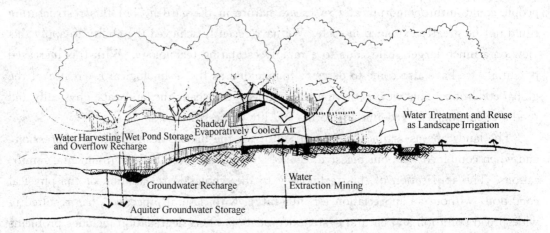

Fig. 1 Landscape as System

The landscape-as-system view sees actions in relation to system dynamics and life-cycle flows. Human behavior and design decisions are considered in their internal and external systemic contexts, and evaluated in terms of reactions (primary, secondary, tertiary, quaternary) and implications to health and productivity of the landscape as system. Good landscape decisions are those that promote management of the landscape and its subsystems and maintains or enhances carrying capacity, health, and productivity.

This viewpoint's popularity has grown with increased cultural awareness of system breakdowns that have resulted from our recent history of anthropocentric behavior. In contrast to the landscape-as-artifact view, the landscape-as-system viewpoint promotes sustainable, culturally relevant landscapes, integrates form and function with landscape dynamics, and maximizes long-term health and productivity of the physical and cultural landscape.

Designers who hold this viewpoint pursue a *systems management* approach, viewing landscape design, first and foremost, as the management of systems. These designers see design as a creative response to systemic behavior, rather than as the expression of the designer's ego independent of context. People holding this viewpoint function in various capacities (private professional firms, nonprofits, public agencies, academic practice), promoting effective management of ecological and human systems, engaging in ecological and human system and impact assessment and mitigation, developing systems-based and performance-based ordinances and development controls, promoting systems-sensitive planning and design, integrating the decisions of diverse people over long periods, and teaching others about systems-sensitive urban and regional planning, landscape architecture, and architecture.

5 LANDSCAPE AS PROBLEM

This view sees the landscape, including its natural and human-made elements, as a situation needing correction. Ozone depletion, polluted air, urban crime, abandoned housing, spoiled beaches, contaminated estuaries, soiled streams, eroded lands, urban blight and sprawl, congestion, and dilapidated buildings are seen as evidence of this problematic landscape. In this view a pervasive and ubiquitous presence of ecological, physiological, and psychological illness is the essence of the landscape.

This mindset can include an appreciation for the preceding four views, including reverence for nature, appreciation of landscape as habitat, sensitivity to landscape as artifact, and response to landscape as system. However, this approach's underlying premise is that all is in disarray. A compelling case is made for this point of view by Rachel Carson in *Silent Spring* (1982), and by the film *koyaanisqatsi* (a Hopi word loosely translating to "life out of balance"). Like the landscape-as-system viewpoint, this is a growing view, owing to the rapid rise in technology and exponentially increasing ability to degrade the landscape and thereby change it from resource to problem.

Expressions of this view range from a shrill cry of alarm to a more optimistic view of many landscape designers. These designers take a problem-solving approach and sometimes regard landscapes as severe problems needing immediate correction, and at other times as merely challenges to create a better world. In this later sense, this view shares ground with the landscape-as-artifact viewpoint.

The landscape-as-problem view is promoted by education addressing landscape design as functional, infrastructural, behavioral, or aesthetic problem-solving. It precludes the opinion that "in this case, nothing should be done!" This mindset dominated most schools of architecture and landscape architecture in the 1970s and continues in some today.

From this viewpoint the landscape designer applies professional skills, scientific knowledge, and aesthetic sensitivity to the correction of environmental ills. Unlike the landscape-as-artifact view that sees value in human expressions, the landscape-as-problem approach emphasizes the problems these expressions represent. This can be a short-term view (existing situation as problem, little attention to secondary, tertiary, and quaternary problems) or can focus on long-term problem-solving.

Applied with a long-term focus, the landscape-as-problem view tends to produce landscapes with few problems. However, applied with a short-term perspective, actions to solve immediate problems often cause reactions even more problematic than the original condition. This viewpoint can also create boring landscapes, characterized by a placelessness that fails to provide the enrichment necessary to sustain the human spirit and promote psychological health.

6 LANDSCAPE AS WEALTH

This view is based upon the perception that people "own" land. The primary value of land is its economic worth; all other landscape measures are secondary to investment potential. Land is a commodity whose value is determined in the marketplace, in units of currency (Fig. 2). This real-estate-appraiser view, seeking "highest and best use," highly integrates various influences via the marketplace to establish land value, and is continually updated in response to new conditions.

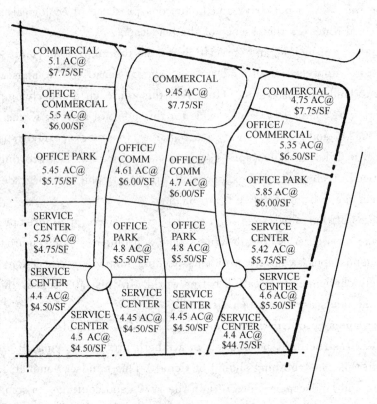

Fig. 2 Landscape as Wealth

This abstract, geographic view translates the landscape into an economic unit, such as square footage of commercial space or number of single family residences. It considers physical land characteristics, market influences, external conditions that influence value, and the intrinsic potential of the land to accommodate the support systems necessary to service the site and promote development. Advocates of this view have a working knowledge of, and appreciation for, the landscape and support systems as economic inputs. Accessibility and the available capacity of support systems (sanitary and storm sewers, electrical and gas service) are often more important than physical characteristics. Sense of place, context, and even the people present are important. Where the rich or poor congregate affect perceived status and economic value; image is a valued economic resource.

Believers in the landscape-as-wealth view consider economic opportunities and constraints intrinsic to the landscape, and those that can be introduced to affect value. They include both landscape as present wealth, and landscape as future wealth. They are futures oriented because the economic value of landscape is, to a large degree, a prediction of its future condition, use, and value.

The landscape-as-wealth viewpoint, strongly seated in our capitalistic ideology, has driven the design of the twentieth-century American landscape. In our materialistic culture and short-term perspective, this approach has enabled us to exploit the environment, grow rapidly, and have a profound impact on landscape efficiency and sustainability. This perspective makes decisions based on economic value rather than landscape carrying capacity. This view served us well during the period of resource abundance created by the exploitation of fossil fuels. But this approach will serve us poorly during the period of resource scarcity, which we have recently entered.

7 LANDSCAPE AS IDEOLOGY

In this view the landscape is seen as a symbol of the values, ideals, aspirations, hopes, and dreams of a culture. People encode and decode landscape meanings about the culture, its underlying philosophies, and its self-perception. The landscape is the physical expression of the culture, and its hopes and dreams. It is rich in associations, and takes on the personality of those who create it. This view sees the landscape as the embodiment of values and asserts that if we are to change the landscape, we must first change the cultural philosophy that creates it.

This mindset maximizes the cultural meaning of the landscape. In homogeneous, slowly changing cultures, and when complete landscapes are created to convey a single ideology, this view can result in landscapes with a strong and integrated sense. Conversely, in heterogenous societies and ones that change very rapidly, such as contemporary America, this view generates a cultural landscape that is spontaneous and stimulating. These highly diverse societies can also produce landscapes in which elements relate poorly to one another, and that lack the relatedness necessary to establish a strong sense. Such societies can create overly stimulating, chaotic, and psychologically unhealthy landscapes.

Part I *Landscape Architecture Interpretation*

8 LANDSCAPE AS HISTORY

The landscape in this view is the complex documentation of the history of natural and human activities in a particular location. It is the cumulative record, documented chronologically. Landscape elements have meaning in context to the chronology, events leading to the creation of the elements, and changes the elements heralded. In this view of landscape, everything is positioned in time and sequence. Settlement patterns, urban form, architectural style, site detail, and other planned and designed characteristics are means for dating elements, and contributing to the chronology.

In this view, the landscape is layers of history. Sometimes these temporal layers are separated in space, as when an entire community is settled during one time period. More commonly, they are interwoven spatially, and the landscape becomes an historically rich, spatial-temporal mosaic. The historical view deciphers this mosaic to develop mental constructs of landscape as living history. To do so, the landscape historian decodes the environment; that is, the historian reads and interprets cues and extrapolates from these cues to reconstruct history. In so doing, the historian is sensitive to which cues normally survive for long periods (such as settlement and urban patterns), and those that are more ephemeral (such as landscape plantings).

The landscape is seen as the record of physical gestures of many generations of people, and of ecological processes structured in time. Proponents decipher this record but usually find it to be an incomplete document. As the landscape historian deciphers the record, organizational patterns, materials, forms, and details tell something about the culture, subculture, and individuals, as well as about the natural forces that created the landscape. To understand the landscape and correctly interpret its elements, the landscape historian views these data in their historical context and in relation to their links with the past and future.

Whereas the landscape-as-system viewpoint seeks to understand the landscape as ecological and human processes that build interactive systems, the landscape-as-history view considers these processes structured in time to explain and interpret changes to physical elements as landscape gestures, and thereby to build a more complete historical record. Landscape gestures are viewed in relation to the cultures and individuals that created them, rather than present-day culture and individuals. Yet, the aggregate of these gestures, that is, the contemporary landscape, is the context within which the historical element is displayed and interpreted, and within which the current drama of life is performed. Therefore, the current landscape affects our perception of history, and the landscape-as-history view affects our current perception and behavior. In this interactive manner, the landscape becomes a living history.

This viewpoint enables us to develop a better understanding of who we are by giving us an understanding of how we came to be. It reinforces our collective consciousness as a culture by focusing on our shared history. However, in our heterogeneous, rapidly changing culture, this view can result in an overly stimulating landscape whose elements lack visual relatedness and can, therefore, be alienating. Also, if focused only backward, this view does not address the relevancy of the individual element to current and future conditions. By looking to the present as living history and the future as history yet to express itself, this view shares ground with the landscape-as-system mindset and becomes an integral part of daily life.

9 LANDSCAPE AS PLACE

This phenomenological view sees the landscape as sensual experience. It focuses not on elements, but on the sensual (sound, smell, tactile) gestalt. This approach also concentrates on the feel, flavor, and ambiance of place; the richness of mental constructs and associations; and the ability of the place to be remembered over time.

Holders of this view take pleasure in the immense variety, uniqueness, and individuality of places. These individuals look beyond generalized understanding and seek to discover the unique sense and value of place that they contend all places have. This can be a powerful view, stimulating numbers of people to travel around the world to experience a special city like Venice or a region like the Alps.

Adherents of this view believe that the person and the environment are inextricably bound in oneness, and that sensing healthy places is an essential dimension of human health and wellness. This viewpoint has been influenced by the philosopher Heidegger (1977) and the architect Norberg - Schulz (1980). Placemaking as human expression and concentration of meaning is seen as one of the essential efforts of human existence.

This view, often held by the geographer, is concerned with the characteristics of places and the analysis of how places are organized, structured, and spatially arranged to create the perceived landscape. It is also of value to the environmental psychologist, who seeks to understand relationships between place and consciousness. Place is also a basic unit of analysis in the area of study known as environmental perception.

The landscape-as-place approach is communicated in many ways. Writers eloquently use words to convey ambiance. Photographers, including Ansel Adams, have produced evocative images, and painters move beyond reproduction to intensify the communication of placeness. Geographers develop cognitive mapping techniques to communicate the mental construct of place, and aerial and locational maps to communicate the spatial arrangement of special places in the landscape.

The landscape-as-place viewpoint focuses on the gestalt rather than on the elements. Landscapes generated by this view downplay the designer's ego and concentrate on landscape character. They tend to be visually coherent, exciting, and sensually rewarding environments. These landscapes, therefore, share characteristics with ones generated by the landscape as system view. Individual gestures integrate with context. They tend not to be pure responses to single issues, but rather to be complex expressions that arbitrate among a multitude of contextual influences.

The landscapes that emerged in slowly changing, low-technology cultures usually had an integrated, systemic sense because of the limited choices available. With our rapidly changing heterogeneous culture and powerful technology, achieving a coherent sense requires a landscape-as-place emphasis and aggressive management of the experiential gestalt.

10   LANDSCAPE AS AESTHETIC

This view places primary emphasis on the artistic quality of landscape features and the landscape as visual scene. In contrast to the landscape-as-place view that sees the landscape experientially, the landscape-as-aesthetic viewpoint takes a detached, abstract approach. It interprets visual forms on the basis of some language of art, such as line, form, color, texture, rhythm, proportion, balance, symmetry, harmony, tension, unity, variety, and so on. This view might synergize with other ones, such as landscape as history, or landscape as place. However, these considerations are seen as secondary to the primary message: the landscape as a vehicle for communicating aesthetic relationships.

The landscape-as-aesthetic approach is a cerebral view of the landscape that holds truth and beauty not to be in function or experience, but as some aesthetic ideal. Human involvement with the landscape is intended to be contemplative rather than experiential. The landscape is seen as object, and the scene is detached from human behavior. Landscapes are endowed with high viewing value. Whether they function properly or have high cultural meaning is of little importance to this viewpoint.

These ten views, of course, are not a complete list of observer biases. These approaches do, however, provide a comprehensive overview and reveal the complexity of landscape interpretation. This complexity becomes more evident as we realize that these views do not exist in isolation. The observer usually espouses and is influenced by more than one bias simultaneously. The individual's interpretation of landscape is usually a complex synergism of several of these (and other) views.

The manner in which we manage, plan, and design the landscape is profoundly affected by how we see the landscape. How we see is, in turn, based on our *world View*: our basic assumptions and beliefs about the potentials and problems of existence, and how we organize ourselves and act to address these potentials and problems. Our world view affects the potentials we see and those we do not see; it affects the problems we solve, and those we exacerbate because they cannot be anticipated through our world view.

WORDS AND EXPRESSIONS

nostalgic [nɔˈstældʒɪk, nə-] *adj.* 恋旧的，怀旧的
vanguard [ˈvænɡɑːd] *n.* （运动或学术研究的）先驱者
seminal [ˈsiːminl] *adj.* 种子的，生殖的；有发展性的
formative [ˈfɔːmətiv] *adj.* 格式化的，影响…的发展
aberrant [æˈberənt] *adj.* 异常的
benign [biˈnain] *adj.* （病）良性的，（气候）良好的，仁慈的，和蔼的
boundary [ˈbaundəri] *adj.* 宽宏大量的，慷慨的
zenith [ˈzeniθ] *n.* 顶点，顶峰，天顶，最高点
paradigm [ˈpærədaim, -dim] *n.* 范例
hydrologic [haiˈdrɔlədʒik] *adj.* 水文学的
ramification [ˌræmifiˈkeiʃən] *n.* 衍生结果，分支（或分枝）
marsh [mɑːʃ] *n.* 湿地，沼泽，沼泽地
metropolitan [metrəˈpɔlɪt(ə)n] *adj.* 首都的，主要都市的，大城市
dilapidated *adj.* 毁坏的，要塌似的，荒废的
decipher [diˈsaifə] *vt.* 译解（密码等），解释 *n.* 密电译文
alienation [ˌeiliəˈneiʃən] *n.* 疏远，转让
eloquently [ˈeləkwənt] *adv.* 善辩地
cognitive [ˈkɔgnitiv] *adj.* 认知的，认识的，有感知的
arbitrate [ˈɑːbitreit] *v.* 作出公断
contemplative [ˈkɔntempleitiv] *adj.* 沉思的，冥想的，[宗] 祈祷的
exacerbate [eksˈæsə(ː)beit] *vt.* 恶化，增剧，激怒，使加剧，使烦恼

Part II

History of Landscape Architecture

LESSON 3

PARADISE ON EARTH: THE ISLAMIC GARDEN

In desert lands, the oasis is typically viewed as a kind of paradise, a respite from the parched land and withering sun. Through conquest and a tolerant religion, the nation of Islam spread westward across North Africa to southern Spain and eastward into Central Asia and India, a territory composed principally of vast dry zones with extremes of heat and cold within which scattered green oases furnished a most precious element, water. In their migrations, Islamic peoples absorbed elements borrowed from other design traditions, which they synthesized into a distinctive style. In desert climates and also where water flowed seasonally, the four heavenly rivers of paradise described in the Quran and the refreshing fountains, as well as the shade and fruit trees to be found there, provided apt symbols for paradise in the oasislike Islamic garden.

Unlike Japanese or English gardens, Persian gardens and their Islamic successors were not constructed as spatial itineraries, places of sequential discovery; rather they were designed to serve the purposes of luxurious ease and sensory delight or, in the case of Mughal tomb gardens, as settings for monuments of commemoration. Water's soothing sound and mesmerizing reflectivity were essential to their ephemeral atmosphere and paradisiacal character. Built mostly in warm climates, they were exterior living spaces, often sumptuous, yet airy. The porticoed palace, the garden pavilion, and the kiosk opened up to the out-of-doors, and often their walls were pierced by grills to admit a filigree of fragmented light, dematerializing interior space. In these spaces, the distinction between inside and out, between architecture and landscape, between the material world and poetry, seems almost to dissolve.

Fruit trees and flowers, birds and animals, shimmering tiles, and the gleam and murmur of running water—these are the vibrant and delicate substances from which, like a beautiful carpet, the Islamic garden is woven. Indeed, Islamic carpet design and garden layout go hand in hand. Garden carpets depict in a stylized manner the *chahar bagh*, or fourfold garden with its intersecting axial watercourses surmounted by a central fountain In addition, they depict symbolically the vegetation planted in actual gardens: the shade-giving plane tree, identified with the Tuba tree in the Quran; the cypress representing death and eternity; and fruit trees standing for life and fertility. The central cartouche can

---

选自 Elizabeth Barlow Rogers Landscape Design: A Cultural and Architecture History Harry N. Abrams, INC, Publishers

be interpreted as a platform, which in real gardens was often surmounted by a pavilion. These form the basic and timeless design formula of the Islamic garden—one or more quadripartite sections defined by narrow watercourses—which has its roots in ancient Persia where the archaeological remains of Achaemenid palaces trace the outlines of pavilions overlooking carved stone channels.

The paradigm of quadripartite landscape space with a defined center, from which energy flows outward in four directions and to which energy returns from the four corners of the cosmos, is a placemaking practice rooted, as we have seen, in prehistoric tradition[1]. But there is a distinction to be made between Islamic and prehistoric cosmological design. Prehistoric societies viewed landscape space in terms that charged *specific* local landscapes with intense religious meaning; their organization of space into quadripartite-center configurations was a declaration of the *actual* residence of divinity within a given landscape. Islamic garden design was rooted in a religion that was also impregnated with cosmological meaning, but because holy literature had begun to supplement and supplant oral tradition, thereby disseminating religion more broadly, a universal cosmological *symbolism* of sacred space, rather than the designation of certain spaces as cosmologically sacred, was now an operative cultural principle guiding landscape design. This observation is true for Hebrewderived, Christian landscape design as well.

EARLY PERSIAN GARDENS

It will be recalled that the word *paradise* was originally used to denote a hunting park. Xenophon(c. 431-c. 352 B. C. E.)[2], the soldier and writer who was a disciple of Socrates, reports on the beauty of the hunting park, the *pairidaeza* at Sardis, of the Achaemenid king Cyrus the Great(died c. 529 B. C. E.). From Xenophon's description we learn that this royal park was both a hunting park and a geometrically planted orchard. At Pasargadae, Cyrus the Great constructed a palace, a separate audience hall, and a garden pavilion overlooking a stone watercourse with square pools at regular intervals.

The shady porticoes of the palace and audience hall at Pasargadae, as well as the garden pavilion itself, overlooked the thin ribbon of water and the orchardgarden that surrounded it. Thus we find in the sixth century B. C. E. the two indispensable elements of Persian garden design: a straight, geometrically elaborated watercourse and a raised platform for garden viewing.

To supply such gardens as this with water, Achaemenid engineers constructed underground tunnels called *qanats* using a method developed as early as the sixth century B. C. E. and still in use today. These were laboriously dug by hand from the point of delivery to the base of a snow-capped mountain in a gentle ever-ascending grade. Shafts for debris removal and air supply created openings at intervals of approximately 50 feet, and these apertures still dot the vast Iranian plain.

After the conquest of Persia by Alexander the Great(356~323B. C. E.), a century of

Hellenizing influence preceded the re-establishment of a persian empire and Persian design traditions under the Parthians (c. 240B. C. E. ~ 226 C. E.). Their capital was Ctesiphon. Between the third and seventh centuries C. E., the Sassanians, successors to Parthian rule, who also made Ctesiphon their capital, continued to express Persian influence in their gardens. As inferred from the design of a legendary Persian carpet measuring 450 feet by 90 feet, which was woven for King Khosrow I Anushirvan (ruled 531~579C. E.), the imagery of the fourfold garden, divided by channels of running water, with a platform overlooking these watercourses, was an established idiom for actual garden construction. This Persian legacy accorded well with the Quranic concept of paradise, providing a readily accessible model for the Islamic garden.

ISLAMIC ORIGINS

In 610 C. E., the prophet Muhammed initiated the Muslim religion. It quickly spread through the Arabian peninsula and into the Middle East and Persia. In 766 C. E., the Abbasid caliphs[3], having asserted their political dominance, founded their capital of Baghdad on the Tigris River. During their rule between the eighth and the thirteenth century, horticulture and technology advanced rapidly. By the early tenth century, the city could boast twenty-three palaces with opulent gardens. One of these fabled, long-vanished palaces was known as the House of the Tree. An artificial tree stood in the middle of a large round pond and had eighteen boughs made of gold and silver hung with precious gems in the form of fruits. This ingenious automata had gold and silver birds perched on its branches, and these emitted musical notes when stirred by the passing breeze.

Simultaneously, beginning in the eighth century, Islamic warriors carried their culture west to Spain. Here Muslim rulers synthesized Hellenistic, Roman, Early Christian, and Persian influences. As the power of the Abbasid caliphs declined, their role shifted from one of political power to one of religious leadership. Baghdad fell to Mongol invaders in 1258, following the campaigns of Genghis Khan and his heirs, but Islamic culture nonetheless remained a unifying force throughout much of Asia, North Africa, and Spain. Within this culture, the essential garden formula of a watercourse and raised platform for sedentary viewing was further developed as a quadripartite space in which the divisions were articulated by narrow water channels that could be thought of as symbolizing the four rivers of paradise.

WORDS AND EXPRESSIONS

denote [di'nəut]	v.	指的是
disciple [di'saipl]	n.	门徒，信徒
Socrates	n.	苏格拉底（公元前 469~前 399，古希腊哲学家）
orchard ['ɔːtʃəd]	n.	果园

Part II *History of Landscape Architecture*

indispensable [ˌindisˈpensəbl]	*adj.* 不可缺少的
qanat [kaːˈnaːt]	*n.* 暗渠，坎儿井
laborious [ləˈbɔːriəs]	*adj.* 费力的；艰难的
shaft [ʃaːft]	*n.* 轴，杆状物
debris [ˈdebriː, ˈdeib-]	*n.* 散落的碎片，残骸
aperture [ˈæpətjuə]	*n.* 窄孔；隙缝
Hellenize [ˈhelinaiz]	*vt.* (使)希腊化；(使)受希腊文化之熏陶
Parthian [ˈpaːθiən, -θjən]	*n.* 帕提亚人；帕提亚语
	adj. 帕提亚的；帕提亚人的
Sassenach	*n.* 撒克逊人，英格兰人
	adj. 撒克逊人的
legendary [ˈledʒəndəri]	*n.* 传奇故事书，传奇文学
	adj. 传说中的
legacy [ˈlegəsi]	*n.* 先人或过去遗留下来的东西
idiom [ˈidiəm]	*n.* 风格，特色
prophet [ˈprɔfit]	*n.* 预言者，先知
Abbasid [əˈbæsid; ˈæbəsid]	*n.* (阿拉伯帝国)阿拔斯王朝(750～1258)的统治者
	adj. 阿拔斯王朝的
peninsula [piˈninsjulə]	*n.* 半岛
Tigris [ˈtaigris]	*n.* 底格里斯河
opulent [ˈɔpjulənt]	*adj.* 华丽的；奢侈的
bough [bau]	*n.* (树的)主枝
perch [pəːtʃ]	*v.* (使)栖息；(使)飞落；(使)暂歇
warrior [ˈwɔriə]	*n.* 战士
Baghdad	*n.* 巴格达(伊拉克首都)
heir [ɛə]	*n.* 继承人，后嗣
sedentary [ˈsedəntəri]	*adj.* (指人)久坐的
articulate [aːˈtikjulit]	*v.* 连接；使成为系统的整体

KEY CONCEPTS

Islamic garden
Porticoed palace
Fourfold garden
Quadripartite landscape space
Orchard garden

NOTES

1. The paradigm of quadripartite landscape space with a defined center, from which energy returns from the four corners of the cosmos, is a place-making practice rooted, as we have seen, in prehistoric tradition.

    由四部分组成的有明确中心的(伊斯兰)园林范例,能量从宇宙的四角回到其中心,这是我们看到的源于史前传统的造园实践。

2. Xenophon

    色诺芬(约公元前434~前355,希腊将军,历史学家,著有《长征记》一书)。

3. caliph

    哈里发(伊斯兰教执掌政教大权的领袖的称号,既是精神上的也是政治观念上的穆斯林领袖),某些穆斯林国家对官员等的尊称。

QUESTIONS FOR REVIEW AND DISCUSSION

1. What is origin meaning of the "paradise"?
2. Describe the Characteristics of the Islamic Garden.
3. When did Islamic culture reach Spain?
4. Please make a further consideration about Islamic developments in Europe?
5. What unique environmental factors led to different/similar development of forms in the Persian and Peristyle Garden styles?

Part Ⅱ *History of Landscape Architecture*

Reading Material

Islamic Gardens of Spain

The leaders of the Muslim army that invaded Spain in 711 C. E. were inspired by the hope of plunder as much as by religious enthusiasm. After defeating the Visigoths, the western Goths who had in the fourth century C. E. claimed the parts of the Roman Empire now occupied by France and Spain, the Arabs established themselves within the remains of their enemies' settlements and the extensive ruins of former Roman colonies. Then, in 750, after a palace revolution, a surviving member of the Umayyad caliphate, the first dynasty of Arab caliphs(661～750), fled Damascus to found the independent emirate of al- Andalus in the southern Spanish region that is known today as Andalusia. Geographically distant, therefore, from Islamic culture in the Middle East, the Arabs in Spain formed their own brilliant and erudite society. Here in Spain, Muslim, Christian, and Jewish communities coexisted under Arab rule. The Arabs had brought with them Persian artistic concepts along with Arabic science, and they married these with Greek philosophy. In this way, Córdoba became in the Middle Ages a center of learning, renowned for such philosophers as Ibn Rushd, known in the West as Averroës (1126～1198), a rationalist who translated Aristotle and anticipated Thomas Aquinas.

While southern Spain has the same hot climate as many other parts of the Islamic geographical sphere, its topography is for the most part more rugged and its land well watered and more fertile. Moorish engineers, rebuilding and extending the remains of Roman aqueducts all around them, created intricate irrigation systems by introducing the *noria*, a bucket-scoop waterwheel that raised water into elevated canals. This greatly increased the amount of arable land and facilitated the construction of numerous gardens. Agriculture prospered, and famous treatises on the subject were written, such as the one by Abu Zakariya, a thirteenth-century agronomist and botanist in Seville. Farmers introduced sugarcane and brought into cultivation rice, cotton, flax, silkworms, and many kinds of fruit. Both the valley of the Guadalaquivir and the plain of Granada became densely settled zones with a rich tapestry of agriculture and gardening, their air fragrant with the scent of orange, lemon, and citron trees.[1]

Topography and contact with the abundant remains of Iberian Rome served to modify the conquerors' Syrian architectural heritage with its previously assimilated Roman and Persian forms. But Spanish Muslim architecture never aspired to the monumental three-dimensionality of architecture in the West. Instead, its aim was atmospheric, and its highest achievement lay in the interweaving of indoor and outdoor spaces in sensuous and sophisticated ways. Thus, in a typical Moorish house and garden, the patio and the structural

---

选自 Elizabeth Barlow Rogers Landscape Design: A Cultural and Architecture History Harry N. Abrams, INC, Publishers

spaces surrounding it interpenetrate one another in a casual yet studied congress of architecture and nature. Ceramic tiles, with their brightly glazed, reflective surfaces, produced an effect of cool airiness.

The spatial interpenetration of indoors and outdoors was not confined to fortress palaces or homes such as are found today in the Albaicín district of Granada, where the durable plan of the Roman peristyle was appropriated and reinterpreted as the *carmen*, the inward-focused house and garden of Arabic Spain. The same planning principle can be seen in the design of the Great Mosque at Córdoba, begun in 785~786. The mosque(now a cathedral), has a hypostyle interior in which the columns supporting a vast number of horseshoe-shaped double arches are evenly placed throughout like rows of trees in an orchard. Originally the wall on this side of the mosque opened via a facade of arches to a 3-acre courtyard planted in avenues of orange trees, which were aligned with the columns of the mosque's interior. An underground cistern supplied the fountains and irrigation channels in this court, called the Patio de los Naranjos, or Court of the Oranges. Unfortunately, the underground cistern has long since been converted into an ossuary, and Christian chapels have filled in the arches that once opened onto this patio.

The Alcázar[2] in Seville, which dates from about a hundred years after the Christian conquest of that city in 1248, exemplifies the extensive Islamic influence upon subsequent Spanish architecture. Using the considerable resources of Islamic craftsmanship, the king of Castile, Pedro the Cruel(ruled 1334~1369), built his fortified palace on the ruins of the former Islamic citadel. The Alcázar gardens consist of a series of enclosed patios. Though altered in subsequent centuries, the Moorish origins of these gardens are evident in their high enclosing walls, geometrical layout, raised paths, numerous fountains, brightly glazed tiles, and plantings of cypress, palm, orange, and lemon trees.

Granada was the last Arabic city recaptured by Christian monarchs, falling to Ferdinand and Isabel in 1492. Its remaining Arabic gardens—the Alhambra and the Generalife—which date from the thirteenth and fourteenth centuries, are among the oldest gardens in the world and enjoy legendary status. Sometime around 1250, Muhammad Ibn Ben Ahmar, the founder of the Nasrid dynasty, who took possession of Granada in 1238, climbed to the top of a bare red escarpment above the valley of the Darro with the spectacular Sierra Nevada rising behind it and laid claim to a site for his palace where there was already standing a building that probably served as a fortress in the late eleventh century. Here he ordered the construction of an aqueduct, the water from which has made possible the gardens of the Alhambra and the Generalife ever since. Built over a period of 250 years, principally during the reigns of Yusuf I(1333~1354) and Muhammad V (1354~1359; 1362~1391), the Alhambra, like the Alcázar in Seville, is an accretion of enclosed garden spaces, some of which were torn away in the sixteenth century when Charles V built a vast square palace with a huge circular interior court.

At the Alhambra, the planted areas of several of the enclosed gardens are defined by

Part II *History of Landscape Architecture*

cross-axial paths. Soil beds were originally sunken well below these walkways and not as we see them today at almost the same grade. planted with flowers, these garden courts would have been read by viewers sitting on carpets and low cushions placed in the surrounding porticoes as brightly colored tapestries. The fragrance of their orange trees, a unique garden design feature of Moorish Spain, would have also perfumed the air. Because one rarely enters directly from the outside into a Spanish-Moorish patio, but rather through a vestibule or twisting corridor, the sight of a beautiful interior garden is unexpected and therefore the impression it makes is powerful, relying as it does on one of the chief tricks of garden art: surprise. For instance, an undistinguished opening off the Court of the Myrtles turns into a small dark corridor leading to the most famous and complex space within the Alhambra, the Court of the Lions.

Here one finds a central fountain and a cruciform pattern of water channels. The fountain is supported by stylized lions with water flowing from their mouths into the basin below, which contemporaries may have linked symbolically with Solomon, or at least with the notion of wise royal rule associated with the Hebrew king[3]. The basin is also fed by water that runs in a silver thread through the narrow white marble canals from the surrounding porticoed spaces. The most magnificent of these pavilionlike structures is the Hall of the Two Sisters flanking the Court of the Lions on the north. Its cupola of stucco blocks set over an octagon is formed into a honeycombed, stalactitelike ceiling of mesmerizing intricacy ascending as a symbolical representation of various levels of the heavens. Adding to the ethereal quality of the architecture are slender alabaster columns, brilliant gilding, and polychrome tiles designed in a rich array of abstract patterns. Here one finds the familiar avoidance of figural imagery and Islamic preference for geometrical forms, believed to embody the mathematical order underlying all creation. For the same reason, topiary was scrupulously avoided and plants in this and other Islamic gardens were allowed to assume their natural forms.

WORDS AND EXPRESSIONS

plunder [ˈplʌndə]   n. 抢劫，偷盗
Visigoth [ˈvizigɔθ, -gɔːθ]   n. 西哥特人（公元4世纪后入侵罗马帝国并在法国和西班牙建立王国的条顿族人）
Goth [gɔθ]   n. 哥特人；粗野的人，野蛮人
Umayyad [uːˈmaijæd]   n. 伍麦耶王朝（阿拉伯哈里发的第一个王朝（661～750），其首都为大马士革）
caliphate [ˈkælifeit]   n. 伊斯兰教国王的职权或其领域
Damascus [dəˈmæskəs]   n. 大马士革（叙利亚首都）
emirate [eˈmiərit]   n. 阿拉伯酋长（贵族、王公）之职位或阶级，酋长国
Andalusia [ˌændəˈluːzjə]   n. 安达鲁西亚

LESSON 3

erudite [ˈeruːdait]	*adj.* 博学的
Cordoba [ˈkɔːdəuvə]	*n.* 科尔多瓦(西班牙)
Averroës	伊斯兰哲学家阿威罗伊
rationalist [ˈræʃənəlist]	*n.* 唯理论者，理性主义者
erudite [ˈeruːdait]	*adj.* 博学的
rationalist [ˈræʃənəlist]	*n.* 唯理论者，理性主义者
Aquinas [əˈkwainæs]	*n.* 阿奎奈(意大利中世纪神学家和经院学家，1226~1274)
rugged [ˈrʌgid]	*adj.* 高低不平的，崎岖的
Moorish [ˈmuəriʃ]	*adj.* 摩尔人的，(建筑，家具等)摩尔人式的，摩尔人风格的
aqueduct [ˈækwiˌdʌkt]	*n.* 沟渠，导水管
intricate [ˈintrikit]	*adj.* 复杂的，错综的
irrigation system	灌溉系统
noria [ˈnɔːriə]	*n.* (西班牙和东方国家的)戽水车
scoop [skuːp]	*n.* 铲子
arable [ˈærəbl]	*adj.* 可耕的，适于耕种的
treatise [ˈtriːtiz]	*n.* 论文，论述
agronomist [əˈgrɔnəmist]	*n.* 农艺学家，农学家
Seville [ˈsevil]	*n.* 塞维利亚，西班牙西南部一港市
sugarcane [ˈʃugəkein]	*n.* [植] 甘蔗，糖蔗
flax [flæks]	*n.* 亚麻
Guadalquivir [ˌgwaːdəlˈkwivə(r)]	*n.* 瓜达尔基维尔河 [西班牙南部]
Granada [graːˈnaːdaː]	*n.* (地名)格拉那达
tapestry [ˈtæpistri]	*n.* 织锦，挂毯
citron [ˈsitrən]	*n.* [植] 香木橼，圆佛手柑
Iberian [aiˈbiəriən]	*adj.* 伊比利亚的，伊比利亚人的
	n. 伊比利亚人，古代伊比利亚人，伊比利亚半岛
Syrian [siriən]	*adj.* 叙利亚的
	n. 叙利亚人
assimilate [əˈsimileit]	*v.* 吸收
sensuous [ˈsensjuəs]	*adj.* 感觉上的，给人美感的
patio [ˈpaːtiəu]	*n.* 天井，院子
airiness [ˈɛərinis]	*n.* 通风
interpenetrate [ˌintə(ː)ˈpenitreit]	*v.* 互相渗透；贯穿；扩散
ceramic [siˈræmik]	*adj.* 陶器的
	n. 陶瓷制品
fortress [ˈfɔːtris]	*n.* 城堡或大的碉堡；要塞；堡垒
peristyle [ˈperistail]	*n.* [建] 绕柱式，列柱走廊，以柱围绕的内院

45

Part II *History of Landscape Architecture*

mosque [mɔsk]	n. 清真寺
cathedral [kə'θi:drəl]	n. 大教堂
hypostyle ['haipəustail]	n. & adj. 多柱式建筑(的)
cistern ['sistən]	n. 水塔, 蓄水池
ossuary ['ɔsjuəri]	n. 藏骨罐; 藏骨堂; 骨灰瓮
chapel ['tʃæpəl]	n. 小礼拜堂, 礼拜
Castile [kæs'ti:l]	n. (地名)卡斯提尔(古代西班牙北部一王国)
fortified ['fɔ:tifaid]	adj. 加强的
citadel ['sitədəl]	n. 根据地, 大本营
monarch ['mɔnək]	n. 君主
Alhambra [æl'hæmbrə]	n. 阿尔罕布拉宫(中古西班牙摩尔人(Moor)诸王的豪华宫殿)
Generalife	n. 赫内拉利费宫(位于阿尔罕布拉宫所在地邻山上的夏宫)
escarpment [i'ska:pmənt]	n. 悬崖, 断崖, 绝壁, 陡斜坡
aqueduct	n. 沟渠, 导水管
sierra ['siərə, si'erə]	n. [地]齿状山脊
accretion [æ'kri:ʃən]	n. 连生, 合生; 增加物, 积成物
portico ['pɔ:tikəu]	n. [建]有圆柱的门廊
tapestry ['tæpistri]	n. 花毯, 挂毯
sunken ['sʌŋkən]	adj. 沉没的, 凹陷的
vestibule ['vestibju:l]	n. 门廊, 前厅
cruciform ['kru:sifɔ:m]	adj. 十字形的
stylized ['stailaizd]	adj. 按固定的传统风格处理的
Solomon ['sɔləmən]	n. 所罗门(?~前932, 以色列国王, 以智慧著称); 聪明人
cupola ['kju:pələ]	n. 圆屋顶
stucco ['stʌkəu]	n. [建]装饰用的灰泥
octagon ['ɔktəgən]	n. 八边形, 八角形
honeycombed ['hʌnikəumd]	adj. 蜂窝结构的
stalactite ['stæləktait]	n. [地]钟乳石
mesmerize ['mezməraiz]	v. 吸引住(某人)
polychrome ['pɔlikrəum]	adj. 彩饰的 n. 多彩艺术品
ethereal [i'θiəriəl]	adj. 轻巧的; 超凡的
alabaster ['æləba:stə]	n. & adj. 雪花石膏(的)
gilding ['gildiŋ]	n. 贴金箔, 镀金
figural ['figjurəl]	adj. 人物形象的, 借喻的
imagery ['imidʒəri]	n. 肖像(总称), 比喻, 雕刻

topiary [ˈtəupiəri, -pjə-]　　　　n. 树木整形术
scrupulously [ˈskru:pjuləsli]　　adv. 小心翼翼地，多顾虑地

NOTES

1. 关于西班牙的伊斯兰世界的(islamic spain)园林/西班牙伊斯兰园林以及它们与周围景观在实际上和象征上的关系的著述，见 D. Fairchild Ruggles, Gardens, Landscape, and Vision in the Palaces of Islamic Spain(Park 大学，宾夕法尼亚：宾夕法尼亚州立大学出版社，2000)。

2. alcázar

　　这个词起源于阿拉伯词语 al-qasr，意为"堡垒"。

3. 根据列王记上 7(1 Kings, 7)：所罗门国王神庙有一个建在 12 头公牛背上的巨大的盆(有十二只铜牛驮海，三只向北，三只向西，三只向南，三只向东。海在牛上，牛尾都向内)。在 1056~1066 年间，Yusuf，一位格拉纳达的犹太教高官建立了一座雄伟华丽的带有喷泉的豪华宫殿花园(palace and garden)，这被同时代的一位诗人认为同所罗门的宫殿花园(that of Solomon)相似，除了"不是建在公牛背上/但是有沿其边缘排列的狮子……/它们的腹部是喷泉之源，水向前喷出/像溪流般涌进它们的口中。"关于 the Court of the Lions 中喷泉的象征意义的著述，见 D. Fairchild Ruggles, Gardens, Landscape, and Vision in the Palaces of Islamic Spain, pp. 163-166, 199-200, 213。

LESSON 4

GARDENS OF SIXTEENTH-CENTURY ITALY

ESTABLISHING THE ITALIAN RENAISSANCE GARDEN PARADIGM: BELVEDERE COURT AND VILLA MADAMA

Encouraged by his reading of Pliny the Younger[1], Petrarch's[2] first somewhat tentative embrace of panoramic perspective on Mont Ventoux heralded the scenic appreciation that would later become a hallmark of Renaissance thought[3]. The Italian word *belvedere*, meaning "beautiful view", is an important one in the history of landscape design because of its association with a particular type of garden structure. Built in various styles, depending upon time and place, a belvedere may be either an independent tower or part of the villa itself. A belvedere is, quite simply, a lookout whose purpose is the enjoyment of scenery. During the Renaissance, belvederes became an important means of enjoying the view of gardens and the surrounding landscape. The papal villa known as Belvedere, built by Innocent VIII (papacy 1484~1492) on a hill within the Vatican is important for our discussion here, however, not only because of its original siting with commanding views of the Roman countryside but also because the subsequent treatment of the ground that lay between it and the Vatican influenced the course of garden history.

Bisected in the late sixteenth century by a structural addition to the Vatican Palace, half of the Court of the Belvedere today serves as a parking lot for Vatican employees, while the remaining half is a pleasant sculpture garden where visitors can stroll. Few today, therefore, comprehend its significance as a pivotal development in the history of landscape design. Perhaps because so much later Italian, and indeed European, landscape design was derived from Bramante's axial terraced composition here, this once-revolutionary garden seems only inevitable, not radical, to us.

The seed for a garden on this spot was sown in the quattrocento. The first humanist pope, Nicholas V (papacy 1447~1455) was deeply interested in architecture, and he employed Alberti[4] as his consultant on such projects as the reconstruction of Old St. Peter's and the integration of this basilica with the Vatican Palace. The plan that Alberti conceived

---

选自 Elizabeth Barlow Rogers Landscape Design: A Cultural and Architecture History Harry N. Abrams, INC, Publishers

included a palace garden. Though considerably smaller in scale, in its ambitious program this garden harked back to Hadrian's Villa rather than to any immediate predecessor, for it was not conceived as a series of outdoor rooms where intimate conversation could take place, as were some of the new villa gardens near Florence, but rather as a space for public gathering and theatrical entertainment. This plan was abandoned at Nicholas's death in 1455, and not until a half century later was a garden program for the Vatican begun in earnest.

Immediately upon his election to the papacy, Pope Julius Ⅱ (papacy 1503~1513) began implementing a plan for a Vatican garden that was part of a political agenda to increase the importance of the papacy as a power in Europe, with the Vatican serving as the seat of a new Roman empire. The revival of the ancient Roman villa tradition within the walls of the Vatican thus served as a symbolical link to imperial times. To perform this work, the pope chose as his architect Donato Bramante (1444~1514), who had recently completed the sophisticated *tempietto* adjacent to San Pietro in Montorio on the Janiculum Hill, and whom he would soon commission to design a new basilica for St. Peter's. Bramante's first commission from the pope was to provide a physical link between the Belvedere of Innocent VⅢ on its hill and the Vatican Palace below, creating sheltered communication between the two buildings. At the same time, he was to provide a setting for the pontiff's fine collection of antique sculpture and an outdoor theater to serve as a suitable space for papal pageantry. In addition, Julius Ⅱ wanted to have a private garden retreat, a place where he could meet and converse with a circle of friends who shared his interest in the rediscovery of the classical world.

In developing his design, Bramante employed Alberti's principles of symmetry and proportion in an axial organization of forms and space that had not been seen since antiquity. He even set about resolving a problem that was generally left unresolved in ancient Roman landscape planning, the harmonization of two colliding axes.

On the uneven terrain between the Vatican Palace and the Belvedere, Bramante placed two parallel loggias, which were three stories on the lowest level adjacent to the palace, then two stories as the rising slope was transformed into an intermediate terrace, and finally one story where an upper terrace joined the villa. The steps necessitated by these grade changes in the terraced hillside became important design elements in their own right, their double staircases celebrations of ascent. Perpendicular to the broad terraces between the loggias (today's museum galleries) was a strong central axis terminating next to the villa in a raised niche—or exedra, so called because of its semicircular form. From the windows of the papal apartments the garden appeared as a stage set or painting demonstrating the principles of single-point perspective, one of the technical discoveries of the Renaissance that theater designers and artists often virtuosically demonstrated in their work. Following Bramante, designers planned gardens with elevated terraces or balconies overlooking them in order that the viewer could readily grasp from this vantage point the axes that enabled and made manifest a perspectival treatment of space.

The elevated niche and its flanking wings screened the awkward juncture of two axes, that of the Belvedere Court and that of the villa. Bramante is believed to have modeled this architectural composition along the lines of the terraced Sanctuary of Fortuna Primigenia at Palestrina. Around 1550, under Pope Julius III (papacy 1550～1555), Michelangelo Buonarroti(1475～1564)[5] replaced Bramante's semicircular Praeneste-like steps with the double flight of stairs we see today. Paired staircases by then had become ubiquitous in Italian garden design as a means of reinforcing axial symmetry and dramatizing the transition from terrace to terrace. Hillsides were therefore the most desirable sites for garden designers after Bramante showed at the Belvedere Court how designers could successfully exploit steep terrain.

The construction of the Belvedere Court did not occur all at once, but proceeded sporadically over half a century. In addition to replacing Bramante's unusual convex-concave stairs in front of the exedra, Michelangelo enclosed the arcade that formed its curving rear and raised the northern wall next to it an additional story. In 1561, Pius IV (papacy 1559～1565) summoned the architect Pirro Ligorio(c. 1510～1583) to finish the project. Ligorio vaulted the niche to create the Nicchione, or Great Niche, and built its surmounting semicircular loggia. At the opposite end of the Court, he added a semicircle of tiered stone seats resembling those of a Roman theater to facilitate viewing the tournaments and other spectacles that took place there.

In 1516, Cardinal Giulio de' Medici, later Pope Clement VII[6], commissioned Raphael (Raffaello Sanzio, 1483～1520)[7] to design the Villa Madama on Monte Mario. Raphael's friend and collaborator Giulio Romano (1492/9～1546)[8] helped with the realization of the design, and Antonio da Sangallo, the Younger(1485～1546), was probably also involved in the project. It was the first villa to be constructed on the outskirts of Rome. Like the Farnesina, the 1508～1511 villa designed by Baldassare Peruzzi (1481～1536)[9] on the banks of the Tiber, it was intended for supper parties attended by popes and cardinals as well as by philosophical noblemen and witty courtesans. These entertainments were an important feature of Roman life during the papacy of Julius II and his successor, Leo X(papacy 1513～1521). Like the Farnesina, the Villa Madama has a beautifully frescoed loggia that serves as the nexus of interpenetrating indoor and outdoor spaces.

Designed in a halcyon era when humanist gatherings and summer entertainments were still the order of the day, the structures of the villa were subservient to the gardens, which stretched out along lengthy axes. From the entrance on the south, one passes into an entry court and beyond through an entry loggia into the large central court. This axis is projected through another loggia in which recessed niches seem to pull the outdoor space into the architecture of the building, while simultaneously pushing the fabric of the building into the adjacent garden. Giovanni da Udine (1487～1561/4), whose beautiful frescoes of garlands embellish the ceiling of the Farnesina, also worked at the Villa Madama, painting the frescoes that decorate the bays of this loggia in the antique style of those found in Nero's Golden House. Originally the loggia, which is now glassed in, opened directly onto the garden. Lofty loggias with the adjacent garden in axial relation to them, the successors of the Villa Medici at Fiesole, help to dissolve the visual separation between building and nature and are among the hallmarks of Italian villa design.

Curiously, the axial orientation of the Villa Madama, unlike that of the Villa d'Este at Tivoli, does not exploit the scenic potential of its lofty site on Monte Mario but runs laterally across the hillside instead of along its gradient. Raphael planned another perpendicular axis that would have accomplished this purpose, but his design for this extension of the garden was never executed. The garden's principal view therefore remains that from the loggia along the villa's main axis as it continues outdoors through a garden of boxwood compartments and a long terrace stretching across the flank of Monte Mario to the north. These two spaces are separated by a tall vine-clad wall pierced with a pedimented gate guarded by a pair of colossal male figures. Parallel to this garden at a lower level is a rectangular fish pond. Fish ponds were common in medieval gardens, but the architectural character of this one introduces us in a preliminary and rudimentary way to what would become one of the chief means of Italian Renaissance garden expression: the use of water as an important design element. Water was employed with great imagination in subsequent sixteenth-century Italian gardens, appearing in fountains, pools, water staircases, water *parterres*, and *giocchi d'acqua*, or droll water games that involved the spectator physically by providing surprise drenchings from concealed jets suddenly activated. Water in these gardens was a means of providing mesmerizing reflectivity, movement, and excitement. It was meant to connote evanescence, insubstantiality, and temporality, while implying the agrarian bounty achieved when humans harness this vital force of nature.

WORDS AND EXPRESSIONS

renaissance	n.	复兴，复活，新生，文艺复兴，文艺复兴时期
Bramante ['bræmbl]	n.	伯拉孟特（意大利建筑家）
belvedere ['belvidiə]	n.	望景楼
villa ['vilə]	n.	别墅；豪华府邸；〈英〉郊区中产阶级的住宅
tentative ['tentətiv]	adj.	试验性的，试探性的，不确定的
panoramic [ˌpænə'ræmik]	adj.	全景的
herald ['herəld]	vt.	宣布（某人/某事物）即将来临
hallmark ['hɔːlmaːk]	n.	特点
papal ['peipl]	adj.	罗马教皇的，教皇制度的
papacy ['peipəsi]	n.	教皇的任期
Vatican ['vætikən]	n.	梵蒂冈，罗马教廷
bisect [bai'sekt]	v.	分成两个（通常为相等的）部分

Part II *History of Landscape Architecture*

stroll [strəul]	v. 闲逛，漫步
pivotal ['pivətəl]	adj. 枢轴的，关键的
terrace ['terəs]	n. 梯田的一层，梯田；阳台，倾斜的平地
quattrocento [ˌkwætrəu'tʃentəu]	n. 15世纪（欧洲文艺复兴的初期）
basilica [bə'zilikə]	n. （古罗马）长方形会堂，长方形基督教堂
hark [ha:k]	vi. 听
hark back to	重新提到或想起原先的问题、旧事等/回溯到
pontiff ['pontif]	n. 罗马教皇，主教，大祭司
pageantry ['pædʒəntri]	n. 壮观，华丽
antiquity [æn'tikwiti]	n. 古代
collide [kə'laid]	vi. 碰撞，抵触
loggia ['lɔdʒə, 'lɔdʒiə]	n. 凉廊
perpendicular [ˌpə:pən'dikjulə]	adj. 垂直的，正交的
niche [nitʃ]	n. （浅的）凹处，（尤指）壁龛
exedra [ik'si:drə, 'eksi-]	n. （古希腊，古罗马）开敞式有座谈话间，半圆形室外坐椅
virtuosi	n. 艺术能手
virtuosic [ˌvə:tju'ɔsitic]	adj. 专家的
balcony ['bælkəni]	n. 阳台
juncture ['dʒʌŋktʃə]	n. 接合点
Fortuna [fɔ:'tju:nə]	n. [罗马神话] 福耳图那（命运女神）
ubiquitous [ju:'bikwitəs]	adj. 到处存在的，（同时）普遍存在的
sporadically [spə'rædikəli]	adv. 偶发地，零星地
convex ['kɔn'veks]	adj. 凸圆的，凸面的
concave ['kɔn'keiv]	adj. 凹的，凹入的
arcade [a:'keid]	n. [建] 拱廊，有拱廊的街道
vault [vɔ:lt]	vt. 盖以圆顶
tournament ['tuənəmənt]	n. 比赛
Tiber ['taibə]	n. 台伯河（意大利中部，流经罗马）
cardinal ['ka:dinəl]	n. 枢机主教，红衣主教
courtesan [kɔ:ti'zæn；(US)'kɔ:tizn]	n. （旧时）交际花
fresco ['freskəu]	n. 在灰泥的墙壁上作的水彩画，壁画 vt. 作壁画于
nexus ['neksəs]	n. 联结，关系
halcyon ['hælsiən]	adj. 平静的，太平的
subservient [sʌb'sə:viənt]	adj. 次要的，从属的
recess [ri'ses]	vt. 使凹进
garland ['ga:lənd]	n. 花环
bay [bei]	n. 隔间部分

LESSON 4

lofty [ˈlɔ(:)fti]	adj. 高高的，极高的
lateral [ˈlætərəl]	n. 侧部，支线
	adj. 横（向）的，侧面的
gradient [ˈgreidiənt]	n. 梯度，倾斜度，坡度
boxwood [ˈbɔkswud]	n. 黄杨木材，黄杨木
clad [klæd]	adj. 被…覆盖的
pedimented [ˌpediˈmentid]	adj. 有人字墙的，人字形的
colossal [kəˈlɔsl]	adj. 巨大的，庞大的
medieval [ˌmediˈiːvəl]	adj. 中世纪的，仿中世纪的，老式的
preliminary [priˈliminəri]	adj. 预备的，初步的
rudimentary [ruːdiˈmentəri]	adj. 基本的；未发展的
parterre [paːˈtɛə]	n. 花坛，花圃
droll [drəul]	adj. 好笑的，滑稽的，逗趣的
drenching [ˈdrentʃiŋ]	n. 湿透
mesmerize [ˈmezməraiz]	v. 施催眠术
connote [kɔˈnəut]	v. 别有含意，意味着
evanescence [ˌiːvəˈnesns]	n. 逐渐消失，幻灭
temporality [ˌtempəˈræliti]	n. 暂时性
agrarian [əˈgrɛəriən]	adj. 有关土地的，耕地的
bounty [ˈbaunti]	n. 慷慨；施与

KEY CONCEPTS

Italian Renaissance garden
Blvedere
Vatican Palace
Sculpture garden
villa
ancient Roman landscape planning
central court
water staircases
axis
symmetry

NOTES

1. Pliny the Younger

　　（小）普林尼(61-112?)罗马作家，以其9卷描述罗马帝国社会生活和私人生活的信札著称。

Part II *History of Landscape Architecture*

2. Petrarch

彼特拉克(1304～1374，意大利诗人，学者、欧洲人文主义运动的主要代表)

3. Encouraged by his reading of Pliny the Younger, Petrarch's first somewhat tentative embrace of panoramic perspective on Mont Ventoux heralded the scenic appreciation that would later become a hallmark of Renaissance thought.

通过阅读(小)普林尼的作品而受到鼓舞，彼特拉克首开先河地试图在蒙特文特克斯运用包含全景透视的(手法)来传达对风景的欣赏，这后来成为文艺复兴思想的主要特点。

4. Alberti Leon Battista

阿尔伯蒂(1401～1472)，意大利艺术家、文艺理论家、建筑师，还从事数学、制图和密码学研究，著有《论绘画》、《建筑十书》等。

5. Michelangelo

米开朗琪罗(1475～1564)意大利文艺复兴盛期雕刻家、画家、建筑师和诗人，主要作品有雕像《大卫》、《摩西》、壁画《最后的审判》；罗马圣彼得大教堂圆顶等。

6. Clement Ⅶ

克雷芒七世(1478～1543)，意大利籍教皇(1523～1534)，与法兰西结盟，反对神圣罗马帝国皇帝查理五世，在面临宗教改革运动时，持比较开明的立场。

7. Raphael

拉斐尔(1483～1520，意大利画家、建筑学家。主要作品有梵蒂冈宫中壁画《圣礼的辩论》、《雅典学派》等。

8. Giulio Romano

朱利奥·罗马诺(1499?～1546)意大利文艺复兴晚期画家和建筑家，拉斐尔的学生，风格主义的奠基人之一。

9. Baldassare Peruzzi

佩鲁奇(1481～1536)，意大利文艺复兴盛期建筑家、画家，主要作品有罗马的法尔内塞行宫等。

QUESTIONS FOR REVIEW AND DISCUSSION

1. How significant was Bramante's axial terraced composition in the history of European garden design?
2. What is the meaning of "Belvedere" in Italian word?
3. Describe the Italian Belvedere Court.
4. Who was the designer of the Villa Madama? Give some examples of his art works.
5. Identify the most important design element of Italian gardens in sixteenth-century.

Reading Material
Axial Planning on an Urban Scale: The Development of Renaissance Rome

PLAN OF SIXTUS V[1]

Although unsurpassed as urban scenography, the Campidoglio and the Via Pia, with their artfully framed vistas, represent a piecemeal approach to city planning. Uniting the city's streets into a well-articulated circulation system and composing its alreday extraordinary existing landmarks into a series of views worthy of Rome's growing reputation as a tourist destination, required a comprehensive vision and forceful leadership for its realization. A visionary leader presented himself in late-sixteenth-century Rome in the person of Sixtus V (papacy 1585～1590). Indeed, all previous efforts to improve the cityscape of Rome were but overtures to the great symphony of urban improvements that was orchestrated during the short Sistine papal term.

Born of Dalmatian peasant stock, the great future pope of the Counter Reformation, Felice Peretti, rose through the ranks of the Church to become Cardinal Montalto, building the Villa Montalto with the revenues that went with his elevation to high office. There he nurtured his plans during the thirteen years of Gregory XIII's[2] papacy. Located in the developing eastern suburb of the settled city at the base of the Esquiline Hill on the site of the present railway station, the Villa Montalto later became the hub of a bold urban design. This plan, which Felice commissioned from the architect and engineer Domenico Fontana (1543～1607)[3] as soon as he was elevated to the papacy, carried the urbanization of Rome to the boundaries of its ancient walls and even, where possible, beyond. No contemporary drawing exists for Fontana's master plan of Rome, but a dramatic, if somewhat inaccurate, bird's-eye rendering of it in fresco decorates one of the walls of the Vatican Library. The web of long arrow-straight thoroughfares had important significance within the context of the Counter-Reformation: linking the Colosseum, the Pantheon, the Forum and other prominent monuments of ancient Rome and, more importantly, its seven major churches, with one another, they inscribed on the face of the ancient city a highly visible itinerary of tourism and pilgrimage that served to enhance its prestige as the original and continuing center of the Catholic Church.

Not since the days of the Roman chariots had equally smooth, wide, and regular urban arteries been built. Moreover, they were to be paved in order to facilitate the movement of the newly invented springsuspension carriage. As yet, there were no sidewalks,

---

选自　Elizabeth Barlow Rogers Landscape Design: A Cultural and Architecture History Harry N. Abrams, INC, Publishers

and pedestrians and vehicles occupied the same street space. The word *corso*, signifying a principal thoroughfare, assumed new meaning in Rome as carriage driving became a fashionable recreation for the upper echelon of society. The Via Pia, the longest straight road built to that date, bore daily witness to Rome's pre-eminence as the world's first city to accommodate these new vehicles in large numbers. Rome indeed was experiencing another modern urban "first": traffic congestion. The cardinals and their immense ecclesiastical retinues, the dignitaries of the embassies from other countries now posted to Rome, the courtesans, the tens of thousands of pilgrims who came every year, the tourist contingent newly awakened to the wonders of the classical past, the foreign artists and artisans—all these thronged the city, congesting its narrow medieval byways and crowding its new thoroughfares. The long-slumbering metropolis was once again lively as horses, carriages, cattle, and pedestrians jostled one another in the burgeoning cosmopolitan setting.

But more than roads were needed to facilitate transportation and stimulate the regrowth of Rome. It was necessary to reconstruct the ancient aqueducts if the untenanted, ruin-studded stretches of the city were to be repopulated. Other popes had begun this process, but none had solved the problem of carrying water to the heights of Rome's famed hills. That was the assignment Sixtus V set for himself, and within only eighteen months, the plan he had nurtured for the Acqua Felice(so named because of the pope's first name, Felice)came to fruition with the completion of a conduit spanning 7 miles of overhead arches and 7 miles of underground tunnels. Its successful opening brought water to the Villa Montalto in 1586 and three years later to twenty-seven public fountains located throughout Rome. Utilitarian at first, many of these were later transformed into the ornamental fountains for which Rome has remained famous.

The Acqua Felice also made possible the construction of a public laundry beside the Baths of Diocletian. And where the already reactivated Acqua Vergine brought water to the site of the present Fountain of Trevi, Sixtus V installed a basin for the washing of wool.[4] With the water problem solved and the nexus of the new street system located in the area where he owned property, he was in a position to gain financially from his program of public works.

As a landscape designer working at a city-planning scale with a visionary patron, Fontana proved his talent in engineering and urban scenography. Together pope and architect created the skeleton of modern Rome, a circulation network of interconnecting streets and focal points, the whole comprising a series of vista corridors punctuated with landmarks old and new. As with the Acqua Felice, Sixtus V bestowed his name on the longest and most important of these unifying thoroughfares, the Strada Felice. This avenue connected Santa Maria Maggiore with Santa Trinità dei Monti on the brow of the Pincio Hill. A final stretch downhill to the Piazza del popolo was never constructed, and the Spanish Steps linking Santa Trinità with the Corso below were not built until the eighteenth century. But the Strada Felice's extension on the other side of Santa Maria Maggiore all the way to Santa Croce in Gerusalemme was carried out, thereby creating a straight span of about 2 miles across the breadth of Rome. Intersecting the Strada Felice at almost a right angle was Michelangelo's Via Pia, the two creating a symbolical cross, referred to as the "*bellissima croce.*"

In the fresco of the Rome of Sixtus V one sees the impulse to untangle the tortuous labyrinth of medieval Rome with the Strada Felice and other roads slashing across the built and as-yet-unbuilt landscape. One also sees the celebration of Rome's incomparable history through the new prominence given to its landmarks. In addition to the pilgrimage churches, the Colosseum and the Columns of Marcus Aurelius[5] and Trajan[6] are focal points of the plan. To set these off, Sixtus V removed the structures around them and regularized the building lines of those remaining to form squares. Elsewhere he created new squares. Fontana and his patron hit upon the happy idea of resurrecting several of the old Egyptian obelisks, exotic souvenirs of ancient campaigns, which had long ago toppled here and there about the city, and using them as markers to center space or temporarily arrest the eye and punctuate its journey along a vista corridor.

The 82-foot-tall obelisk marking Nero's racetrack near St. Peter's had, remarkably, remained standing throughout the Middle Ages next to the south side of the church. Fontana directed the feat of moving this 320-ton monument to its present position in front of St. Peter's, thus defining the center of the ovoid piazza, which Bernini[7] later embraced with his great curving fourfold colonnades. Fontana had the obelisk lying in the Circus Maximus erected in the center of the space that became the Piazza del Popolo, giving focus to its converging trident of new streets. Two more obelisks were set up along the Strada Felice, one at its midpoint in front of Santa Maria Maggiore, the other at its southeastern terminus in front of Santa Croce in Gerusalemme. To incorporate them into the religious symbolism of the Counter-Reformation's triumphant Catholicism, the pope had each of the four Sistine obelisks surmounted with a globe bearing a cross. Thus, an ancient Egyptian form, developed to stand in sentinel pairs at tomb entrances, became an isolated freestanding object centering urban open space, a felicitous borrowing that would be copied in other times in other lands, often without the Church's triumphant cross.

Sixteenth-century Italian landscape design not only manifested the humanists' interest in reviving ancient forms and themes, but it also served as a means of asserting prestige and displaying wealth and power. The same humanist iconographies into which were encoded messages of family and personal pride within a garden setting could be applied on an urban scale to proclaim the power of the Church or of a ruler. The garden, in effect, served as a design studio wherein problems of axial layout and scenography were solved in ways that were simultaneously applied to city planning. For example, Fontana's development of the triangular piazza in front of Pope Sixtus V's Villa Montalto as a garden *trivio* with three avenues radiating outward from an open space near the Church of Santa Maria Maggiore, in a manner that both ennobled the entrance to the *casino* and suggested the breadth of the gardens behind it, shows how closely connected were the principles of landscape design within and without the garden.

This means of stabilizing architectural forms in relationship to a particular setting and suggesting territorial possession through spatial extension, developed here as part of Fontana's plan for the villa, became a widely used device wherever monumental planning occurred. Fontana's role as city planner is thus pivotal. He conceived the design of the Villa Montalto's *trivio* within the comprehensive frame of cityscape. By linking it and other radial compositions of axes, such as those emanating from the *trivio* at the Piazza del Popolo, to form a transurban network, he created a plan for an entire city, something that had not occurred in the West since ancient Roman times and then only for colonial cities and not the capital.

As the unification of garden space through axial layout became increasingly the objective of garden designers in the seventeenth century, their royal employers saw the symbolic value of reordering old cities and building new ones according to the same principles. It is not surprising that these principles, which served effectively as a spatial metaphor for princely grandeur and dominion, were eagerly absorbed by ambitious monarchs elsewhere, notably in France. However, before the lessons of Sixtus V's plan were applied in an urban setting in that country in the early seventeenth century during the reign of Henry IV (ruled 1589~1610), a gradual process of replacing French medievalism with the new Renaissance style imported from Italy had necessarily ensued. This stylistic evolution, begun in the Loire Valley, reflected the political relations between the two countries over the course of the sixteenth century as Italian influence in France alternated with the development of an independent French Renaissance style.

WORDS AND EXPRESSIONS

Sistine ['sistain, 'sisti:n]	*adj.*	西克斯图斯(罗马教皇)的
unsurpassed [,ʌnsə(:)'pa:st]	*adj.*	未被凌驾的,非常卓越的
scenography [si:'nɔgrəfi]	*n.*	透视法,配景图法
vista ['vistə]	*n.*	狭长的景色;街景;深景(尤指人透过如两排建筑或树木之间空隙看到的远景或视觉感受)
piecemeal ['pi:smi:l]	*adj.*	一件件的;一个个的;零碎的
visionary ['viʒənəri:(US)'viʒəneri]	*adj.*	有远见的;有洞察力的
overture ['əuvətjuə]	*n.*	提议;建议
symphony ['simfəni]	*n.*	交响乐,交响曲;和谐(的东西)
orchestrate ['ɔ:kistreit, -kes-]	*v.*	编管弦乐曲;使…协调地结合在一起
nurture ['nə:tʃə]	*vt.*	培养;教育;发展
hub [hʌb]	*n.*	中心;焦点
rendering ['rendəriŋ]	*n.*	透视图;示意图

LESSON 4

thoroughfare [ˈθʌrəfɛə]	n. 通路，大道
Colosseum [ˌkɔləˈsiəm]	n. 罗马大角斗场
Pantheon [pænˈθi(:)ən]	n. (古希腊、罗马供奉众神的)万神殿(罗马一圆顶庙宇，建于公元120～124)
forum	n. 古罗马城镇的广场(或市场)，论坛，法庭，讨论会
chariot [ˈtʃæriət]	n. 敞篷双轮马车(古时用于战争或竞赛)
echelon [ˈeʃəlɔn]	n. 等级，阶层
ecclesiastical [iˌkli:ziˈæstikl]	adj. 教会的，牧师的，神职的
contingent [kənˈtindʒənt]	n. 参加某集会的一批具有某共同点的人；代表团
throng [θrɔŋ]	v. 群集；挤进；塞满
slumber [ˈslʌmbə]	n. 不活跃或休眠的状态
	v. 睡眠；处于休眠的或静止的
jostle [ˈdʒɔsl]	v. 挤，推，撞
cosmopolitan [ˌkɔzməˈpɔlitən]	n. 四海为家的人，世界主义者
	adj. 世界性的
aqueduct [ˈækwidʌkt]	n. 沟渠，导水管
untenanted [ˌʌnˈtenəntid]	adj. 无人租赁的，未被租用的，未被租赁者占用的
famed [feimd]	adj. 著名的，闻名的
fruition [fru(:)ˈiʃən]	n. (希望、计划等的)实现；完成
conduit [ˈkɔndit]	n. 管道，导管，沟渠
laundry [ˈlɔ:ndri]	n. 洗衣店
bestow [biˈstəu]	v. 给予；赐赠
brow [brau]	n. 脊；(山的)坡顶；(悬崖的)边缘
intersect [ˌintəˈsekt]	v. 贯穿；横切；和……交叉
right [rait]	adj. 垂直的，直角的
untangle [ˈʌnˈtæŋgl]	v. 解开
tortuous [ˈtɔ:tjuəs]	adj. 曲折的，复杂的
labyrinth [ˈlæbərinθ]	n. 迷宫，错综复杂
slash [slæʃ]	v. 猛砍，乱砍(通过有力的、彻底的打击来切割或形成)
resurrect [ˌrezəˈrekt]	v. 复兴；恢复实施、受注意或重新起用
obelisk [ˈɔbilisk]	n. [建] 方尖碑
exotic [igˈzɔtik]	adj. 外来的
souvenir [ˈsu:vəniə]	n. 纪念品，纪念物
topple [ˈtɔpl]	v. 倒下；倾覆
ovoid [ˈəuvɔid]	adj. 卵形的
piazza [piˈætsə]	n. 广场，走廊，露天市场
colonnade [ˌkɔləˈneid]	n. 柱廊
converge [kənˈvə:dʒ]	v. (使)集中于一点；(使)会聚

Part II *History of Landscape Architecture*

trident [ˈtraidənt]	n. 三角叉
sentinel [ˈsentinl]	n. 哨兵
freestanding [ˈfriːstændiŋ]	adj. 独立式的，不需依靠支撑物的
felicitous [fəˈlisitəs]	adj. 适当的；得体的
pivotal [ˈpivətəl]	adj. 枢轴的，关键的
emanate [ˈeməneit]	v. 散发，发出，发源
metaphor [ˈmetəfə]	n. 隐喻，象征
ensue [inˈsjuː]	v. 跟着发生，继起

NOTES

1. Sixtus V

    西克斯图斯五世(1520～1590)，意大利籍教皇，整顿教廷中央行政机构，进行反宗教改革运动。

2. Gregory XIII

    格列高利十三世(1502～1585)意大利籍教皇，整顿天主教会，推进反宗教改革运动。

3. Domenico Fontana

    丰塔纳(1543～1607)，意大利建筑师，设计了梵蒂冈图书馆(1587～1590)、水乐宫(1587)等，并将公元1世纪时运至罗马的埃及方尖碑从梵蒂冈的广场移至圣彼德大教堂前(1586)。

4. 为了通过丝绸和羊毛布匹生产刺激罗马经济，Sixtus 五世颁布了一项法律，要求大范围种植桑树并且在罗马大剧场内建立一座羊毛纺织厂，这个项目因为他的去世而被搁置。

5. Marcus Aurelius

    马可·奥勒利乌斯(121～180)罗马皇帝，新斯多葛派哲学的主要代表，宣扬禁欲主义和宿命论，著有《自省录》12篇。

6. Trajan

    图拉真(53？～117)古罗马皇帝，改革财政，加强集权统治，大兴土木，修建城市、港口、道路和桥梁。

7. Bernini

    伯尔尼尼，意大利建筑家、雕塑家和画家。巴洛克艺术风格的代表人物。

FRANCE LANDSCAPE DESIGN: SIXTEENTH AND SEVENTEENTH CENTURIES

The Paris basin comprehended the Seine and the Loire and was a natural geographical unit. This focusing on Paris was largely responsible for the centralization so characteristic of French life and history. Similarly, all French classical landscape was focused upon this one unit, for the Loire, with its subsidiary capital at Orléans, was the romantic complement to the Seine. The scenery of the basin as a whole was one of peaceful undulating corn-lands interspersed with cathedral or market towns, with here and there a château set in its canalized moat. Near Paris there were hardwood forests criss-crossed with straight rides for hunting. The climate was Atlantic-European with an average annual rainfall of twenty-four inches and a summer warm enough for vines. Paris itself was a densely populated and thriving city set on lines of continental communications, reshaped in the second half of the sixteenth century by the change of royal residence from the Île de France. Established in the Louvre (original royal residence c.1400) and the Tuileries, the monarchy thenceforth never ceased to be attracted towards the west. In the Touraine lay the source of all the splendid water conceptions of seventeenth-century France.

In 1453 the English were practically expelled from French soil; France emerged as a united nation; and Charles VIII, invading Italy in 1495, experienced the first flush of the Renaissance. Francis I (r.1515~47) obtained parity of power with Spain, and became the first French king to rule 'au bon plaisir'. Cultivated, elegant and appreciative of the Italian Renaissance, Francis invited eminent Italian artists and craftsmen to his court at Amboise on the Loire; among these were Vignola and Leonardo da Vinci. Following a period of instability, Cardinal Richelieu(1585~1642)[1] came to power under Louis VIII (r.1610~43) and virtually ruled France from 1624 to 1642, overcoming internal disorders rising from the Reformation, promoting national security abroad, and ruthlessly establishing the foundations of an absolute monarchy. On this basis Louis XIV (1661~1715) ruled for fifty years, shrewdly and efficiently, enlarging French influence abroad to become the dominant power in Europe, encouraging the arts and sciences at home, and creating in his Court at Versailles a civilization of pleasure that has had no equal. The vast expenditure

---

选自　Geoffrey Jellicoe, Susan Jellicoe. The Landscape of Man: Shaping the Environment from Prehistory to the Present Day, Thames & Hudson 1995

Part II History of Landscape Architecture

involved was met by taxation from which the nobility and the Church were exempt, an injustice that led to the French Revolution in 1789.

Civilization as expressed by the monarchy was superficially one of delightful materialism. In this it differed from that of Italy, where there had always existed a passionate desire that art should convey something of the unknown world that lay beyond the senses. In contemporary France this was not so apparent: civilization centred upon the Sun King and the arts were in principle expressive of the pleasures of living. The acceptance and support by the public of such a monarchy at such a time was only possible because the majority still remained docilely Catholic. The Papacy itself was in general friendly to the French becoming an agreeable instrument of policy. The philosopher whose theories were studied and put into practice, especially by Richelieu, was the Florentine Machiavelli: that princes were absolute, and that to ensure this the end justified the means. Light writers such as Molière (1622~1673)[2], were encouraged, provided they were in accord with the régime. Beneath this facade of uniformity, concern for moral values was expressed by Jansenism(Cornelius Jansen, 1585~1638).[3] Blaise Pascal(1623~1662),[4] natural philosopher and mathematician, evolved the transformation of geometrical figures by conical and optical projection, and may thus have encouraged the three-dimensional geometry of Le Nôtre. The great original French philosopher of the period was Descartes(1596~1650), who settled in more liberal Holland.

Few churches were built, the energy being directed towards new country estates for monarch and nobility. The sixteenth century saw the creation in the Loire Valley of an almost total romantic water landscape stretching for over a hundred miles. Thereafter classicism gained control, great country layouts becoming more ordered and symmetrical. Cardinal Richelieu laid out perhaps the first domestic landscape design to comprehend a whole new town, named after himself. Influence continued to filter through from Italy but there was no daring innovation in space design until Vaux-le-Vicomte[5] and the advent of Le Nôtre(1613~1700). His brief for the grand country-house was simple: to organize the landscape into one mighty scene that would express the dignity and elegance of man and delight his senses. All nature should conform. The supreme moments were those of carnival, with barges on the canals, fireworks and countless guests in the gardens. The concept of comprehensive landscape-planning, apparent at Richelieu, was fully realized in the gardens, palace and town of Versailles, which came to symbolize the power of a united nation.

Sixteenth-century architecture grew from French Gothic with Italian grafted upon it. The moated château gave rise to an imaginative water relationship from which sprang Chenonceau(1515)and later inspired both moated house and independent canal at Vaux-le-Vicomte(1661). Gothic gave way to classic about 1600 but the spirit within was that of monarchist France rather than Italian Baroque.[6] It is not surprising that Bernini's design for the Louvre in 1665 was rejected; although reliant upon environment, Italian Baroque architecture was still violently individual. In France the tendency to wards total space organization made the individual building subservient to the whole. The French grouping of buildings might be likened to a military parade where all ranks were properly positioned and moved only on instruction; the Italian to a fashionable party, where eloquent and not so eloquent were in common medley and movement. This concept of the ordered assembly of buildings transformed Paris and inspired town-planning until the present century. It created the vast idea of town, palace and gardens of Versailles whose unity was subsequently impaired by the architect Hardouin-Mansart(1646～1708),[7] apparently unappreciative of the composition as a whole.

Fig. 1   Vaux-Le-Vicomte, Designed by Le Nôtre. 1656～1661

André Le Nôtre revolutionized French garden design, abolishing the idea of compartments and substituting that of totally organized space. The principles of composition were simple: (a)the garden no longer to be a mere extension of the house, which itself became part only of a great land composition; (b)solid as opposed to two-dimensional geometry based on axiality, related to an undulating site; (c)shape as though carved out of ordered woodlands and crisply defined by *charmilles*(clipped hedges); (d)the Baroque quality of unity with sky and surroundings achieved by water reflection and avenues leading indefinitely outwards; (e)the scale expanding as it receded from the house; (f)sculpture and fountains, themselves works of art, to provide rhythm and punctuate space; (g)the science of optics to direct the eye firmly without power to roam, and illusionist devices to make distance seem nearer or further; (h)the apparent revelation of the whole project in a glance, and the later element of surprise and contrast mainly in intimate woodlands; (i) the disposal of all parts, and especially of steps and stairways, for the dignity and enhancement of persons in movement; their scale to be larger than life, and thus to give a sense of being within an heroic landscape of the gods.

Part II   History of Landscape Architecture

   Marie de Médicis married Henry IV in 1600, giving a superficial impetus to Italian influence upon French culture. A comparison between the form of the Boboli Gardens, her home in Florence, and the Luxembourg Gardens shows a nostalgic similarity. The detail, however, was original and French. The compartments de broderie, for instance, were first introduced here by Boyceau (d. 1638), executed in box, flowers and coloured sands. Cardinal Richelieu(1585~1642), on the other hand, who unified France and laid the foundations of absolute monarchy, ushered in a new and pure French concept of comprehensive planning and space design. The landscape of the Château de Richelieu in Touraine was a unified design carved out of woods, with decorative canals arising from drainage, and inclusive of a town as a subsidiary element. The concept, designed 1627~37 by J. Le Mercier, prepared the way for the work of Le Nôtre.

   Vaux-Le-Vicomte, completed 1661 for Fouquet, Finance Minister of Louis XIV, was the first major work of André Le Nôtre. The predecessor of both château (Le Vau, architect) and landscape was Richelieu, whose simple conception of space was transformed by Le Nôtre into an accomplished work of art. In principle, a single woodland compartment of gently falling and rising land has been sculptured to present at a glance a majestic scene of ground architecture. Apart from the skilful proportioning and subdivision by cross axes that disappear into the woods, and the rich carpeting, the design develops two important new principles: (a) architecture is secondary to landscape architecture and the scale expands outwards from the buildings to become heroic rather than domestic; and (b) the element of surprise withholds the grandest single feature, the sunk canal, from the first glance.

   At chantilly le nôtre carried his principles a stage further than at Vaux. The original site comprised an old castle, triangular in plan, surrounded by a lake, without any conscious shaping of the landscape. Le Nôtre's plan created a new main axis, but unlike Vaux did not feature the house as the central accent; here the castle has become secondary. A canal, similar to that of Vaux but even larger in dimensions, is again placed at right angles to the axis, but there is no element of surprise. Water embraces both castle and parterre gardens, and the project is primarily one of the spectacle of water pageantry. The scale of Le Nôtre's layout, as can be seen in the air view, is vast in relation to the historic castle. The two elements-castle and axis-are linked by the equestrian statue of the Grand Condé, for whom it was built. Looking south, one sees the canal in the foreground, the statue above its flight of steps in the middle distance; the vista is closed by the avenue approach.

   Although versailles was the culmination of the work of Le Nôtre, greatly exceeding Vaux and Chantilly in magnificence, it suffered from a late change in the shape of the palace which proved harmful to the concept of château, town and gardens as a single unit of landscape architecture. The process of evolution was as follows. A relatively modest hunting lodge was begun in 1624 for Louis XIII. This was reconstructed after 1661 by Louis XIV; the painting by Patel(c. 1668) shows that service wings have been added to the original moated château and that Le Nôtre has developed the main lines of the layout. In 1669 the

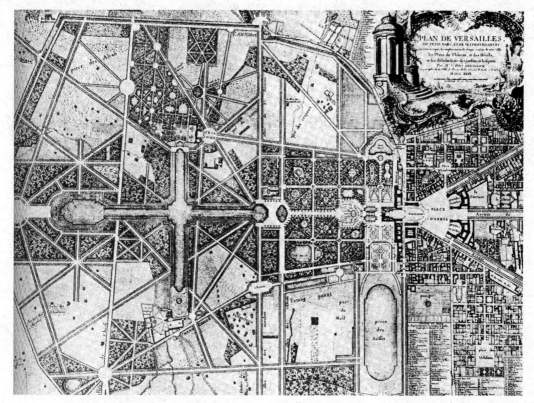

Fig. 2

moated château was embedded in a new front by Le Vau. In 1678 Hardouin-Mansart displaced Le Vau as architect, closed the central elevational recess and added the enormous wings. The plan of the palace reconstructs the stages. The plan of 1746 made by the Abbé Delagrive shows Versailles as completed by Le Nôtre before 1700.

The most splendid expression of absolute monarchy in history: from the palace of Versailles, the distance passes into infinity. The shape is defined by trees and punctuated by sculpture seen against the clipped *charmilles* or hedges. The smaller views show the grand canal across the fountain of Apollo, seen from the *tapis vert*; the fountain of Apollo in play against the light; and the cross canal from the Grand Trianon. Secretly within the woodlands are garden features that were in constant change, among them the water colonnade by Mansart, the obelisk fountain and the children's fountain, behind which is seen a *charmille* in the making. Schools of open-air sculpture and fountain design ensured a consistent standard of detail that has never been surpassed in landscape.

WORDS AND EXPRESSIONS

Loire [lwa:]   n. 卢瓦尔河［法国中部］（或译罗亚尔河，发源于塞文山脉，经中央高原，西流注入大西洋的比斯开湾，是

Part II *History of Landscape Architecture*

	法国最长的河流）
subsidiary [səˈsidjəri]	*adj.* 辅助的，补充的
Orleans [ɔːˈliənz, ˈɔːl-]	奥尔良（法国中部城市）
undulate [ˈʌndjuleit]	*v.* 波动，起伏，成波浪形
	adj. 波浪形的，起伏的
château [ˈʃɑːtəu]	*n.* 城堡
crisscross [ˈkriskrɔs]	*n.* 十字形
	adj. 十字形的
thrive [θraiv]	*v.* 兴旺，繁荣，茁壮成长，旺盛
monarchy [ˈmɔnəki]	*n.* 君主政体，君主政治，君主国
thenceforth [ˌðensˈfɔːθ]	*adv.* 从那时，其后
expel [iksˈpel]	*v.* 驱逐，开除，排出，发射
shrewdly [ˈʃruːdli]	*ad.* 机灵地
Versailles [vɛəˈsai, vəˈseilz]	*n.* 凡尔赛（法国北部城市），凡尔赛宫
exempt [igˈzempt]	*v.* 免除
	adj. 被免除的
superficially [ˌsjuːpəˈfiʃəli]	*adv.* 表面地，浅薄地
passionate [ˈpæʃənit]	*adj.* 充满热情的
docilely [ˈdəusaili]	*adv.* 听话地，驯良地
Machiavelli [ˌmækiəˈveli]	*n.* 马基雅弗利（意大利新兴资产阶级思想政治家，历史学家）
regime [reiˈʒiːm]	*n.* 政体；政权；政权制度
conical [ˈkɔnikəl]	*adj.* 圆锥的，圆锥形的
Le Nôtre	*n.* 勒诺特尔（1613～1700），法国17世纪著名造园师
Descartes [deiˈkɑːt, dɛkart]	*n.* 笛卡尔（法国哲学家、数学家，1596～1690）
mighty [ˈmaiti]	*n.* 有势力的人
	adj. 有势力的，强大的
	adv. 很，极，非常
carnival [ˈkɑːnivəl]	*n.* 狂欢节，饮宴狂欢
graft [grɑːft]	*n.* 嫁接，（接枝用的）嫩枝
	v. 嫁接，接枝，移植（皮肤等）
moat [məut]	*n.* 护城河，城壕
	v. 挖壕围绕
eloquent [ˈeləkwənt]	*adj.* 雄辩的，有口才的
crisply [ˈkrispli]	*adv.* 易碎地，清楚地
dignity [ˈdigniti]	*n.* 尊严，高贵
Luxembourg [ˈluksəmˌbəːg]	*n.* 卢森堡公国（西欧国家）
Fontainebleau [ˈfɔntinbləu]	*n.* 枫丹白露［法国北部城镇］（在巴黎东南，有著名的宫殿）

majestic [məˈdʒestik]   adj. 宏伟的，庄严的

KEY CONCEPTS

French garden style
Parterre garden
Axial allées
French Gothic
Italian Baroque
Versailles
château
monarchy

NOTES

1. Richelieu [ˈrɪʃəluː]
   黎塞留（1585～1642），法国王路易十三的国务秘书兼御前会议主席、枢机主教，擅权巩固专制统治，镇压贵族叛乱和农民起义，对外参加三十年战争，扩张法国势力。
2. Molière [ˈmɔliɛə]
   莫里哀（1622～1673），法国著名剧作家，演员，首创法国现实主义喜剧和喜剧的新风格。
3. Jansenism [ˈdʒænsənIzəm] 宗］
   詹森主义（17世纪天主教詹森教派的神学主张，认为人性由于原罪而败坏，人若没有上帝恩宠便为肉欲所摆布而不能行善避恶）。
4. Pascal [ˈpæskəl]
   帕斯卡（Blaise，1623～1662，法国数学家、物理学家、哲学家，概率论创立者之一。著有《思想录》等）。
5. Vaux-le-Vicomte
   沃-勒-维贡特府邸花园，园主为尼古拉·福开（Nicolas Fouquet）。勒诺特尔的成名作。
6. Gothic gave way to classic about 1600 but the spirit within was that of monarchist France rather than Italian Baroque.
   在1600年代哥特主义让位于古典主义，但其内在思想却是法国的君主制思想而非意大利的巴洛克风格。
7. Hardouin-Mansart
   n. 芒萨尔（1646～1708），法国宫廷建筑师和城市规划师，负责凡尔赛宫的重建、扩建工程，规划巴黎旺多姆广场和胜利广场。

Part II History of Landscape Architecture

QUESTIONS FOR REVIEW AND DISCUSSION

1. Describe the geographical characteristics of Paris basin.
2. What were the impacts of Charles VIII invading Italy on the French culture?
3. Who was the designer of the VAUX-LE-VICOMTE ? Describe his main design principles.
4. Discuss the Baroque style of Le Nôtre's works.
5. What unique environmental factors led to different development of garden forms in the French and Italian Renaissance gardens?

Reading Material

Power and Glory: The Genius of Le Nôtre and The Grandeur of The Baroque[1]

In seventeenth-century France, the nature of monarchy changed in a functional way. Feudal kings in the late Middle Ages had traveled with their retinues, holding court in castles scattered throughout their kingdoms or enjoying the hospitality of vassal lords. The Renaissance princes of the fifteenth and sixteenth centuries were peripatetic, enjoying the pleasures of the hunt in several royal forests and performing affairs of state while entertaining in the *châteaux* of the Loire Valley and the Île de France. It was not until the rule of Louis XIV (ruled 1643-1715) that this situation changed. Although the king and his retinue traveled to various royal seats—Fontainebleau, Saint-Germain-en-Laye, Chambord, and, later, Marly—residing in these for considerable periods of time, the court of France increasingly revolved in the orbit of Versailles, as Louis's attachment to his father's old hunting lodge and his determination to make it the radiant center and symbol of his reign grew. It was here that a distinctive style expressing authoritarian order and elegant rationality matured.

This style might never have gained pre-eminence as an international design idiom had not Louis XIV heeded Cardinal Jules Mazarin's deathbed recommendation and appointed Jean-Baptiste Colbert(1619~1683)as his finance minister. Colbert soon reformed the system of taxation, making it more honest, and during the first part of the king's long reign, Colbert's brilliant reorganization of finance and industry increased the prosperity of France. Louis was able during most of his reign to enjoy its benefits and turn them to both personal and national advantage.

Through the elevation of all the arts to new heights of excellence, as well as through astute political diplomacy, Louis XIV established France as the leading power in Europe, making it a great state and also the exemplar of style. Both Colbert and the king understood well the role that all the arts, especially the fine arts—architecture, painting, and sculpture—would play in that process. Colbert belonged to the prestigious Académie Française, established by Cardinal Richelieu and incorporated in 1635, and was instrumental in founding several academies for the advancement of the arts and sciences. The establishment of these ushered in an era of important building projects sponsored by the king[2].

The king gave dance, music, and theater new dignity and status. He founded the Académie Royale de Danse in 1661, and the Académie Royale de Musique(the Paris Opera)

选自 Elizabeth Barlow Rogers Landscape Design: A Cultural and Architecture History Harry N. Abrams, LNC, Publishers

in 1669. Molière's troupe of actors was the precursor of the Comédie Française, which was officially chartered by the king in 1680. Louis himself was a dancer and performed in several ballets in his youth. Thus, Louis over the years, with the assistance of Colbert, supported and institutionalized the diverse talents that were responsible for forging a rich and sophisticated culture within which the French seventeenth-century style flourished as a powerful political and social statement and tangible manifestation of the power and glory of monarchy.

We have seen how readily the French appropriated the idiom of the Italian Renaissance and how thoroughly they transformed it into a style with a distinctly French inflection. Building upon this French Renaissance style, the architects and planners who served Louis XIV now took inspiration from contemporary Italian Baroque art and architecture, adapting it into yet another distinctive style. It is a style of sober grandeur, which is differentiated from the robust plasticity and exuberant theatricality of its Italian models by its linear elegance and by the application of mathematical principles to produce designs of eminent rationality.

There was a moment, however, at the beginning of the young king's reign when this outcome may have been in doubt. Colbert understood that work on the unfinished Louvre Palace should be recommenced as a first major building project of the new regime. In 1665, displeased with the plans submitted by French architects, he summoned to Paris the distinguished Italian architect and sculptor Gianlorenzo Bernini(1598~1680)in order to commission a design that would glorify the young king with the same kind of dynamic, robustly theatrical architecture that Bernini had brought to papal Rome. But the Italian's three proposals, vast in scale, would have demolished the existing palace. His solution, moreover, although also neoclassical in its inspiration, would have taken French architectural aesthetics in a dynamically Baroque direction rather than the more chaste one advocated by the king's advisors.

Louis, ceding to Colbert's counsel after several months of consideration, dismissed Bernini's proposals and put the problem in the hands of a committee consisting of Claude Perrault(1613~1688), an expert on the architecture of antiquity, the architect Louis Le Vau(1612~1670), and the painter Charles Le Brun(1619~1690). The East Front of the Louvre, which represents the solution their collaboration produced, has a central Roman-style pavilion, colonnaded wings with paired columns, and symmetrical pavilions at each end. The whole architectural composition is upheld by a ground-floor podium. In choosing an architectural vocabulary that directly linked Louis XIV symbolically with the might of imperial Rome, especially with the cool Olympian grandeur of the classicizing styles of emperors Augustus and Hadrian, the Louvre design committee substituted its own brand of neoclassicism for that of the Italian Baroque. Even though the architects who worked for Louis used such Italian Baroque forms as high domes and curving walls with verve and skill, the path of austere grandeur that is represented by the term *French classicism* is one that they never relinquished, and the Baroque elements that they did appropriate were submitted to its firm authority.

Except for the Louvre and a few other projects, Louis XIV, unlike Henry IV, took only a secondary interest in beautifying the capital, concentrating instead upon making the palace and gardens of Versailles into a cynosure of universal renown. That he was able to accomplish this astonishing feat is due not only to the circumstances of patronage that he and Colbert established but also to the presence of genius at his side. That genius belonged to a remarkable generation of French designers, in the front rank of whom stood André Le Nôtre(1613~1700), a man who throughout his long life was honored to bear the title of king's gardener.

In Le Nôtre's hands, Renaissance garden style—which we today frequently characterize as "formal"—assumed a new scale and, as it did so, forsook small-scale compartmentalization and intricate effects in favor of unified spatial composition and monumentality expressive of the evolving French style of regal grandeur in landscape terms. Formal order was made to merge with nature, and boundaries appeared to dissolve into distant prospects. The walled gardens of Catherine de Médicis, though large by Renaissance standards, were suddenly dwarfed by the dimensions of the new gardens. The former are composed of axially arranged, visibly contained spaces, inwardly focused and walled, whereas the latter are commensurate with their illusion of limitlessness—that is, large enough to have distant and generally imperceptible boundaries and axes that carry the eye to the horizon line.

This illusion of indeterminate axial extension provides a landscape analogue to the spatial concepts of René Descartes(1596~1650), the French philosopher, mathematician, and founder of analytical geometry. Descartes believed that starting from skepticism the human intellect could comprehend the mathematical principles underlying God's creation. His rigorous methodology viewed the natural world in mechanistic terms, as objectively measurable. With Descartes, the scientific enterprise itself became boundless, and this new mode of open-ended inquiry helped establish fresh cosmological premises. The seventeenth-century cosmology, which Descartes's philosophy synthesized, provided the groundwork for modern physics. Descartes built his cosmology on that of the German astronomer, physicist, and mathematician Johannes Kepler(1571~1630), who explained how planets moved in eliptical orbits. To Kepler's theories Descartes added the concept of a heliocentric universe previously expounded by the Polish astronomer Nicolaus Copernicus (1473~1543). Because of the invention of the telescope by Galileo Galilei(1564~1642), the universe was now known to be much vaster than previously imagined. Descartes held that space was indefinitely divisible and that all movement is in a straight line. Accordingly, extension(*extensio*)is the essence of both space and matter, which are equated with each other and which determine the nature of quantity, dimension, and the measurement of distance. This meant in effect the abandonment of the Aristotelian notion of *topos*, the idea that place is coterminous with contained and defined space. Cartesian space, by contrast, is boundless and, with regard to the concept of place, value-neutral, since space could now be conceived as a universal grid of mathematical coordinates with places existing merely as locational points along its infinitely extensible planes.[3]

In this view, place is secondary to matter and space. Its nondistinctive status helps account for the abstract character of Le Nôtre's designs, which express Descartes's attempt to geometricize all nature rather than to explicate *topos*. The geometric formality of Le Nôtre's designs is also due to his employment of Cartesian analytic geometry as a practical compositional tool; the precisely calculated proportions of their component parts and his calculation of the effects of perspective on the viewer manifest an understanding of Cartesian mathematics. Although Le Nôtre may not have intended explicitly to portray the Cartesian vision of heliocentric cosmic space, an impossibility in any case, Cartesian philosophy is implicit in the indefinitely extended axes of the serenely grand gardens he designed for France's Sun King.

In addition to giving expression to a new cosmology, Descartes assisted in the overthrow of Aristotelian Scholasticism by espousing a philosophy based upon the belief that the human mind could, through deductive reasoning, grasp and control the world. The optimism inherent in the Cartesian belief that, through their own powers of intellect, human beings could master the inner workings of nature and direct these toward progressive ends is echoed by the confident grandeur of Le Nôtre's gardens. It was the Sun King's duty to symbolize in his divinely appointed person and to project through his royal authority France's position as the intellectual lader of the modern Western world, and it was Le Nôtre's job to portray this absolute power through landscape design. Both king and gardener realized, however, the difference between reality and suggestion. Le Nôtre created a garden that implied rationality yet was based on an illusion, human dominance over nature; for his part, the king realized the limits of rationalism as a tool of power and means to accomplish his political goals in a world filled with passion and intrigue.

While it is often assumed that William Kent in eighteenthcentury England was the first designer to "leap the wall" of the garden to embrace all of nature, Le Nôtre, operating under the cultural influence of Descartes, had performed this feat nearly a century earlier. But unlike the naturalistic style of the English garden formulated by Kent and his followers, the confident, world-embracing idiom of the French classical style with its extended axes and geometrically derived layouts celebrated absolute monarchy, not libertarian values.

The work of transforming ordinary countryside into stepped terraces, grand canals, artificial cascades, and axial promenades was accomplished at the price of villages and fields laid waste and peasants relocated. It was also achieved at a huge monetary cost, even at the low prevailing wage rates. It was certainly seen as impressive just for that reason; the enormous expenditure was an important aspect of the seventeenth-century French gardens'message, demonstrating the king's economic power and superior taste. Furthermore, these gardens were designed to serve as stages upon which the members of an aristocratic society played out the dramas of their lives with theatrical ritual as they met one another upon balustraded terraces, walked along sweeping *allées*, or trysted within the relative privacy of *bosquets*.

Theaters of social life, the gardens of seventeenth-century France often served as real stages for the performing arts. Within them, concerts, ballets, plays, fireworks, and banquets took place with increasing regularity. Theatrical entertainments were part of Louis XIV's means of keeping an otherwise bored nobility in check. Le Nôtre knew the composer Jean-Baptiste Lully(1632~1687) and the playwright Molière(Jean-Baptiste Poquelin, 1622~1675) and organized his spaces with their performance requirements in mind.

French classical gardens were theatrical in yet another sense. Had they been merely expositions of Cartesian logic, elegantly defined empty stages for aristocratic intercourse and entertainment they would have been boring. But with their abundant water jets and populations of stone gods and goddesses, they provided the spectator with movement and a rich mythological companionship. Like the Renaissance villa gardens of Italy from which they are derived, they were programmatic texts in stone, water, and vegetation. Le Nôtre and his collaborators(notably Le Brun, whose express charge was the sculptural program of the gardens at Vauxle-Vicomte and Versailles) had a sufficient humanistic education to continue the Renaissance practice of garden arrangement according to elaborate programs of allegorical allusion.

The elegant rationality of the style Le Nôtre forged in collaboration with the architects, artists, and artisans of his day influenced courts throughout Europe. Just as France under Louis XIV became the dominant military power in Europe, so the French classical landscape style became prevalent during and after his reign. Although inflected according to regional conditions of taste and topography, it rapidly spread to the Netherlands, England, Germany, and Russia.

The French classical garden was influential even in Italy, as is apparent a century later in the scale and plan of the royal gardens of Caserta near Naples. But Italian landscape design was so imbued with the robust theatricality of local taste that French classicism was never thoroughly integrated into it. Rather, the currents of Italian Baroque style continued to flow northward as various European monarchs and princes summoned artists and craftsmen to mingle their talents with those of French designers. In Italy itself, a wealthy clergy and its related aristocracy brought the art of villa garden building to a triumphant and spectacular close. Humanistic iconography, at first in the service of the princes of the church and state, was finally abandoned altogether and ornament became an end in its own right. Thus, the elaborate symbolical programs that informed such gardens as the Villa d'Este gave way to the kind of sculptural tableaux one finds at Caserta.

Grand-scale geometrical landscape composition in the French manner initiated another

Part II History of Landscape Architecture

tradition, that of monumental city planning, beginning already in the time of Louis XIV and carried forward in the eighteenth century in Washington, D. C. and St. Petersburg, and in the nineteenth century, most spectacularly in Paris itself. And although they may work with an entirely contemporary sensibility and no longer have as their primary philosophical reference the Cartesian cosmological view that was a principal *raison d'être* for axial extension in the seventeenth century, many of today's French landscape designers stand squarely in Le Nôtre's long shadow as they rebuild the public spaces of Paris and other French cities. For all of these reasons it is worthwhile to examine more closely the career of this remarkable royal servant.

WORDS AND EXPRESSIONS

vassal ['væsəl]	n. 诸侯，封臣，附庸
peripatetic [ˌperipə'tetik]	adj. 到处走的，漫游的，巡回的
Chambord [ʃa'bɔ:]	n. 尚波尔（法国中北部一村庄）
radiant ['reidjənt]	adj. 光芒四射的，光辉灿烂的
heed [hi:d]	n. & v. 注意，留意
astute [ə'stju:t; (US)ə'stu:t]	adj. 机敏的，狡猾的
exemplar [ig'zemplə]	n. 模范，榜样，标本
usher ['ʌʃə]	v. 导引，引进
usher sth. in	开创、开始或引进某事物，预示
troupe [tru:p]	n. （演出的）班子，团，队
precursor [pri(:)'kə:sə]	n. 先驱，前辈
charter ['tʃa:tə]	vt. 特许
ballet ['bælei, bæ'lei]	n. 芭蕾舞（团）；芭蕾舞剧，芭蕾舞乐曲
institutionalize [ˌinsti'tju:ʃənəlaiz]	v. 把（某人）置于公共机构照料之下
tangible ['tændʒəbl]	adj. 明确的，切实的，确实的
appropriate [ə'prəupriit]	v. 拿（某事物）为己所用
inflection [in'flekʃən]	n. 变形
sober ['səubə]	adj. 严肃的，冷静的，郑重的
robust [rə'bʌst]	adj. 有活力的，强健的
plasticity [plæs'tisiti]	n. 可塑性，塑性
exuberant [ig'zju:bərənt]	adj. 丰富的，足够的
theatricality [θiˌætri'kæliti]	n. 戏剧风格
Louvre [lu:vr, 'lu:və]	n. 卢浮宫
neoclassical ['ni:əuklæsikəl]	adj. 新古典主义的
chaste [tʃeist]	adj. （风格）简单的，不修饰的
cynosure ['sinəzjuə]	n. 引起众人注视的人（或事物），赞美

LESSON 5

	的目标；北极星，小熊星座
feat [fi:t]	n. 功绩，壮举
patronage [ˈpætrənidʒ]	n. 资助，赞助，支持
forsake [fəˈseik]	vt. 放弃 抛弃
compartmentalization [ˌkɔmpɑːtˈmentəlaizeiʃən]	n. 区分，划分
regal [ˈriːgəl]	adj. (似)帝王的，为帝王而设的，王室的
dwarf [dwɔːf]	n. 矮子，侏儒
	v. (使)变矮小
commensurate [kəˈmenʃərit]	adj. 相称的，相当的
imperceptible [ˌimpəˈseptəbl]	adj. 觉察不到的
indeterminate [ˌindiˈtəːminit]	adj. 不确定的，模糊的
analogue [ˈænəlɔg]	n. 相似物，类似情况
skepticism [ˈskeptisizəm]	n. 怀疑态度，怀疑主义
premise [ˈpremis]	n. 假定，假设
astronomer [əˈstrɔnəmə(r)]	n. 天文学家
elliptical [iˈliptikəl]	adj. 椭圆形的
Copernicus	n. 哥白尼
heliocentric [ˌhiːliəuˈsentrik]	adj. 以太阳为中心的
Aristotelian	adj. 亚里士多德的
expound [iksˈpaund]	v. 详细说明，解释
coterminous [kəuˈtəːminəs]	adj. 与…有共同边界的(with)

NOTES

1. Baroque（也作 Baroque）巴洛克风格的：约 1550~1700 年间盛行于欧洲的一种艺术和建筑风格。

2. 见 Robert W. Berger，太阳王的花园：对路易十四时期的凡尔赛园林的研究(In the Garden of the Sun King：Studies on the Park of Versailles Under Louis XIV. Washington, DC. Dumbarton Oaks，1985)第二章，关于对小学院派(the Petite Academie)(后被重新命名为 the Academie Royale des Inscriptions et Medailles)在决定凡尔赛的肖像画项目中作用的著述。Petite Academie 是一个致力于开发以赞颂皇室为主题的肖像画作的学院，负责设计纪念君王事迹的纪念章以及皇家建筑的装饰。黎塞留(Richelieu)在贵族中引发了一场建筑热，17 世纪上半叶间，在巴黎建成了 300 多座新的贵族宅邸和花园，法国人对其首都的引以为傲就始于这一时期。

3. 关于笛卡尔"空间世界要作为一个无限的、浑然一体的物质领域范围来理解领会，这些物质的本质在于它们的扩展延伸"的理论，见 Edward Casey，地方的命运：哲学历史(The Fate of Place：A Philosophical History. Berkeley：University of California Press 1997)，p. 154。

LESSON 6

THE LANDSCAPE GARDEN IN ENGLAND

The landscape garden was an entirely different concept and its origins were varied. The English countryside with large fields made possible by enclosure, rolling hills, winding streams, and scattered trees, inherently unsuited to the French garden, was an important element in English country life. The formal gardens of France were associated with despotic government distasteful to the democratic and rightsconscious Englishmen of the eighteenth century. An antithesis to the formal garden would thus be more acceptable. The emerging Romantic movement produced poetry, and paintings which extolled the beauties of nature and landscape. The grand tour which all cultured Englishmen made through the Alps to Italy brought them in contact with rugged, picturesque scenery. Scenes such as they would see on the tour were represented on the canvases of Nicolas Poussin, Salvador Rosa, and Claude Lorrain. The paintings were not actual views but compositions of typical elements selected and arranged for emphasis—craggy mountains, rivers, pastoral plains, ruined castles and monuments, lakes, and windblown trees. Many included classical temples and groups of allegorical figures. In addition to the landscape and its stylization in the paintings, the visitor to Italy saw the famous villas and their gardens in an appealing, romantic state of disrepair. The travelers began to see landscape through the eyes of the painter and consequently on their return to England found their stiff formal gardens uninteresting and unattractive. One other influence was the Orient, which was opened to trade in the seventeenth century. Scenes on imported porcelain and lacquer work depicted natural gardens, lakes, and waterfalls and the aesthetic and attitude which they represented were influential in the development of a new system of gardening in England.

The landscape garden was a product of the Romantic movement. Its form was based on direct observation of nature and the principles of painting. Surprise, variety, concealment, and the development of idyllic prospects became the goals of the art of landscape. The manipulation of nature's undulating contours according to Hogarth's[1] serpentine "line of beauty" and the articulation of light and shade much as a painter would do became the preoccupation of all men of taste and culture in eighteenth-century England and ultimately all over Europe and in America in the nineteenth century. Where they existed,

---

选自 Laurie Michael An Introduction to Landscape Architecture 2nded. New York, NY: Elsevier

the parterre and terrace of the formal garden were replaced with rolling grassland, clumps of trees, lakes, meandering rivers, and serpentine drives(Figs. 1 and 2). In the early examples the scene was embellished at suitable points with temples, bridges, and sculptures.

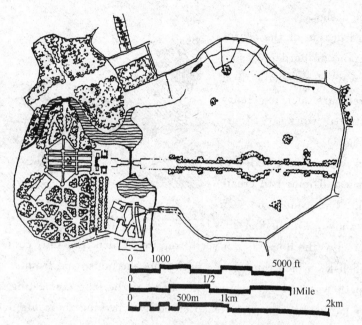

Fig. 1   Blenheim Palace as laid out by Henry Wise in 1705
Note (1)the straight entrance from the village,
(2)the parterre in front of the house and
the radiating avenues in the woodland

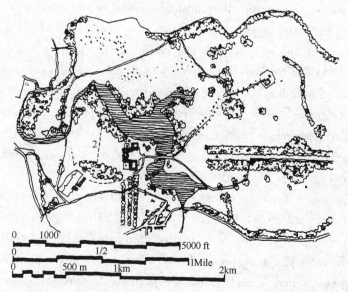

Fig. 2   Blenheim Palace as altered by Lancelot Brown in 1758
Note (1)the new winding approach from the village,
(2)the irregular plantings and the sunken fence in
front of the house replacing the parterre

Of fundamental importance was the elimination of the visual break between garden and landscape. One of the techniques for eliminating this break was the sunken fence. This allowed the eye to see straight out to the countryside while at the same time keeping deer and stock out of the garden proper. It is a technique with potential for use today in contemporary landscape design.

By the third decade of the century, the revolution in garden design was well under way. It was led at first by so-called amateurs such as Henry Hoare, who started work at Stourhead[2] in 1743(Fig. 3).

The garden was set in a valley in which a stream was dammed to create an irregular lake. This cannot be seen from the house above, a Palladian villa, and, conversely, the house is not seen from the garden. The only connection between the two is an obelisk, which can be seen both from the house and from a specific point in the garden. A path was laid out around the shore of the lake connecting a series of "events," and the garden was properly experienced by following the route in the prescribed direction. The tour might take a day even though the distance was not great. The garden was arranged according to the rules of landscape painting, and in fact in this particular case the garden was based on a painting by Claude Lorrain. The bridge at the starting point, the Temple of Flora, and the Pantheon set out in the garden are similar in form and disposition to those in the painting.

Fig. 3　Stourhead, England(1744)

A further level of appreciation was the mythological or literary allusions associated with each feature. As one walked, new vistas and views were revealed and the visitor was brought obliquely to buildings and places seen earlier. At one point the path leads underground into a cool grotto with a moss-covered statue of Neptune, ferns, and the sound of running water. It is a conscious change in environment to evoke physiologically, as well as intellectually, images of a legendary underwater kingdom. A rocky opening at water level reveals the Temple of Flora across the lake already visited.

Stourhead is thus a sequence of experiences. Many have intellectual meaning and are conceived and appreciated on the basis of a knowledge of mythology and poetry. In addition, the environmental qualities of light, temperature, texture, and sound together with visual impressions add sensations which, combined with the first level of reaction, make a complete experience. A modern movie is perhaps the closest comparison in which an image, the meaning associated with it, and the response can be predetermined.

Bright flowering plants were not favored in the landscape garden. The rhododendrons that can be seen at Stourhead today were not part of the original planting. These were planted later and now stimulate a controversy between "purists" and the National Trust, who own and maintain the garden for the public. The National Trust say that the visiting public like azaleas. The purists would like the rhododendrons removed.

William Kent[3] was the first professional to design gardens in the new manner. At Rousham, built between 1738 and 1740, Kent planned the entire view from the existing house and built a miller's cottage and a ruin on a distant hill to complete the romantic composition. Thus the design consideration extended to the entire landscape visible from the house. The cumulative effect of this approach has resulted in the way the English landscape looks today. It has been designed and is a composite of views from many country houses. The garden at Rousham lies to one side of the house and includes a classical arcade, a serpentine rivulet, a grotto, cascades, and evocative statues placed within clearings in a woodland and connected with vistas and walks.

By the mid-eighteenth century, the new style in gardening was widely accepted. Lancelot Brown[4], called Capability Brown, became the leading exponent and was in great demand. Unlike Kent, he did not approve of architectural features in the garden. Terraces and parterres were to be cleared away from the base of the house until nothing was left except grass, which came right up to the foundations. A sunken fence would eliminate the visual boundary, and the seemingly contiguous landscape would be planted irregularly with trees in clumps or groups on undulating ground. If possible, a stream would be dammed to form a lake as at Blenheim, and made to fit naturally without awkwardness into the landscape(Fig. 4). The appearance of these landscapes depended on good estate management and productive agriculture, for they encompassed working farms and fields. In addition, the making of picturesque landscapes which would blend visually into the existing natural system depended on an understanding of ecological principles.

Fig. 4 Blenheim, England(1758)

In the late eighteenth and early nineteenth century Humphry Repton[5] published a theory of landscape gardening and became the leading exponent of the style. Repton modified Brown's ruthless formula and favored the restoration of the terrace to connect the house to the garden. In a satirical essay Repton was referred to as Mr. Milestone because of a trick

Part II History of Landscape Architecture

whereby the milestones set on the driveway leading to the house were set at less than a mile apart. In this we see evidence of appreciation based on quantity and size reflecting on the prestige of the owners. A technique of more importance were his "redbooks", which illustrated his proposals with "before" and "after" drawings or watercolors(Figs. 5 and 6). Comparison of these showed how a quiet, uninteresting meadow and stream could be transformed into a beautiful landscape with serpentine lake and irregular plantations as an environment for a castlelike establishment set on a broad terrace.

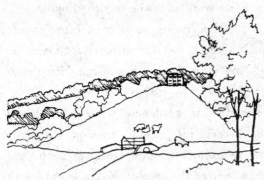

Fig. 5 An impression of Redbook drawing by Repton showing a house in a bland landscape—a parody of Brown's formula(1803)

Fig. 6 The "after" illustration by Repton showed the introduction of a terrace and outbuildings, a romantic lake and picturesque planting(1803)

WORDS AND EXPRESSIONS

scattered ['skætəd]　　　　　　adj. 离散的，分散的
despotic [des'pɔtik]　　　　　　adj. 专制的，暴虐的
antithesis [æn'tiθisis]　　　　　n. 对立面
extol [iks'tɔl]　　　　　　　　　v. 赞美
Alps [ælps]　　　　　　　　　　n. 阿尔卑斯山
canvas ['kænvəs]　　　　　　　n. 帆布
craggy ['krægi]　　　　　　　　adj. 多峭壁的，崎岖的
pastoral ['pɑːstərəl]　　　　　　n. 牧歌，田园文学，田园诗
　　　　　　　　　　　　　　　adj. 牧人的，田园生活的，牧师的
allegorical [ˌæli'ɔrikəl]　　　　　adj. 寓言的，讽喻的
orient ['ɔːriənt]　　　　　　　　n. 东方，东方诸国(指地中海以东各国)
　　　　　　　　　　　　　　　adj. 东方的，上升的，灿烂的
　　　　　　　　　　　　　　　vt. 使朝东，使适应，确定方向
porcelain ['pɔːslin, -lein]　　　　n. 瓷器，瓷
　　　　　　　　　　　　　　　adj. 瓷制的，精美的，脆的
lacquer ['lækə]　　　　　　　　n. 漆，漆器

LESSON 6

	vt. 用漆涂于…，使表面光泽
idyllic [aiˈdilik，iˈdilik]	*adj.* 田园短诗的，牧歌的，生动逼真的
contour [ˈkɔntuə]	*n.* 轮廓，周线，等高线
serpentine [ˈsəːpəntain]	*adj.* 蜿蜒的
preoccupation [pri(ː)ˌɔkjuˈpeiʃən]	*n.* 当务之急
meandering [miˈændəriŋ]	*n.* 蜿蜒的河流，漫步，聊天
	adj. 蜿蜒的，漫步的，聊天的
Palladian	(16世纪意大利建筑家)帕拉第奥（A. Palladio）的帕拉第奥建筑形式的［希神］智慧女神帕拉斯(Pallas)的
disposition [dispəˈziʃən]	*n.* 部署
grotto [ˈɡrɔtəu]	*n.* 洞穴，岩穴，人工洞室
moss [mɔs]	*n.* 苔，藓
fern [fəːn]	*n.* ［植］蕨类植物
rivulet [ˈrivjulit]	*n.* 小河，小溪，溪流
clearing [ˈkliəriŋ]	*n.* 空旷地
exponent [eksˈpəunənt]	*n.* 解释者，说明者，代表者，典型，指数
blend [blend]	*vt.* 混合
	n. 混合
satirical [səˈtirik(ə)l]	*adj.* 好讽刺的，爱挖苦人的

KEY CONCEPTS

landscape garden
Romantic Movement
garden design
landscape painting

NOTES

1. William Hogarth
   贺加斯(1697~1764)，英国油画家、版画家、艺术理论家。
2. Stourhead
   斯托海德(公园)，位于威尔特郡，在索尔斯伯里平原的西南角。1717年，亨利·霍尔一世（Henri Hoare I）买下了这里的地产。
3. William Kent
   威廉·肯特(1686~1748)，是真正摆脱了规则园林的第一位造园家，也是卓越的建筑师、室内设计师和画家。曾在意大利的罗马学习绘画，并结识英国的伯林顿伯爵，回国后，就负责伯爵府邸的装饰工作。还为肯辛顿宫做过室内装饰，以后成为皇室的肖像画家，同时也从事造园工作。

Part II History of Landscape Architecture

4. Lancelot Brown

朗斯洛特·布朗(1715～1783)，英国风景园的代表人物，被称为"万能布朗"(Capability Brown)。

5. Humphry Repton

胡弗莱·雷普顿(1752～1818)，继布朗之后18世纪后期英国最杰出的风景园林师。

QUESTIONS FOR REVIEW AND DISCUSSION

1. What are the main factors influencing the English garden style in 18th century?
2. Give a general description of William Kent's design style.
3. What are the main difference between Lancelot Brown's design and William Kent's?
4. Why was Repton referred to as Mr. Milestone in an essay?

Reading Material

The Landscape Garden in The United States

In due course the romantic landscape garden was adopted in America. Thomas Jefferson's remodeling of the Monticello gardens(Fig. 1) and the simple lawn and plantations introduced at Mount Vernon in 1737(Fig. 2) are early indications of a change in American taste. Some of the first completely new landscape gardens were designed by Andre Parmentier, a Belgian who established a nursery in Brooklyn in 1824. In 1828 he wrote an essay praising the picturesque style and opposing the formalism then prevalent in America. He subsequently laid out the grounds of several large estates along the Hudson River before his death in 1830.

Fig. 1 Monticello, Virginia(1796)

Parmentier was succeeded by Andrew Jackson Downing as champion of the landscape garden. Downing's theory, published in 1841, was based on the work of Repton and embodied the same theory of the picturesque. His arguments in favor of the beauties of natural landscape, woods, and plantations and the aesthetic and moral values to be obtained from them were so convincing that all new gardens in association with the increasing number of suburban villas were laid out in the Romantic idiom(Fig. 3). His book was moralistic in tone, stressing the refinement and sophistication needed to appreciate the subtleties of natural forms. By the middle of the nineteenth century Downing had established himself

---

选自 (Laurie Michael An Introduction to Landscape Architecture 2nded. New York, NY: Elsevier)

Part II *History of Landscape Architecture*

as a tastemaker in gardening matters on the East coast in America. He was adopted by the wealthy owners of estates on the Hudson River. Here he created very creditable landscapes in the English manner but with care to emphasize the particular qualities of each site. Illustrations in his book show prototypical villas for people of middle income(Fig. 4). Families are seen posed somewhat awkwardly or having tea on a lawn enclosed with conifers and shrubberies or commanding a view of a distant mountain landscape.

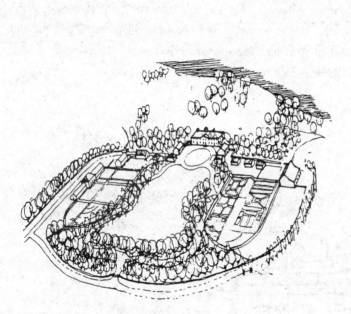

Fig. 2 Mount Vernon(1737)

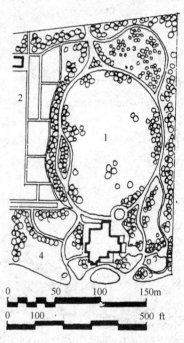

Fig. 3 Plan of suburban Villa Garden by Andrew Jackson Downing(1841)
(1)lawn, (2)kitchen garden, (3)picturesque garden, (4)flower garden.

Fig. 4 Villa and landscape garden as advocated by Andrew Jackson Downing(nineteenth century)

LESSON 6

Downing established and popularized the Romantic landscape garden as a tradition in America. It was part of a larger interest in nature and the American landscape. In the adoption of an informal and natural style of landscape design which recognized the constraints and potentials of each site we can detect the roots of a landscape philosophy held and advocated strongly by Frederick Law Olmsted as he entered practice in 1856. This East coast tradition, which emphasized nature and natural looks with soft edges and curving lines as a contrast to urbanism, persisted well into the twentieth century and remains popular today in contrast to the modern garden.

WORDS AND EXPRESSIONS

Belgian ['beldʒən]   n. 比利时人；adj. 比利时的
prevalent ['prevələnt]   adj. 普遍的，流行的
embody [im'bɔdi]   vt. 具体表达，使具体化，包含，收录
moralistic [mɔrə'listik；(US)mɔːr-]   adj. 道学的，说教的，教训的
subtlety ['sʌtlti]   n. 稀薄，微妙，精明

LESSON 7

LANDSCAPE DESIGN IN THE EAST: CHINA

The notion of landscape as a text with encoded meaning, a place of memory and association, an experiential space in which to stroll and enjoy the unfolding of sequential views or to sit quietly and ponder the thoughts prompted by the impressions of scenery upon the senses—these fundamentals were common to both East Asian gardens and the gardens developed in England in the eighteenth century.[1] The reciprocal association between landscape design and painting that was first developed in China and then later adopted in Japan is similar to the eighteenth-century English sensibility that found in Claude Lorrain's seventeenth-century paintings an appropriate idiom for the layout of the parks of great estates. Similarly, an affinity for landscape themes, prevalent in eighteenth-and nineteenth-century English literature, is especially common in the poetry of China and Japan. The Romantic appreciation for the sublime in nature, which caused William Wordsworth to attune his soul to "the sounding cataract ... the tall rock, the mountain, and the deep and gloomy wood," was akin to the reverence for nature of Chinese scholars and mystics many centuries before.

But in spite of this apparent similarity between East and West, at a certain point in time with regard to each culture's philosophical attitude toward landscape, the underlying differences between the historic gardens of Asia and those formed in Europe and America are fundamental and profound. Western environmentalists attempting to reforge the broken human contract with nature, who try to reason the causes for its rupture in the first place, must reckon with the Judeo-Christian tradition of a jealous God who tolerates no rivals and is situated in a remote Heaven, the true paradise as compared to the "false" paradise of this world. The ancient Greeks, who had dreamed their gods out of the ground and placed them in the sky upon Olympus, did not so thoroughly depopulate the earth of its divinities as did the monotheistic cultures of Judaism and Christianity. They journeyed to sacred places in nature, seeking oracular wisdom at Delphi and spiritual initiation at Eleusis. But it is to nature-oriented religions like Daoism and Shinto that one must look to find a more direct bond between people and Earth. In China and Japan, although nature was as thoroughly harnessed to serve human economic ends as in the West, the scholarly and ruling elites espoused and expressed through landscape design Buddhist precepts informed by Daoist and Shinto ideals emphasizing life lived in spiritual harmony with nature. Chinese

---

选自 Elizabeth Barlow Rogers Landscape Design: A Cultural and Architecture History Harry N. Abrams, INC, Publishers

Daoist thought fostered perceptions of *qi*, the "breath", or inherent energy, possessed by all phenomena. In Japan, Shinto religion led participants to reverence *kami*,[2] the spirits found in nature.[3] Garden design in both countries reflected and nourished these ideals.

Rocks—the mineral substance of nature—had as strong an aesthetic and associative value in East Asian gardens as representational sculpture in carved stone and cast bronze did in Western ones. In China, garden designers employed carefully selected, waterworn rocks with clefts and fissures. These spatially intricate rocks were usually intended to evoke the mist-shrouded mountain ranges of the larger landscape, for the Chinese attributed to their country's peaks the same in-dwelling mystery and connection with the divine as did other early civilizations. Such scenery might be termed *sublime* according to the aesthetics of the West.

In Japan, where mountains are less dramatically formed, designers sometimes employed rocks in compositions that intentionally evoked scenes from Chinese painting, but more often rocks were placed in water or gravel "streams" as metaphorical islands. Japanese garden designers also displayed particular ingenuity in their selection of beautifully shaped flat stepping stones, positioning them so as to form, in conjunction with moss, ground-plane patterns of highly pleasing pattern and texture. Like the rocks in Chinese gardens and their somewhat smaller counterparts displayed in the studies of Chinese scholars, Japanese garden rocks were often associated with mythical or real animals of symbolical import. In both cultures, the viewer was encouraged to enjoy the abstract beauty of these mineral forms while also imagining their resemblance to other things.

JI CHENG'S GARDEN MANUAL: THE YUAN YE

By the end of the Song period, the conventions of Chinese garden design were well established. As Chinese merchants prospered during the Ming dynasty, they, like the emperor himself, emulated the cultural elite, the mandarin class of scholar-officials. To help these arrivistes avoid the aesthetic blunders of the uneducated, garden designers began to write treatises that codified garden style and served as manuals for landscape builders.

Foremost among these was the *Yuan ye*, or *The Craft of Gardens*, by Ji Cheng (b. 1582) of Wujiang in the province of Jiangsu. A noted garden builder himself, as well as a poet and painter, he completed his comprehensive three-volume classic on landscape theory and practice in 1634.

Ji Cheng's book is unusual, and perhaps unique, among garden manuals in its blend of practical advice and pattern-book instruction with poetic visualization and mood painting. Although specific in discussing the appearance of various kinds of stones and offering abundant diagrams for window and railing lattices, together with numerous door shapes and paving designs, the *Yuan ye* offers no static prescription for garden planning. The author firmly states that "there is no definite way of making scenery; you know it is right when it stirs your emotions," stressing that it is *qi*, the pulsating breath of life that must be the result of the designer's efforts.

Good siting is a primary ingredient of Ji Cheng's prescription for garden making. A garden designer must screen out what is ugly and offensive and make use of "borrowed scenery" (*jie jing*), whether a distant view of misty mountains, the rooflines of a nearby monastery, or the flowers of a neighbor's garden. A small piece of ground beside a dwelling can be turned into a garden by digging a pond, collecting stones with which to build up a "mountain," and making a welcoming gate for guests. Willows, a stand of bamboos, and some luxuriant trees and flowers are all that are needed to complete the picture and set the mood for poetry-writing parties and sitting in the company of one's favorite concubine melting snow water for tea.

In Ji Cheng's manual, in the chapter "The Selection of Stones," he discusses in reverent detail the highly prized Lake Tai stones with their hollows and holes. He recommends that these be given pride of place like fine sculpture in front of big halls, within large pavilions, or beneath a stately pine tree. It is clear from the *Yuan ye* that stone selection was a highly developed skill limited to a small number of individuals who could successfully quarry fine specimens from the mountains or find them in river and lake beds. Sometimes to be found in museum collections of Chinese art today, these prize stones, with light and shade directing the eye as it travels in and out of their folds and hollows and up the flanks of an imagined mountain precipice, do appear to possess *qi*; their vibrancy is akin to that found in works of painting and calligraphy in the same galleries.

Ji Cheng also writes about wall design. The walls in Chinese gardens provide an important means of segregating space, screening from sight the mundane workaday reality of city streets while making the garden invisible to passersby, except for glimpses gained through latticed openings composed of thin tiles or cast bricks. The walls of Chinese gardens often rise and fall according to the elevation of the ground. Curved roof tiles, sometimes following a wavy line, produce a sense of animated movement, while basrelief friezes frequently add ornamental interest.

Walls outline various courts and corridors within the garden, subdividing it into discrete though linked scenic units. These are often pierced by windows with tracery, for which Ji Cheng provided many patterns. Carefully placed windows and circular "moon gates" and vase-or gourd-shaped doors frame views of adjacent garden spaces. The whitewashed surfaces of these walls are often brush-rubbed with ground yellow river sand mixed with a small amount of chalk to give them a lustrous waxy polish. The function of a Chinese garden wall is not, however, ornamental; rather, it is meant to serve, like the neutral silk or paper of a painting, as a background, capturing shadows in calligraphic patterns and acting as a foil for the rocks and plants in front of it.

In plan, a typical Southern Chinese scholar-garden, built in the manner codified by Ji Cheng, arranges the functional parts of the mansion and its adjacent series of courts around the edges of the site. The principal hall faces a central pond, which occupies approximately three-tenths of the site(see Fig. 1). Like the arms of a lake in nature, the ends of

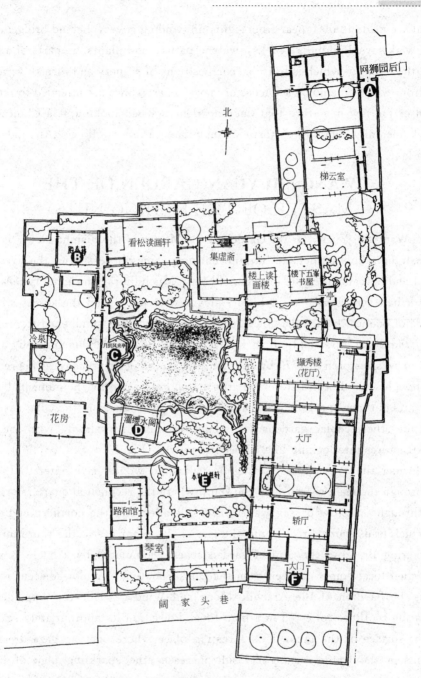

Fig. 1 Plan of Wang Shi Yuan (Garden of the Master of the Fishing Nets), Suzhou. Qing Dynasty

- **A** Visitors' Entrance
- **B** Cottage to Accompany Spring
- **C** Pavillion of the Arrving Moon and Wind
- **D** Waterside Hall for Washing the Tassels of One's Hat
- **E** Hall of Small Mountains and Osmanthus Spring
- **F** Main Entrance

the pond are made to disappear from sight, in winding coves, behind bridges, or beyond covered walkways. Buildings, rocks, water, paths, and plants are parts of a harmonious whole, the intent of which is to frame compositions of scenery and furnish various vantage points from which to enjoy a sequence of views. These views are intended to remind one of the kind of journey in nature that one experiences when looking at a Chinese landscape painting, mentally climbing up tortuous mountain paths or following the indented shoreline of a lake.

WANG SHI YUAN(GARDEN OF THE MASTER OF THE FISHING NETS)

The Wang Shi Yuan, or the Garden of the Master of the Fishing Nets, is one of several remaining scholargardens in Suzhou that give some impression of the lives led by the educated and bureaucratic elite in imperial China. Much literary meaning is packed into this one-and-a-half-acre garden of idyllically arranged scenery, and the spaces within it bear the kinds of poetical names that Jia Zheng's son Bao-yu was summoned to provied in *The Story of the Stone*. First laid out in 1140, in early Southern Song times by a high court official, it was restored in 1770 by another official, Song Zongyuan, as his retirement retreat. Though altered both before and after its appropriation by the municipal government in 1958, its outlines and principal features remain the same as in the Qing period (1644~1911). Like other scholar-gardens, it is highly compartmentalized, with courtyards and roofed structures interlocking like pieces of a puzzle (Fig. 1).

In former times, visitors arriving by palanquin would have entered the Wang Shi Yuan through the main entrance on the south where the residential quarters are. Today access is through a narrow passageway from a side alley into the northern end of the complex, which leads more directly into the garden. In either case, the route into the Place for Gathering Breezes—the central garden space, dominated by a lake—is a circuitous one. Its chief focal point, as seen from the Duck Shooting Corridor adjacent to the family halls, is the Pavilion of the Arriving Moon and Wind, a delicate, six-sided structure with soaring rooflines collected in a high finial. Poised on its appropriately scaled rockery above the surface of the lake, it is a resting place where one can gaze dreamily at the reflections in the water. A mirror inside increases the sparkling play of light on its surfaces.

The visitor does not arrive by an obvious path to this spot but is diverted along the way by other pavilions and their adjacent courtyards. The Hall of Small Mountains and Osmanthus Spring is completely screened from the lake by a tall mountain of earth and rockwork. From inside, one views this composition through windows framed with lacy fretwork. On the south side of this structure lies a small courtyard containing many fine specimens of Lake Tai rocks placed in an undulating composition. The bright white wall of this courtyard constitutes the pictorial ground upon which the shadows of the fragrant osmanthus trees are cast, forming a tracery pattern that complements the fretwork of the small openings in it as well as that of the windows of the pavilion.

The Waterside Hall for Washing the Tassels of One's Hat sits at the water's edge on the south side of the lake opposite the Veranda for Viewing Pines and Looking at Paintings. The latter pavilion has a lake view seen through old pines and cypresses, which are set in a rockery. Besides these lakeside summerhouses, there are other garden pavilions, several of which serve the needs of the scholar. The Five Peaks Study, for instance, is a library. Since interior stairs are not favored in ornamental Chinese architecture, access to its second story was gained via steps set into a rockery next to its east wall. Adjacent to it is the House of Concentrated Study. Another study, the Cottage to Accompany Spring, had its own private pebble-paved courtyard garden to the south as well as another tiny courtyard on the north. The latter, which is framed from inside by beautifully carved window surrounds, contains a delicate composition of bamboo, rocks, and flowering plants.

IMPERIAL BEIJING

By 1279, Khubilai Khan, the grandson of Genghis Khan, had toppled the Jin dynasty in the northern part of China, captured Hangzhou, and gained control of the entire country at an estimated cost of 30 million lives. Khubilai moved the capital of his Mongol empire to Beijing and assimilated the more sophisticated culture of the people he had conquered. The Yuan dynasty, as the Mongol rulership was styled, lasted until 1368. Like other disaffected Chinese civil servants before them, a number of the mandarin elite went into permanent retirement rather than serve the foreign conqueror, some finding careers as artists whose works were in demand by the growing merchant class. Others went north to carry on their traditional duties, including artistic ones, at court.

The Jin emperors, whose occupancy of Beijing preceded that of the Mongols, had excavated a canal and a marshy lake, the nucleus of the three contemporary lakes around which "sea palaces" and pleasure parks were built. Khubilai Khan further excavated this lake, which is known as Bei Hai, or Northern Sea, setting up hunting preserves around it and embellishing its shores with many trees and costly buildings. At its southern end he formed an island from the dredged spoil upon which he erected a "mountain" studded with rocks of lapis lazuli. To Marco Polo, this Green Hill presented a wondrous sight. According to him, the trees planted upon it were transported there by elephants.

The first emperor of the Ming dynasty(1368～1644)located the capital at Nanjing where it remained until the third emperor, Yongle(ruled 1403～1424), reestablished the court at Beijing. For fourteen years Yongle's builders labored to erect a city modeled on the previous Ming emperor's capital at Nanjing. Guided by geomancy, Confucian symbolism, and cosmology, they gave physical representation to the emperor's rule under the "mandate of heaven". This was expressed as a hierarchical ordering of space in which were

Part II *History of Landscape Architecture*

nested three rectangular walled enclosures containing the Inner City, the Imperial City, and the Forbidden City, all of which were centered on a great north-south axis punctuated by ceremonial gates.

In 1420, Yongle's vast complex of walled enclosures and palatial buildings was ready for occupancy, and Beijing officially became the Ming capital. The Altar of Heaven was also built in the reign of Yongle to the south of Qian Qing Men(Gate of August Purity), the great Front Gate of the Inner City. It was flanked by two circular temples, the Temple of Heaven and the Hall of Prayer for Good Harvests. During the reign of Jiajing(ruled 1522~1566)in the next century at the cardinal points just outside the Inner City additional magnificent altars were raised to the Earth, Sun, Moon, and Agriculture. At that time, about 1550, another walled rectangle was constructed, enclosing the district to the south of the Inner City. Called the Outer City, it encompassed the Altar of Heaven and the Altar of Agriculture(replaced by a Worker's Stadium in the 1950s).

WORDS AND EXPRESSIONS

muse [mjuːz]   *n.* 艺术家(尤指诗人)的创作灵感，灵感的源泉
encode [inˈkəud]   *vt.* 译成密码
reciprocal [riˈsiprəkəl]   *adj.* 互相给予的，互惠的，相互的
affinity [əˈfiniti]   *n.* 强烈喜爱(某人/某事物)
sublime [səˈblaim]   *n.* 庄严，崇高
attune [əˈtjuːn]   *vt.* 使调和，使相合
cataract [ˈkætərækt]   *n.* 大瀑布，奔流
akin [əˈkin]   *adj.* 类似的
reverence [ˈrevərəns]   *n. & v.* 尊敬，(尤指宗教的)崇敬
mystic [ˈmistik]   *n.* 神秘家，神秘主义者
rupture [ˈrʌptʃə(r)]   *n.* 破裂，决裂，敌对
reckon [ˈrekən]   *v.* 考虑到或重视某人/某事物
depopulate [diːˈpɔpjuleit]   *v.* (使)人口减少
divinity [diˈviniti]   *n.* 神，神学，神性，上帝
monotheistic [mɔnəuθiːˈistik]   *adj.* 一神论的
Judaism [ˈdʒuːdeiizəm]   *n.* 犹太教
oracular [ɔˈrækjulə]   *adj.* 神谕的，明哲的
Delphi [ˈdelfai]   *n.* 特尔斐(希腊古都，因 Apollo(太阳神)的神殿而著称)
Eleusis [ˌeljəˈθirin]   *n.* 依路西斯(古希腊中东部一城市)
Shinto [ˈʃintəu]   *n.* 日本之神道教
precept [ˈpriːsept]   *n.* 准则，戒律，箴言
Kami [ˈkaːmi]   *n.* 〈日〉(神道教的)神
cleft [kleft]   *n.* 裂缝，隙口

LESSON 7

fissure [ˈfiʃə]	n. 裂缝，裂沟
evoke [iˈvəuk]	v. 唤起，引起
shroud [ʃraud]	v. 覆盖
metaphorical [ˌmetəˈfɔrikəl]	adj. 隐喻性的，比喻性的
ingenuity [ˌindʒiˈnjuːiti]	n. 心灵手巧；善于发明创造
emulate [ˈemjuleit]	v. （竭力）仿效/赶超某人，与某人竞争
mandarin [ˈmændərin]	n. 官僚的，保守知识界的
arriviste [ˌæriːˈvist]	n. 暴发户，新贵
blunder [ˈblʌndə]	n. 大错，失误
codify [ˈkɔdifai, ˈkəu-]	vt. 编成法典，使法律成文化
foremost [ˈfɔːməust]	adj. （位置或时间）最先的，最初的，最重要的
	adv. 首要地，首先
railing [ˈreiliŋ]	n. 栏杆，围栏
lattice [ˈlætis]	n. 格子，格子窗，格子门
static [ˈstætik]	adj. 静态的，固定的
pulsate [pʌlˈseit, ˈpʌlseit]	vi. 搏动，（有规律的）跳动
misty [ˈmisti]	adj. 有薄雾的
concubine [ˈkɔŋkjubain]	n. 妾
stately [ˈsteitli]	adj. 庄严的，堂皇的
quarry [ˈkwɔri]	vt. 采（石），挖掘
precipice [ˈpresipis]	n. 悬崖，峭壁
vibrancy [ˈvaibrənsi]	n. 振动，振动性，活跃，响亮
calligraphy [kəˈligrəfi]	n. 书法
mundane [ˈmʌndein]	adj. 世俗的，平凡的
workaday [ˈwəːkədei]	adj. 工作日的
animated [ˈænimeitid]	adj. 生气勃勃的，活跃的，活泼的
bas-relief [ˈbæsriliːf]	n. 浅浮雕，低浮雕
frieze [friːz]	n. 雕饰，（墙头或建筑物上端的）带状装饰
discrete [disˈkriːt]	adj. 不连续的，离散的
tracery [ˈtreisəri]	n. [建] 花饰窗格，窗饰
gourd [guəd]	n. 葫芦类植物
whitewash [ˈ(h)waitwɔʃ]	v. 用石灰水把…刷白，粉刷
lustrous [ˈlʌstrəs]	adj. 有光泽的
neutral [ˈnjuːtrəl]	adj. 浅色的，无色的，非彩色的
foil [fɔil]	n. [建] 烘托，衬托
cove [kəuv]	n. 小（海）湾，（河）湾/〈美〉小峡谷
tortuous [ˈtɔːtjuəs]	adj. 曲折的，盘旋的
indented [inˈdentid]	adj. 锯齿状的，犬牙交错的
bureaucratic [ˌbjuərəuˈkrætɪk]	adj. 官僚政治的

Part II History of Landscape Architecture

poetical [pəuˈetikəl]	adj. 诗的，诗意的
municipal [mju(ː)ˈnisipəl]	adj. 市政的，地方性的，地方自治的
outline [ˈautlain]	n. 轮廓，外形
interlock [ˌintəˈlɔk]	v. 连接，组合；连锁，互锁
palanquin [pælənˈkiːn]	n. 轿子
alley [ˈæli]	n. 小路，巷，（花园里两边有树篱的）小径
circuitous [sə(ː)ˈkju(ː)itəs]	adj. 迂回线路的
finial [ˈfainiəl]	n. [建] 叶尖饰，尖顶饰，物件顶端的装饰物
poise [pɔiz]	v. （使）平衡，（使）悬着
osmanthus [ɔsˈmænθəs]	n. [植] 木犀属植物
rockwork [ˈrɔkwəːk]	n. 假山；天然岩石群
lacy [ˈleisi]	adj. 花边的
fretwork [ˈfretwəːk]	n. [建] 浮雕细工
pictorial [pikˈtɔːriəl]	adj. 有图画的，用图画表示的
tracery [ˈtreisəri]	n. [建] 花饰窗格，窗饰
tassel [ˈtæsl]	n. 穗，缨
veranda [vəˈrændə]	n. 阳台，走廊
summerhouse [ˈsʌməhaus]	n. 凉亭，亭子
study [ˈstʌdi]	n. 书房
pebble [ˈpebl]	n. 小圆石，小鹅卵石
Genghis Khan	n. 成吉思汗（中国元太祖）
topple [ˈtɔp(ə)l]	v. 使倾覆，推翻
assimilate [əˈsimileit]	v. 吸收
disaffected [disəˈfektid]	adj. 抱不平的，有叛意的，不服的
excavate [ˈekskəveit]	v. 挖掘，开凿
marshy [ˈmɑːʃi]	adj. 沼泽般的
nucleus [ˈnjuːkliəs]	n. 核心，中心，基点
dredge [dredʒ]	v. 挖掘，捞取
stud [stʌd]	v. 散布，点缀
lapis lazuli [ˈlæpisˈlæzjulai]	n. 天青石，青金石
geomancy [ˈdʒi(ː)əumænsi]	n. 泥土占卜（抓沙散地，按其所成象以断吉凶）
hierarchical [ˌhaiəˈrɑːkikəl]	adj. 分等级的
nest [nest]	v. 置于巢中，重叠放置
rectangular [rekˈtæŋgjulə]	adj. 矩形的
ceremonial [ˌseriˈməunjəl]	adj. 礼仪的，仪式的，正式的

KEY CONCEPTS

Scholar-garden

borrowed scenery
Chinese garden design
Paving design
Stone selection
Calligraphy
Geomancy

NOTES

1. The notion of landscape as a text with encoded meaning, a place of memory and association, an experiential space in which to stroll and enjoy the unfolding of sequential views or to sit quietly and ponder the thoughts prompted by the impressions of scenery upon the sense—these fundamentals were common to both East Asian gardens and the gardens developed in England in eighteenth century.

    景观的概念作为一种具有编码意义的题目,作为记忆和联想的地方,作为漫步和享受系列风景展开的体验空间,或者坐下来静静地沉思风景对感觉所带来的印象——这些基本要素对于东亚园林以及后来18世纪在英国所发展的园林是共同的。

2. *Kami*

    只有通过信仰才能辨知的(神道教的)神,向人类生活施加了一种神秘的有创造性的、和谐的影响。与个体宗族相联系的守护神在神社中接受崇拜,他们向崇拜者展现真正的办法和意愿。

3. 虽然中国园林与西方风景园林(Picturesque garden)对于不规则和自然的效果有共同的偏爱,但它作为一件艺术品更为简洁紧凑,充当着整个自然界的一个象征。这一艺术转而为日本庭园的设计提供了推动力,在日本庭园中,艺术和自然之间的关系被神道教的传统和来自中国的佛教思想所支持。佛教没有破坏和消灭神道教,而是与它并存,这加强了日本与自然的联系。这一发展始于公元6世纪末期,表现了日本人有意识地将外来影响融入其文化核心的能力,在这一过程中将它们改造成为真正本土化的表现形式。

QUESTIONS FOR REVIEW AND DISCUSSION

1. Discuss Jicheng's prescription for garden making.
2. Explain what is the scholar-gardens, using some examples.
3. Discuss the influence of Chinese culture on Japanese garden.

Part II *History of Landscape Architecture*

Reading Material

The Influence of Chinese culture on Japanese Garden(Part one)

By the time Chinese teachings reached Japan in earnest in the sixth century, the Chinese had already developed a comprehensive and sophisticated understanding of the physical universe. To the literate Chinese, who had developed knowledge in the areas of astronomy, mathmatics, civil engineering, and other fields, the landscape had meanings beyond the animistic sacredness attributed to it by the Japanese. In landscape the Chinese saw the working of great universal forces and laws. Observation of nature not only provided spiritual inspiration but offered a key to cosmic understanding.

Unlike the Japanese of the time, the Chinese were great builders, and their cities, temples, tombs, and homes were modeled after their conceptions of the universal order. In addition, the arts of landscape gardening and painting were meant to exemplify the action of cosmic design.

LANDSCAPE PHILOSOPHY: THE HARMONIC IDEAL

Certain ideas run like main currents throughout the course of Chinese philosophy. There is a central assumption that the universe is in constant change, a continuing process of growth and decay, creation and destruction, life and death. Everything is subject to this process, and nothing remains static: Just as the clouds change shape in the wind and the stars move in the heavens, so too do the mountains and valleys change, though they move too slowly for human observation. Two great opposing forces are revealed in this constant process, and since time immemorial they have been called yin and yang.

Yin is female, mother, negative, dark, damp, deep, and destructive. Yang is male, father, positive, bright, hard, high, penetrating, and constructive. Between these opposite poles, the great oscillations of the universe take place. Neither can exist independently, for all things yang contain some small element of yin and vice versa. In the extreme of one we see the creation of the other in a pattern much like a sinusoidal wave: Strong activity results in rest, as extreme winter coldness gives way to spring warmth. Thus creation is seen as a multitude of cyclic processes represented by black-and-white diagrams that express these whirling patterns of change.

A goal in life, as well as in art, for many was to achieve harmony: harmony of forces within an individual and of those without. Internally, various practices(yoga) were used to manipulate and balance breathing and sexual energy, which were considered direct

---

选自　Mitchell Bring, Josses Wayembergh Japanese Gardens Design and Meaning McGraw-Hill Book Company

LESSON 7

human manifestations of yin and yang forces. Externally, people sought to integrate their homes and ancestral tombs with the energy in the environment. Landscape was invested with sexual attributes, and every element could be classified, depending on shape and quality, into yin or yang. The very word for landscape, a combination of the Chinese characters for mountain(yang)and water(yin), implies this dualism. Landscape art, both painting and gardening, sought to represent ideal harmony. The "opening and closing" relationships of hills and valleys, positive and negative shapes, horizontal and vertical, were invoked as evidence of balanced yin and yang.

Other symbols were also used to express the workings of yin and yang. A primary idea of Chinese culture was the division of the universe into three parts: heaven, earth, and man. The problems of human existence could be solved by reconciling the claims of heaven (yang)and earth(yin). Heaven, represented by a circle, was seen as the source of the various energies that worked through the passive earth(represented by a square)where people labored to effect favorable changes for themselves in their present life and after death. The old-fashioned Chinese coin—a circle pierced by a square with an Imperial inscription between the two forms—represents this fundamental relationship. A chief function of the Emperor was to serve as an intermediary between the two realms. By performing rites in his palace and city, which were specifically designed for this purpose, he attempted to reconcile the claims of each. A major natural diaster was an almost certain sign that the Emperor was unsuccessful in fulfilling his duties.

Chinese landscape art always depicted elements of heaven, earth, and people, or something man-made(such as a path or bridge), implying that no matter how small the human element seemed in comparison to the majestic mountains and seas, the scene was not complete without some indication of human presence. Landscape painting tried to show the harmonic ideal, and great engineering feats—which imply the subjugation of nature—are usually not pictured. Conversely, ruins or wrecks such as those painted in romantic European landscapes, suggesting the domination of nature over people, never appear in East Asian landscape paintings. Such paintings instead pictured a person in complete harmony with the environment: hence the recurring figure in painting and literature of the scholar hermit in his retreat. Freed from the petty concerns and intrigues of an official career, the hermit scholar was able to find inspiration, insight, and fulfillment amid the mountains and rivers of the countryside. Most often pictured alone—or with a single attendant—living in a simple thatched hut, the recluse represented an ultimate in tranquillity and harmony.

This ideal image had a lasting impact on garden form in Japan. Indeed, later on this was a principal reason for building a garden in the first place. As the Japanese tried to recreate the setting of a retreat amid the "wildness" of nature, architecture and landscape gardening were designed to meet this purpose. Even the most elaborate Japanese structures were little more than pavilions, easily opened to the garden outside, while the humble

Part II History of Landscape Architecture

ceremonial tea house of the Japanese tea garden takes its form directly from the hut of a retreat. The buildings and the garden surroundings attempted to recreate this ideal, which reflected the harmony and balance of the cosmos.

WORDS AND EXPRESSIONS

literate [ˈlitərit]	adj. 有文化的
sacred [ˈseikrid]	adj. 神的，宗教的，庄严的，神圣的
sacredness	n. 神，宗教
animistic [ˌæniˈmistik]	adj. 万物有灵论的
animistic sacredness	泛神论
oscillation [ˌɔsiˈleiʃən]	n. 摆动，振动
sinusoidal [ˌsaɪnəˈsɔɪdəl]	adj. 正弦曲线的
dualism [ˈdjuːəlizəm]	n. 二重性，二元性
depict [diˈpikt]	vt. 描绘
majestic [məˈdʒestik]	adj. 雄伟的，庄严的
subjugation [ˌsʌbdʒuˈgeiʃən]	n. 征服，克制
hermit [ˈhəːmit]	n. 隐士

LESSON 8

LANDSCAPE DESIGN IN THE EAST: JAPAN

Chinese garden concepts arrived in Japan along with Buddhism in the sixth century. Although sharing a similar aesthetic approach, the gardens built in the small, Well-watered island nation of Japan would ultimately differ from those of China, a country of vastly greater dimensions, a land of contrasting wide plains and mountainous precipices. After appropriating Chinese garden concepts, instead of continuing to create "recollections" of famous scenes in nature in the Chinese manner, Japanese garden designers increasingly sought a generic ideal of nature in conformity with the scale and topography of their own natural landscape.

The eleventh-century treatise known as the *Sakuteiki*, presumably written by Tachibana no Toshitsuna(1028~1084), is Japan's earliest known manual of garden rules.[1] In it one finds prescriptions for the handling of stones set within moving water in the socalled "large river style." The *Sakuteiki* counsels that, in order to make a proper garden, one should travel widely and become acquainted with beautiful scenes in nature, indicating that by this time the Japanese had singled out various famous views as prized components of their country's natural landscape. Besides giving precise instructions for building waterfalls and other garden features, the author encourages gardeners to orient their buildings to the south according to the principles of geomancy. Logically, streams should be placed on this, their most open, side. He prescribed that these flow from east to west in order to cleanse the evil air emanating from the northeast and ward off demons. In addition to following these prescriptions of the *Sakuteiki*, Japanese garden designers often incorporated a distant vista in their designs in order to enlarge the visual sphere of the usually quite small garden and to reinforce its connection with the natural world. They referred to this technique of borrowing scenery as *shakkei*.

Buddhist creation mythology and Daoist belief in the paradisaical Isles of the Blest furnished the lakeand-islands motif that underlies the composition of many Japanese gardens, even those compressed visions of a Zen Buddhist universe known as *kare sansui*, or dry landscapes[2]. Beginning in the thirteenth century, members of the newly imported Zen sect designed these spare, almost austere, gardens as aids to meditation. These are minimalist compositions of carefully positioned stones, which are meant to be read as islands in a dry

---

选自 Elizabeth Barlow Rogers Landscape Design: A Cultural and Architecture History Harry N. Abrams, INC, Publishers

"river" of carefully raked gravel or sand or as mountains in a landscape of mosses. Such Zen-inspired gardens played an important role among members of the ruling classes; certain emperors and even some shoguns—powerful military dictators who ruled under the nominal authority of the emperor—found garden-making to be a satisfying escape from court politics and civil strife. The tea ceremony, developed in the late fifteenth century, was not a religious exercise, but it nevertheless provided a disciplined experience of concentration and aesthetic and spiritual refreshment for which passage along a garden path of moss and stones offered a prescribed prelude and conclusion.

The Japanese combined their penchant for cultural appropriation with a talent for reinvention. Japan's island geography and a semi-isolationist policy during much of its history fostered the assimilation and transformation of those ideas and forms that were adopted from the outside into a vigorous native expression. The arrival of Commodore Matthew Perry's American ships in Tokyo Bay in 1853~1954 ended the country's previous two centuries of closure to all but Dutch and Chinese traders, whose access was strictly limited. Increasing transactions with the West started Japan on a path of profound change. Without some degree of cultural isolation and the focused aestheticism that matured the Japanese garden into a great art form, the slow but creative evolution that counts as development within a traditional artistic idiom came to a standstill. Its assimilative energies directed toward building a powerful economy and its political life reshaped since 1945 as a capitalist democracy, Japan has become today a conservator of its cultural heritage. As in other countries where the government and cultural institutions protect a "golden age" of previous artistic accomplishment, in Japan the state and the religious establishments of Kyoto maintain the incomparable imperial and Buddhist temple gardens as much-appreciated heritage icons and tourist attractions.

The talents of Japanese landscape designers today contribute to the pluralistic internationalism of garden art rather than to the continued development of a specifically indigenous style. The *vocabulary* of Japanese garden design—its abstract compositional harmonies, its elegant rusticity, its "borrowed" views, its asymmetrical configuration of design elements, its attention to ground plane patterns and textures in the arrangement of moss and stones—has furnished inspiration to modern garden designers in other countries. To appreciate more fully the richness of simplicity in this carefully matured language of landscape, we must now review the history of Japanese gardens.

THE NARA AND HEIAN COURTS

Buddhism was introduced from China into Japan in 552. Under the regent, Prince Shotoku(573~621), who promoted it and built temples, it gained the kind of institutional status enjoyed by Christianity in the West after the reign of Constantine the Great. The acceptance of Buddhism, together with contacts with Korea and the first official Japanese embassy to China in the early seventh century, stimulated the adoption of Chinese artistic and architectural forms. Formerly, rulers had constructed their dwellings in the vernacular style of the structures at the Ise Shrine. Moreover, because of the premium put upon spatial purification and ritual rebuilding, the capital was moved at the beginning of each new reign. In 710, however, the court was established at Nara, and there it remained for the next seventy-five years through several reigns.

The plan of the city, with its hierarchical ordering of space within a grid layout, was, at a lesser scale, a conscious imitation of that of Chang'an, the Chinese Tang dynasty capital. The temples constructed to house large images of Buddha were unlike any previous Japanese architectural forms. The spatial layout of their surrounding compounds also followed Chinese models.

Korean craftsmen were brought to Nara to help develop imperial gardens in the Chinese manner, with lakes and rock arrangements forming islands. From archaeological excavations, as well as from paintings and poetry of this period, we surmise that these were similar to the Tang models they sought to imitate, being *yarimizu*, or river-style gardens. Their meandering streams furnished the opportunity to organize poetry competitions like the ones popular in contemporary Chinese gardens.

Upon ascending the throne in 781, Emperor Kammu decided to move the capital once more, probably in order to separate the government from the influence of priests at Nara, who, to his distress, had amassed considerable political power. After ten years of building this new capital, Nagaoka-kyō, the not-yet-finished city was abandoned in favor of another site nearby, Heian-kyō, meaning the Capital of Peace and Tranquility, the original name of Kyoto. Once established, Kyoto became the imperial capital of Japan for more than a thousand years until the Meiji Restoration in 1868, when Tokyo was made the capital.

In Kyoto, as at Nara, the gridiron plan of Chang'an formed the model for a new city roughly half Nara's size, or 3.5 miles(5.6 kilometers) north to south by 3 miles(4.8 kilometers) east to west[3]. Also, as at Nara, the imperial enclosure, known as the Daidairi, was placed at the end of a broad axis at the city's northern end. The surrounding city was subdivided into 76 large squares, measuring approximately 400 feet(122 meters) to a side. The eastern half of this residential grid became the location of choice for the nobility; however, the western half was never developed in accordance with its original outlines. In an attempt to avoid the political tensions that had existed at Nara, the emperor mandated that new temples be sited outside the city, and these were therefore built on the lower slopes of the surrounding hills, as were estates of the powerful nobility.

In the Heian period(781~1185), a golden age for Kyoto, all the arts, including landscape design, were held in high esteem. Gardens in this period were ampler than later ones, and the lakes in them were generous in size. Fortunately for posterity, Murasaki Shikibu(970?~1026?), a lady of the court, chronicled the aesthetic pursuits of the elite during the Heian era in *The Tale of Genji*, a novel written around the year 1000. In it we

Part II *History of Landscape Architecture*

read of Prince Genji in many beautiful garden settings as he enjoys such pastimes as rowing in Chinese-style boats around the islands in the lake or going on an outing to admire the fall foliage. Inspired by Chinese models, these islands consisted of arrangements of rocks, some intended to suggest the form of a symbolically meaningful tortoise or crane. Pavilions in the style known as *shindenzukuri* stood at the edge of the water. These structures, derived from Chinese architectural norms, were elegant in their lines but rustic in character, with reticulated two-part shutters that could be raised in summer. Their floors were polished wood, as tatami mats and other specifically Japanese conventions had not yet become established. These viewing platforms were actually projecting wings of a large central pavilion, or *shinden*, that faced the lake. A swath of white sand at the lake's edge served as a stage for mime and dance performances, which could be enjoyed from a *shindenzukuri* pavilion. Raised covered passages linked the separate pavilions with each other and with the *shinden*.

Within Japan's feudal social structure, the powerful Fujiwara clan had gained supremacy by 850, and in their role as regents for emperors in their minority, members of this family gradually appropriated much of the imperial power and married into the imperial family. Their chief, Fujiwara no Michinaga(966~1027), held the title of *kampaku*, a high governmental position in which he mediated between the emperor and court officials in affairs of state. As respected but powerless figureheads, emperors typically spent their lives engaged in cultural pursuits. Making a virtue of their relatively raduced circumstances, they refined their chosen style, which was derived from rustic vernacular architecture, into a vocabulary of elegantly crafted details and beautifully proportioned parts. By contrast, the Fujiwara, like the shoguns who followed them, liked to display their power in works of magnificence. The splendor of the Heian period is found in the Byōdō-in, built as a villa by the *kampaku* Fujiwara Yorimichi(992~1074)on his estate south of Kyoto and converted into a temple in 1052. The pond garden(now severely compromised in size)and serene *shinden*-style Phoenix Hall(Hōō-dō)of 1053 at Byōdō-in—so named because its soaring wings evoke those of the mythical bird as it alights—were meant to depict Amida Buddha's Paradise. It is the sole remaining structure of the twenty-six halls and seven pagodas that were once grouped around the pond at the Byōdō-in.

As they became increasingly interested in cultural rather than military pursuits, the Fujiwara regents were challenged by other powerful clans, the Taira and Minamoto, and the emperor now more than ever governed in name only. Power first fell to the Taira, but their authority was upset by the Minamoto clan and their *samurai* army. The Minamoto established headquarters at the town of Kamakura, which gave ist name to the period of their ascendancy. Shoguns, in whom hereditary military command rested, continued to exert authority more or less continuously from the late twelfth century until the Meiji Restoration of 1868.

LESSON 8

WORDS AND EXPRESSIONS

generic [dʒiˈnerik]	adj. 一般的，通有的
precipice [ˈpresipis]	n. 悬崖
cleanse [klenz]	v. 使纯洁，使纯净
emanate [ˈeməneit]	v. 散发，发出，发源
vista [ˈvistə]	n. 狭长的景色；街景；深景（尤指人透过如两排建筑或树木之间空隙看到的远景或视觉感受）
mythology [miˈθɔlədʒi]	n. 神话
blest [blest]	adj. 神圣的
motif [məuˈtiːf]	n. 主题，主旨；图形
sect [sekt]	n. 宗派，教派，教士会，流派
meditation [mediˈteiʃən]	n. 沉思，冥想
rake [reik]	v. 用耙子耙
shogun [ˈʃəuˌɡuːn]	n.〈日〉幕府时代的将军
nominal [ˈnɔminl]	adj. 名义上的，有名无实的
strife [straif]	n. 斗争，冲突，竞争
prelude [ˈpreljuːd]	n. 前奏，序幕
penchant [ˈpɑːŋʃɔːŋ]	n.（强烈的）倾向，爱好，嗜好
commodore [ˈkɔmədɔː]	n. 海军准将，船队队长
Kyoto [kiˈəutəu]	n. 京都（日本古都）
transaction [trænˈzækʃən]	n. 办理，处理；交易，事务
assimilative [əˈsimilətiv]	adj. 同化的，同化力的
icon [ˈaikɔn]	n. 图标，肖像，偶像
pluralistic [ˌpluərəˈlistik]	adj. 多元文化的
indigenous [inˈdidʒinəs]	adj. 本土的
asymmetrical [ˌæsiˈmetrikl]	adj. 不均匀的，不对称的
rusticity [rʌˈstisəti]	n. 乡村式，田园生活
furnish [ˈfəːniʃ]	vt. 供应，提供，装备，布置
	v. 供给
Nara [ˈnɑːrə]	n. 奈良（日本本州岛中西部城市）
Heian [ˈheiən, ˌheiˈɑːn]	adj.〈日〉平安时代的（指日本历史上以文艺兴旺发展著称的时期，794～1185）
regent [ˈriːdʒənt]	n. 摄政者
institutional [ˌinstiˈtjuːʃənəl]	adj. 制度上的；法律的；社会事业性质的
vernacular [vəˈnækjulə]	adj. 本国的
premium [ˈpriːmjəm]	n. 奖励，奖赏

Part II *History of Landscape Architecture*

put a premium on	奖励，鼓励，重视，助长
lesser ['lesə]	adj. 较小的
excavation [ˌekskə'veiʃən]	n. 挖掘，发掘，挖掘成的洞，出土文物
surmise ['sə:maiz]	v. 推测，猜测
furnish ['fə:niʃ]	vt. 供应，提供
amass [ə'mæs]	vt. 积累，积聚
Nagaoka ['na:ga:'əuka:]	n. 长冈［日本本州岛中北部城市］
Meiji ['meidʒi:]	n. 明治（日本明治天皇睦仁）
Meiji Restoration	明治维新
gridiron ['gridˌaiən]	n. 铁格架，格状物
mandate ['mændeit]	vt. 命令，要求
ample ['æmpl]	adj. 大的，宽敞的
posterity [pɔs'teriti]	n. 子孙，后裔
chronicle ['krɔnikl]	v. 记事，叙述；记录，记载
pastime ['pa:staim]	n. 消遣，娱乐
outing ['autiŋ]	n. 外出，户外散步
foliage ['fəuliidʒ]	n. 植物的叶子（总称）；叶子及梗和枝
reticulated [ri'tikjulitid]	adj. 网状的
shutter ['ʃʌtə(r)]	n. 遮蔽物；百叶窗；窗板
tatami [tə'ta:mi]	n.〈日〉榻榻米（日本人铺在室内地板上的稻草垫）
swath [swɔ:θ]	n. 长而宽的地带；长而宽的一条
mime [maim]	n. 哑剧
supremacy [sju'preməsi]	n. 地位最高的人，至高，无上，霸权
figurehead ['figəhed]	n. 有名无实的领袖
serene [si'ri:n]	adj. 平静的，宁静的
soaring ['sɔ:riŋ 'sɔər-]	adj. 高飞的；高耸入云的
alight [ə'lait]	vi. 下来，飞落
samurai ['sæmurai]	n.（封建时代的）日本武士，日本陆军军官
Kamakura [ˌka:ma:'kura]	n.［日］镰仓，日本本州岛东南部一城市，濒临横滨南部太平洋的一个海湾。该市可能建于公元7世纪，如今为旅游胜地、住宅区和宗教中心。
hereditary [hi'reditəri]	adj. 世袭的
ascendancy [ə'sendənsi]	n. 优势，支配（或统治）地位

KEY CONCEPTS

Geomancy practice
Vantage point
tracery
Japanese garden design
Central pavilion
Rustic vernacular architecture

NOTES

1. 对于造园 the Sakuteiki or Treatise on Garden Making 的一个精彩概括，见 Loraine Kuck，日本园林世界：从中国起源到现代景观艺术（*The World of the Japanese Garden：From Chinese* Origins to Modern Landscape Art（纽约：Weatherhill，1968），pp. 91～93。Kuck 的日本园林史中一部珍贵的参考文献。

2. Buddhist creation mythology and Daoist belief in the paradisaical Isles of Blest furnished the lake-and-islands motif that underlies the composition of many Japanese garden, even those compressed visions of Zen Buddhist universe known as *kare sansui*, or dry landscape.

　　佛教所创造的神话及道教福地仙岛的信念形成的湖-岛主题成为很多日本园林的基本构成，即便是被广泛认知的禅宗凝炼视觉的枯山水也是如此。kare sansui 日文音译，即枯山水。

3. 唐代长安东西跨度大约 6 英里（9.7km），南北长度约 5.25 英里（8.5km）。被丘陵包围的京都只能向南扩展。

QUESTIONS FOR REVIEW AND DISCUSSION

1. What unique environmental factors led to different/similar development of garden forms in the Chinese and Japanese gardens?
2. How are the design expressions related to Japan unique cultural, social or political forces of each period?
3. Of what value is learning the fundamentals of garden's long history?

Part II History of Landscape Architecture

Reading Material

The Influence of Chinese culture on Japanese Garden(Part two)

LANDSCAPE PRACTICE: GEOMANCY

Given this expressed goal of harmony, these questions must be asked: How did the Chinese, and later the Japanese, conceive of nature(heaven and earth)and how did they try to harmonize with it when building cities, homes, and gardens? Analysis of Chinese geomancy provides answers to both questions in summary form. Defined as "the art of adapting the residences of the living and the dead so as to cooperate and harmonize with the local currents of the cosmic breath," geomancy has been the subject of considerable interest and controversy. Ernest Eitel, writing in 1873, called geomancy(*feng-shui*, Chinese, and *fusui*, Japanese—literally meaning wind and water)the "rudiments of Chinese natural science," and he recorded the strong objections voiced by the Chinese of Hong Kong to British planned improvements such as telegraphs, railroads, and even church spires because they violated geomantic principles. Joseph Needham called geomancy a "far reaching pseudo science" and acknowledged its contributions to modern science, such as the invention of the magnetic compass and the attention to landscape that resulted in topographical mapping. Loraine Kuck in her study of Japanese gardens ignored geomancy completely, believing it had misled josiah Conder in his first explanations of the gardens; but she recognized the role it played in the "secret" manual of Japanese gardeners. It is now thought to be a principal foundation of urban planning in the Chinese realm with geomantic ideas closely incorporated into early garden making practice.

The concern of geomancy for integrating structures of human origin with the great forces of nature made it the "ecology" of its day. The "wind and waters" of Chinese geomancy refer to the cosmic breath of energy(*ch'i*)of heaven and earth, which had to be determined for a particular site before anything could be built. Earth here means the living biological earth where seasonal cycles of plant and animal life seemed to demonstrate the fixed mathematical laws seen in the motions of the heavenly bodies. The fundamental energy of *ch'i*, which flows through the heavens, was similarly perceived to be flowing through the bodies of all living things, including the "body" of earth. Just as humans have veins and acupuncture sites where *ch'i* can be stimulated and adjusted, the earth too had veins(surface and subterranean watercourses)and centers of *ch'i*. This is graphically described by a fourteenth-century Chinese scientist:

The body of the earth is like that of a human being... Ordinary people, not being able to see the veins and vessels which are disposed in order within the body of man, think that it is no more than a lump of solid flesh. Likewise, not being able to see the veins and vessels which are disposed in order under the ground, they think that the earth is just a homogeneous mass.

Just as a person should be judged for signs of sickness or health by physical appearance, so could a prospective building site. This was extremely important, for the health of human beings was seen to be directly interrelated with the health of their environment:

Now if the ch'i of the earth can get through the veins, then the water and the earth above will be fragrant and flourishing; and all men and things will be pure and wise... but if the ch'i of the earth is stopped up, then the water and earth and natural products will be bitter, cold and withered... and all men and things will be evil and foolish.

This relationship between people and the earth was considered very delicate and easily damaged or repaired:

When Hideyoshi's [d. 1598] soldiers of Japan invaded Korea, they set up camp in Sonsan for a time. A Japanese geomancer of the army unit observed the form of the mountains and realized that the place would produce many great men and that Korea would be prosperous.

For this reason, the Japanese geomancer advised the soldiers to burn an important place on the mountain in the back of Sonsan town and to drive in a great iron piling. In this way he killed the vital energy for the mountain.

After that time, strangely, no great men were born in Sonsan or even in the neighbouring counties.

Thus, until a few decades ago it is said that people were roaming around in the mountains of Sonsan County in order to find the iron bar.

The key factor affecting the energy of a site was its orientation, and the magnetic compass was first developed in service to geomancy. It was used by the Chinese for site reading and planning centuries before they used it for navigation. The original compass consisted of a square plate(representing the earth)marked with the main compass points beneath a polished circular disk(representing heaven); a magnetic spoon made from lodestone modeled after the shape of the Big Dipper was placed on the disk to indicate direction. Subsequent developments saw the spoon replaced by the familiar dry pivot compass, which was surrounded by numerous concentric rings pertaining to both the positions of the heavens and the conditions of the landscape. One ring, for example, is based on the twelve-year cycle of Jupiter, with each year represented by an animal. On the compass dial, each of the twelve divisions also pertains to a month, a direction, and a two-hour period of the day. Time and direction were thus inseparably linked in the Chinese classification, and the compass, like the calendar year, was divided into $365\frac{1}{4}$ units. The geomantic compass embodied large portions of the Chinese understanding of natural processes.

In building site selection, ideally the geomancer would be free to choose the most auspicious spot in the landscape. Often, however, such selection was not possible and, in these cases, the geomancer was called upon to evaluate and provide instructions for site improvements(Fig. 1). The compass was aligned and calculations were made regarding positions of the heavens. Next, important landscape features were observed and their relative position noted. A tally was kept of all these important celestial and terrestrial factors, and the final computations resulted in a formula for building: Perhaps a pond had to be dug or an artificial mountain built; a too-yang angular hill might have to be rounded by bushes or a too-yin site might need some prominent trees or stones. Like a giant acupuncture needle, a pagoda might be erected to stimulate the local currents of *ch'i*.

When reading the actual landscape, geomancers found significance in many things. Mountains, often called "dragons" in the geomantic literature, were the most powerful determinants of *ch'i*. In general, geomancers sought to avoid disturbing the sleeping dragons. Just before his death, a builder of the Great Wall remarked, "I could not make the Great Wall without cutting through the veins of the earth." Stones (and dinosaur bones) were often called the bones of the dragons and were considered to harbor great concentrations of energy.

The origin and flow of watercourses was next in importance in determining the *ch'i* of a site. Water could block the flow of *ch'i* and thus could be harmful if it prevented *ch'i* from entering a site, or good if it helped concentrate the *ch'i* by slowing its exit. Underground watercourses were also carefully noted, as were wind and soil conditions.

This attention to natural phenomena resulted in some practical benefits. The first thing recommended by a geomancer was a southfacing site, preferably protected by a horseshoe-shaped mountain closed on all sides except the south. In terms of sun exposure and protection from bad weather, this makes sound sense environmentally, as does the predilection for flowing water near dwellings. Geomantic practice placed the dwelling in the "belly of the dragon", i.e., inside the bend of a river, where it was not prone to the eroding action that cuts away the outside bank. A strong aversion to underground seepage led to careful observation of terrain and soil, which was examined for "inauspicious" insects at the same time. This careful site selection was practical, as was the planting of trees to

Fig. 1 The geomancer Consulting his compass when selecting a city site.

form a windbreak in accord with the geomantic preference for a calm site. Trees were also often planted simply to balance the energy of a site.

A large part of geomancy—its less functional side—was concerned with allegorical readings of meaning in the landscape. Land forms were given descriptive poetic names such as the "sitting general" or "horses standing still," and the needs and functions of landscape were assessed in allegorical terms as illustrated by this story from Korea, where Chinese geomancy was also practiced:

The Kim family of Sangchon lived in Mokchon village with great prosperity and power. Whenever a new governor of Andong County arrived, he had to visit the family first and greet them. When Maeng Sasong came to Andong as the governor of the county, he thought that this visit was not the right thing to do for a person who was in the position of governor. Therefore, he changed the direction of a stream to Sangchon village in order to suppress the auspiciousness of Mokchon. This was done because the landscape of the Kim village was the type of a silkworm's head, and therefore the silkworm could not cross the stream to reach the mulberry grove. In addition, he removed the mulberry trees and planted lacquer trees in order to kill the silkworm. After that, the Kim family lost its fortune and declined.

This allegorical understanding of landscape was also an aesthetic evaluation. Geomancers saw "beauty" as a clear indication of auspiciousness, and often modifications were made to the landscape principally to improve its appearance and thus one's fortune. Indeed, Needham credits geomancy with responsibility for the "exceptional beauty of the positioning of farmhouses, manors, villages and cities throughout the realm of the Chinese culture."

Because the garden was built within the context of a greater landscape, its siting had to be integrated with the macropatterns of the region. And because it used the real substances of earth—stones, trees, and water—the micropatterns of *ch'i* had to be coordinated within the garden. The garden artist had to discern the veins of energy contained within the stones and harmonize the currents between them. Paths, river courses, and other shapes generated their own currents which also had to be fully harmonized with each other.

Thus seen through the eyes of a geomancer, the artificially constructed environment which we today call a garden had many different levels of meaning. It was made to be the most ideal of landscapes, designed to bring the best possible luck. It was both beautiful, for beauty is a sign of good fortune, and functional, as it manipulated the local currents of *ch'i* for maximum benefit. The beautiful landscape was the geomantically correct landscape.

WORDS AND EXPRESSIONS

lodestone ['ləudstəun]   *n.* 天然磁石
Jupiter ['dʒu:pitə]   *n.* 木星

Part II History of Landscape Architecture

terrestrial [tiˈrestriəl]	adj. 地球(上)的；陆地的
predilection [ˌpriːdiˈlekʃən]	n. 偏爱，偏好
immortal [iˈmɔːtl]	adj. 不朽的 流芳百世的
oscillate [ˈɔsileit]	v. 摆动，振动
crane [krein]	n. 鹤
pilgrim [ˈpilgrim]	n. 香客，朝山进香的人
sinusoid [ˈsainəˌsɔid]	n. 正弦曲线
manifestation [ˌmænifesˈteiʃən]	n. 表明，表现形式；现象
reconcile [ˈrekənsail]	v. 使和解，调解，调和
inscription [inˈskripʃən]	n. 铭刻，碑文
intermediary [ˌintəˈmiːdiəri]	n. 中介物，手段，工具
majestic [məˈdʒestik]	adj. 庄严的，雄伟的，壮丽的
retreat [riˈtriːt]	v. 退隐
recluse [riˈkluːs]	adj. 隐居的，遁世的；孤寂的
	n. 隐士，遁世者
humble [ˈhʌmbl]	adj. 谦卑的，恭顺的

LESSON 9

CONSERVING NATURE: LANDSCAPE DESIGN AS ENVIRONMENTAL SCIENCE AND ART

CONSERVING NATURE: LANDSCAPE DESIGN AS ENVIRONMENTAL SCIENCE AND ART

The roots of today's environmental consciousness lie in nineteenth-century earth science. In 1863, the British geologist Charles Lyell(1797~1875)published *Geological Evidences of the Antiquity of Man*.[1] Charles Darwin(1809~1882)was aware of Lyell's work, which promoted and helped confirm his theory of evolutionary biology as in *Origin of Species* (1859). The observations recorded by the German naturalist and explorer Alexander von Humboldt(1769~1859) during his voyages to South America, Cuba, and Mexico advanced the nascent field of ecology.[2] Early geographers such as the German Karl Ritter(1779~1859)and the Swiss-born Arnold Henry Guyot(1807~1884) studied the earth in relation to human activity.[3] But it was an American, George Perkins Marsh(1801~1882), who attempted to show the extent to which human intervention was altering climate, topography, vegetation patterns, soil, and the habitats of species, often with consequences inimical for future generations. In his landmark book *Man and Nature* (1864) Marsh, who claimed no scientific expertise but a great deal of practical experience as a farmer, industrial investor, and diplomatic traveler, set out to show "that whereas Ritter and Guyot think that the earth made man, man in fact made the earth."[4]

A native of Vermont, Marsh saw firsthand how clear-cutting of forested slopes had promoted erosion and how these actions had caused the silting of former wetlands and decimated many animal species. In biblical cadences, Marsh described how man the destroyer of nature has felled forests whose network of fibrous roots bound the mould to the rocky skeleton of the earth,... has broken up the mountain reservoirs, the percolation of whose waters through unseen channels supplied the fountains that refreshed his cattle and fertilized his fields,... has torn the thin glebe which confined the light earth of extensive plains, and has destroyed the fringe of semi-aquatic plants which skirted the coast and checked the drifting of sea sand,... has warred on all the tribes of animated nature whose

---

选自 Elizabeth Barlow Rogers Landscape Design: A Cultural and Architecture History Harry N. Abrams, INC, Publishers

Part II History of Landscape Architecture

spoil he could not convert to his own uses, and... not protected the birds which prey on the insects most destructive to his own harvests."⁵

Marsh fully approved of canals, dikes, river embankments, and other means of engineering that channeled the forces of nature toward human ends. But he believed that such controls could be productive in the long term only if nature's regenerative forces were encouraged, not stymied. His book was influential in begetting awareness of the environment as an organic system in which all the parts were interdependent. Motives of overweening human greed persisted in his day as they do in ours, and in an aside, he railed against "the decay of commercial morality" and "unprincipled corporations, which not only defy the legislative power, but have, too often, corrupted even the administration of justice." Although his urgent message sowed the seeds of forestry and land management practices that eventually became part of government, only in recent years have the dire effects that Marsh predicted—multiplied by pressures of population growth and forces of industrial mechanization that he could hardly have imagined—prompted political protest and legislative actions leading to pollution controls and some positive steps toward the responsible regeneration of degraded natural environments.

As we have seen, inherent in modernism was a celebratory attitude toward feats of engineering and little regard for their environmental consequences. Although modernist landscape architects following Christopher Tunnard intended and usually inflicted no serious environmental harm, their objectives were essentially aesthetic as they wished to bring their profession in line with the exciting new developments in architecture, painting, and sculpture. In terms of planning, the urban-rural balance that Lewis Mumford preached in opposition to metropolitanism, with greenbelt communities scattered throughout a region, went generally unheeded. Only since the 1970s has a belated awareness of the need to reconcile human objectives with the operation of natural ecosystems become general and influential upon the practice of landscape design. It was at the University of Pennsylvania where Mumford taught for a period in the early 1960s that the ground was laid for a landscape architecture that conjoined the regionalism of the 1920s with the emerging environmental consciousness.

LANDSCAPE AS ENVIRONMENTAL SCIENCE

"We need nature as much in the city as in the countryside," wrote Ian L. McHarg (b. 1920) in 1969 in his now-classic book, *Design with Nature*.⁶ In the wake of Rachel Carson's⁷ eloquent call to environmental conscience in *Silent Spring* (1962), McHarg articulated with similar fervor a conservation strategy that sought to unseat the mind-set condoned by the Judeo-Christian biblical injunction encouraging humanity to subdue the earth. He enjoined planners, developers, and landscape architects to view Earth not as an exploitable resource but as the very source of life, the terrestrial miracle in space, an intricate organism of which humanity is an inseparable part. A gifted teacher, as chairman of

LESSON 9

the Department of Landscape Architecture and Regional Planning at the University of Pennsylvania from 1964 until 1986, McHarg became a leading exponent of an enlightened land-planning strategy that sought to make the constraints and opportunities presented by natural ecosystems an integral part of design and development. Informing his philosophy is his personal experience of the contrast of countryside to industrial city, of wartime landscape devastation to great landscape beauty, and of post-World War II convalescence in both grim and exhilarating environments.

As a landscape architect, McHarg came to feel that it was not enough to simply ameliorate the conditions found in the Glasgow slums of his youth. Practicing in Philadelphia in the firm he founded in 1963, he recognized that "providing a decorative background for human play" did not address the larger environmental threat posed by rings of suburbs encroaching upon rural and wild landscapes and the increasing divorce of human beings from wild nature. Further, the environment as a whole was being made toxic with pesticides and industrial wastes, and by then humans had sown the dire seeds of massive planetary devastation by producing the atomic bomb. He believes that urban planners and landscape architects can significantly alter this supremely dangerous course of science and technology and stem the harmful forces within industrial capitalist society.

As we have seen, other landscape architects—notably Charles Eliot and Jens Jensen—had preceded McHarg in advancing the cause of nature preserves in metropolitan areas, in studying native plant ecologies, and in forging a design idiom that expressed the simple beauties of regional locality. Stanley White(1891~1979)and Hideo Sasaki (b.1919), both gifted teachers of landscape architecture, were instrumental in bringing environmental science into the student curriculum. For instance, Sasaki had his Harvard students study a site in terms of its soil conditions, drainage patterns, and vegetation character and ground-plane coverage. These then became the determinants in locating development and assigning preservation value. To this analytical approach based on principles of ecological determinism, McHarg added an intuitive methodology incorporating personal values that evinced his affinity for Japanese culture and the metaphysics expressed in the Zen garden as well as his respect for the architecture of Louis Kahn(1901~1974), who taught architecture at the University of Pennsylvania when McHarg led the landscape architecture program there. McHarg appreciated Kahn's notion of design as a poetic expression of space and light and of the essential, inherent qualities of material and site.

In an age of scientific rationalism that puts a premium on nonsubjective measures, McHarg felt compelled to further a science-based approach to designing with nature. He made the natural sciences an essential foundation for his department's curriculum at the University of Pennsylvania, with courses in plant ecology and geology. In his geophysical and environmental approach to landscape design, McHarg developed a coordinated mapping system with overlays to render analyses of ecological, climatic, geological, topographical, hydrological, economic, natural, scenic, and historical features. Assigning

Part II *History of Landscape Architecture*

categories of social value to these, he has been able to chart optimum development paths and preservation zones according to the carrying capacity of the land and its fitness for specific uses. Put as simply as possible, a McHarg plan, such as the ones he prepared for the Philadelphia Metropolitan Area, the Baltimore Region, the Potomac River Basin, and for relocating the highway planned through the Staten Island Greenbelt, assigns levels of density and development and categories of land use based upon suitability. Flood and hurricane vulnerability and water conservation are paramount considerations. Overlay analysis shows invariably that valleys with their biologically and hydrologically important river basins and wetlands should be preserved, development on slopes should be minimized to allow groundwater to drain properly and recharge the subsurface aquifer, and uplands where settlement is least damaging allowed to become the zones of most intense occupation. Between 1970 and 1974, McHarg's firm, Wallace McHarg Roberts and Todd, applied this planning methodology to the development of Woodlands, an 18,000-acre new town built by developer George Mitchell north of Houston, Texas.

Sustainability is a new word in the lexicon of planners and designers. Woodlands, where the homes are clustered in a natural woodland setting rather than on conventionally landscaped lots, demonstrates McHarg's synthesis of human ecology and natural ecology in an economically viable plan that measures social and environmental costs together with dollar costs is hardly widespread in America. But to date, the incentives to build similar communities are not widespread. Government's role in terms of environmental improvement remains principally regulatory. To plan on a large regional scale in the manner McHarg and others have suggested requires governmental effectiveness and creativity backed by elected officials and policy makers at all levels.

Without such environmental planning, social and economic demands—for jobs, for public access, for equity—result in higher political value being assigned to individual and class interests than to those of society at large. Yet elsewhere sustainable communities are being promoted however imperfectly, particularly in northern European countries such as the Netherlands, Sweden, and Germany where there is a stronger ethic and more ingrained politics of responsible land use and urban husbandry than in America.[8] Directing the policies of contemporary industrial capitalism and the consumer society toward this end in all countries is one of the most important challenges of the twenty-first century.

WORDS AND EXPRESSIONS

nascent ['næsnt]   *adj.* 发生中的，初期的，新生的
inimical [i'nimikl]   *adj.* 有害的，不利的
diplomatic [diplə'mætik] *adj.* 外交的，老练的
Vermont [vəː'mɔnt]   *n.* 佛蒙特州（美国州名）
silt [silt]   *n.* 淤沙，淤泥

LESSON 9

	v. (使)淤塞，充塞
decimate [ˈdesimeit]	vt. 毁掉大部分，大批杀害
fibrous [ˈfaibrəs]	adj. 纤维(状)的
percolation [ˌpə:kəˈleiʃən]	n. 渗透，浸透，过滤
glebe [gli:b]	n. 田，土地
animate [ˈænimeit]	v. 鼓舞
	adj. 生气勃勃的
dike [daik]	n. 堤防
embankment [imˈbæŋkmənt]	n. 堤防，(河或海的)堤岸
stymie [ˈstaimi]	v. 阻碍，妨碍
beget [biˈget]	vt. 产生，引起
overweening [ˌəuvəˈwi:niŋ]	adj. 骄傲的，自负的/过分的，极端的
dire [ˈdaiə]	adj. 可怕的，可悲的，悲惨的
inflict [inˈflikt]	v. 造成，使遭受(损伤、苦痛等)
preach [pri:tʃ]	v. 鼓吹
reconcile [ˈrekənsail]	vt. 使和谐，使一致，使符合
fervor [ˈfə:və]	n. 热情，热烈
unseat [ˈʌnˈsi:t]	vt. 使失去资格；使退位
condone [kənˈdəun]	vt. 宽恕，赦免
Judeo-Christian [dʒu:ˈdi:əuˈkristjən]	adj. 兼犹太教与基督教的，犹太教与基督教所共有的
biblical [ˈbiblikəl]	adj. 圣经的，有关圣经的，按照圣经的
injunction [inˈdʒʌnkʃən]	n. 命令，指令，训谕
subdue [sʌbˈdju:]	v. 征服
terrestrial [tiˈrestriəl]	adj. 陆地的
devastation [ˌdevəsˈteiʃən]	n. 毁坏
convalescence [ˌkɔnvəˈlesəns]	n. 逐渐康复
grim [grim]	adj. 严酷的
exhilarating [igˈziləreitiŋ]	adj. 使人愉快的，令人振奋的
ameliorate [əˈmi:ljəreit]	v. 改善，改进
slum [slʌm]	n. 贫民窟
encroach [inˈkrəutʃ]	vi. (逐步或暗中)侵占，蚕食
toxic [ˈtɔksik]	adj. 有毒的
pesticide [ˈpestisaid]	n. 杀虫剂
planetary [ˈplænitri]	n. 行星的，地球(上)的
stem [stem]	v. 阻止
evince [iˈvins]	vt. 表明，表现
metaphysics [ˌmetəˈfiziks]	n. 玄学
rationalism [ˈræʃənəlizəm]	n. 理性主义，唯理论

overlay [ˌəuvəˈlei]	n. 覆盖物，涂盖层
render [ˈrendə]	v. 表达；描绘
optimum [ˈɔptiməm]	adj. 最佳的，最适宜的
Baltimore [ˈbɔːltimɔː]	n. 巴尔的摩，美国马里兰州的一城市
Potomac [pəˈtəumək]	n. 波托马克河（美国东部重要河流）
hurricane	n. 飓风，狂风
paramount [ˌærəˈpɔŋɡə]	adj. 极为重要的
aquifer [ˈækwifə]	n. 含水土层，蓄水层
lexicon [ˈleksikən]	n. 词典
upland [ˈʌplənd]	n. 丘陵地，高地，
synthesis [ˈsinθisis]	n. 综合
viable [ˈvaiəbl]	adj. 可行的
ingrained [inˈɡreind, ˈinɡreind]	adj. 彻底的，根深蒂固的

KEY CONCEPTS

Greenbelt
Urban-rural balance
Natural ecosystems
Natural preserves
Carry capacity
Overlay analysis
Sustainability
Human ecology
Environmental planning

NOTES

1. Charles Lyell
    赖尔（1797～1875），英国地质学家，认为地球表面特征是不断缓慢变化的过程中形成的，主要著作有《地质学原理》。
2. Alexander von Humboldt
    洪堡（1769～1859），德国自然科学家，自然地理科学家，近代地质学、气候学、地磁学、生态学创始人之一，著有《1799～1804 新大陆亚热带区域旅行记》。
3. Arnold Henry Guyot
    19 世纪瑞士籍美国地理学家和气象学家。
4. 见 David Lowenthal，乔治．珀金斯．马奇保护者先驱（George Perkins Marsh：Prophet of Conservation Seattle：University of Washington Press，2000），p. 267
5. 乔治．珀金斯．马奇，人与自然（Man and Nature）。或者，人类活动改变的自然地理

LESSON 9

(*Physical Geography as Modified by Human Action* 1864), David Lowenthal 编辑 (Cambridge, Massachusetts: The Belknap Press of Hardvard University 1965), pp. 38

6. Ian McHarg

  设计结合自然(*Design With Nnature*, 25 周年纪念版 New York: John Wiley & Sons Inc., 1992)p. 19。

7. Rachel Carson

  卡森(1907~1964),美国女生物学家,以有关环境污染和海洋自然史方面的著述闻名,如《寂静的春天》。

8. 见 Anne Whiston Spirn, 岩石园:城市自然和人性化设计 The Granite Garden: Urban Nature and Human Design(纽约: Basic Books, 1984)。又见 Timothy Beatley, 绿色城市:欧洲城市典范(*Green Urbanism*: *Learning from European Cities* 华盛顿特区: Island 出版社, 2000)。

QUESTIONS FOR REVIEW AND DISCUSSION

1. Who is George Perkins Marsh? What contribute of his effort to environment conservation?
2. Discuss the McHarg's science-based approach to designing with nature.
3. Explain the meaning of the word "sustainability".
4. Why are preservation planning principles so important?

Part II *History of Landscape Architecture*

Reading Material

Landscape Design as Environment Art

McHarg has been the most eloquent academic exponent of ecological landscape design in America, and Lawrence Halprin (b. 1916) has been one of its most active. Whereas McHarg has felt the need to put environmental planning within a rational natural-science framework, Halprin has honored the values of environment more in the manner of an artist, celebrating human creativity and community life within the context of nature and using environmental motifs metaphorically in his designs, which include several powerful evocations of nature in downtown public places.

Halprin's long and productive career has been nourished by degrees in plant sciences and horticulture from Cornell and the University of Wisconsin, Madison, study at Harvard with his adopted mentor Christopher Tunnard after discovering Tunnard's *Gardens in the Modern Landscape*, and employment in the San Francisco office of Thomas Church where he worked on the Donnell Garden. Important to Halprin's work has been his understanding of landscape design as process rather than unchanging product. He calls this process "scoring," a musical metaphor implying his intention to create spatial frameworks that allow for change over time and within which others can play participatory riffs. His legacy includes, besides his landscape designs, books that elucidate his design approach, including *The R. S. V. P. Cycles: Creative Processes in the Human Environment* (1969).

Between 1962 and 1965, Halprin was responsible for making San Francisco's Ghiradelli Square, an early effort at urban revitalization, into a vibrant public space animated by fountains, outdoor lighting, and landscaping, where people come for alfresco eating, shopping, socializing, and participating in performances, which are often impromptu. His "Take Part" design workshops elicit citizen collaboration in shaping a project's final program. Even as several other prominent landscape architects such as Hideo Sasaki and Peter Walker (b. 1932) have adopted the corporate-management style of successful large architectural firms, Halprin—like Roberto Burle Marx or Halprin's former employer, Thomas Church—has maintained his practice using an earlier model, that of the studio, because he finds the creative synergy of its collaborative atmosphere especially congenial.

With a strong interest in making landscape architecture transcend the functional and social to attain a spiritual dimension, Halprin has studied Jungian psychology in search of symbols and archetypes that hold universal meaning. Echoing Olmsted's notion of the fundamental benefit of parks as an uplifting of the spirit through the senses, Halprin has

---

选自 Elizabeth Barlow Rogers Landscape Design: A Cultural and Architecture History Harry N. Abrams, INC, Publishers

said, "What we are after is a sense of poetry in the landscape, a magnificent lift which will enrich the lives of the people who are moving about in the landscape."[1] He has nourished his own spiritual roots by maintaining a strong connection over the years with Israel, where he spent some time after high school living on a kibbutz. His most notable project in that country is the Walter and Elise Haas Promenade built in the mid-1980s in Jerusalem on a hill overlooking the Old City.

In the United States, Halprin designed the 7.5-acre Franklin Delano Roosevelt Memorial located in West Potomac Park, a 66-acre peninsula beside the Tidal Basin in Washington, D. C.. Dedicated on May 2, 1997, the memorial to the thirtysecond president of the United States consists of a richly planted 1,200-foot-long(365.8-meter-long) sequence of four interconnected garden spaces with narrative sculpture and fountains.[2] With his strong sense of landscape as theatrical performance and employing the storyboard technique used by filmmakers to plot what he called "Roosevelt's[3] journey of life," Halprin scripted a sequence of 21 quotations, brief texts from famous speeches by Roosevelt, which are incised into the memorial's walls of rusticated pink and red granite. He combined these inscriptions with sculptures by Tom Hardy, Neil Estern, Leonard Baskin, George Segal, and Robert Graham in a chronological narrative of Roosevelt's presidency and leadership during two of the nation's gravest ordeals, the Great Depression and World War II. The memorial also contains hope for world peace as symbolized by the inclusion of a statue of Eleanor Roosevelt as a delegate to the United Nations.

Halprin's connection with McHarg's approach to environmental planning is perhaps most evident in his "ecoscore" for Sea Ranch, a planned community of weekend and vacation homes and condominiums developed in the mid-1960s by Oceanic Properties on property occupying a 10-mile stretch of northern California coastline, which was once used for sheep grazing. Halprin conceived the plan for the first 1,800 acres to be developed of the original 5,300acre parcel in collaboration with MLTW, the architectural firm of Charles Moore, Donlyn Lyndon, William Turnbull, and Richard Whitaker. As was later true of Seaside's plan, Halprin's plan for Sea Ranch put a premium upon communal spaces, and only about 50 percent of the land was sold to private owners.

By clustering the sites for houses and condominiums adjacent to existing cypress hedgerows, Halprin was able to leave the former sheep pastures as open meadows with views to the ocean across the beach bluffs. Trails throughout enable residents to experience the landscape as a totality. The meadows are held as commons and their maintenance made a community responsibility. Unlike Seaside, where low picket fences manifest an ambience of yard-to-yard neighborliness, at Sea Ranch owners' rules specify that properties be kept unfenced. The clustered houses without visible property lines or landscaping appear to merge with their natural setting. This intention is furthered by Sea Ranch's rustic architectural vocabulary—unpainted redwood or cedar siding and eaveless shed roofs of shingle or sod, which are positioned to deflect the Pacific winds.

Part Ⅱ   *History of Landscape Architecture*

As an innovative effort in environmentally harmonious place making and an expression of the 1960s idealism that motivated the careers of both McHarg and Halprin, Sea Ranch deserves a place in the history of landscape design. Both of these landscape architects have seen city and country as a continuum, and their influence in furthering a new moral imperative by bringing ecological considerations to the fore has been influential within their profession.

As much of the aging industrial infrastructure of cities falls into disuse because of new transportation and manufacturing technologies, landscape architects have been engaged in the reclamation of *brownfields*, former factory sites and decaying waterfronts. Notable among those who have attempted to poeticize the industrial past through landscape design is Richard Haag(b. 1923), an early Postmodern contextualist whose Gasworks Park(1970~1978)on the shores of Lake Union in Seattle, Washington, and Bloedel Reserve, Bainbridge Island, Puget Sound, Washington(1985~), demonstrate concern for environmental healing through bioremediation.

Although contemporary landscape architects have not entirely abandoned the principles of the Picturesque, Arts and Crafts, Neoclassical, and Modernist design traditions that have constituted their training during the past century, and although they still rely on some of the principles of these design styles as well as upon McHargian environmentalism to inform their work, several are adopting an approach that seeks the same kind of creative freedom granted to Conceptual artists. Thus, they look to their own imaginative resources as they manipulate stones, earth, and water to produce land art, forms in and of the landscape. At the same time, Earthworks artists share some of the same concerns as environmentalists, and they work in a similar manner and at the same scale as landscape architects. As they, too, seek to manifest beauty within a brownfields context, the distinction between art and landscape design tends to dissolve.

WORDS AND EXPRESSIONS

evocation [ˌevəuˈkeiʃən]	n. 唤出，唤起
Wisconsin [wisˈkɔnsin]	n. 威斯康星州(美国州名)，威斯康星河(密西西比河支流)
mentor [ˈmentɔː]	n. 导师，指导者
participatory [ˈpɑːtisipeitəri, pə-]	adj. 供人分享的
riff [rif]	n. (爵士音乐中的)即兴重复段
vibrant [ˈvaibrənt]	adj. 有活力的，活跃的
elucidate [iˈljuːsideit]	vt. 阐明，说明
alfresco [ælˈfreskəu]	adv. & adj. 在户外(的)，在露天(的)
impromptu [imˈprɔmptjuː]	n. 即席演出，即兴曲
	adj. 即席的

LESSON 9

	adv. 即席地，未经准备地
elicit [i'lisit]	*vt.* 引出，诱出
synergy ['sinədʒi]	*n.* 协同，配合，共同合作
congenial [kən'dʒi:njəl]	*adj.* 适合的，意气相投的
Jungian ['juŋiən]	（瑞士心理学家，精神病学家）
	adj. 容格的，容格之学说的
	n. 支持容格的人，研究容格学说的人
archetype ['ɑ:kitaip]	*n.* 原型
kibbutz [ki'bu:ts, -'buts]	*n.* 以色列的集体农场
Jerusalem [dʒe'ru:sələm]	*n.* 耶路撒冷
dedicate ['dedikeit]	*vt.* 献（身），致力，题献（一部著作给某人）
storyboard ['stɔ:rɪbɔ:d]	*n.* （电影、电视节目或商业广告等的）情节串连图板
incise [in'saiz]	*vt.* 切割，雕刻
rusticate ['rʌstikeit]	*v.* [建] 使成粗面石工
chronological [ˌkrɔnə'lɔdʒikəl]	*adj.* 按年代顺序的，按时间顺序的
narrative ['nærətiv]	*n.* 叙述，讲述
ordeal [ɔ:'di:l, -'di:əl]	*n.* 苦难经历；严峻考验
condominium [ˌkɔndə'miniəm]	*n.* （产权为居住者自有的）公寓（的单元）
grazing ['greiziŋ]	*n.* 放牧
premium ['primjəm]	*n.* 额外费用，奖金，奖赏，保险费
put a premium on...	奖励，重视
hedgerow ['hedʒrəu]	*n.* 灌木篱墙
bluff [blʌf]	*n.* 断崖，绝壁
picket ['pikit]	*n.* 尖板条（做篱笆或拴马用的）
ambience ['æmbiəns]	*n.* 周围环境，气氛
neighborliness ['neibəlinis]	*n.* 亲切，友善
eave ['i:v]	*n.* 屋檐
further ['fə:ðə]	*vt.* 促进，增进，助长
cedar ['si:də]	*n.* 雪松（木材）
shingle ['ʃiŋgl]	*n.* 木（片）瓦，盖屋板
sod [sɔd]	*n.* 草皮
deflect [di'flekt]	*v.* （使）偏斜，（使）偏转
imperative [im'perətiv]	*n.* 必须履行的责任，义务
reclamation [ˌreklə'meiʃən]	*n.* 开垦，改造，（废料等的）收回
waterfront ['wɔ:təfrʌnt]	*n.* 水边地码头区，滨水地区
healing ['hi:liŋ]	*n.* 康复，复原
remediation [riˌmidi'eiʃən]	*n.* 补救，纠正

NOTES

1. 见 Peter Walker 和 Melanie Simo, 无形的花园：现代美国景观研究 *Invisible Gardens: The Search for Modernism in the American Landscape*（Cambridge, Massachusetts: MIT 出版社, 1994), pp. 258~259。
2. 对于富兰克林·罗斯福(Franklin Delano Roosevelt)纪念碑历史的相关内容，作者十分感谢 Reuben M. Rainey, 叙述性园林：劳伦斯·哈普林的罗斯福纪念地(*The Garden as Narrative: Lawrence Halprin's Franklin Delano Roosevelt Memorial*) 未发行手稿, 1995。
3. Franklin Delano Roosevelt

   罗斯福(1882~1945), 美国第 32 任总统(1933~1945), 民主党人, 第二次世界大战爆发时支持英国和法国, 太平洋战争(1941)爆发后对建立反法西斯同盟做出重大贡献。

Part III

Design Elements and Methods

LESSON 10

DESIGN AND PLANING METHODS

Design results from methods of working. A sculpture of welded steel differs from one chipped from granite or modelled with clay. Rodin was a modeller. Brancusi a carver. Picasso a constructor. Look at their work: different methods produce different results. A modern planned town is not like an organic town. A garden that is made by using a drawing to fix every detail before starting work will differ, markedly, from one that is made by choosing the plants and stones one at a time. year after year. Means influence ends.

Rough hands and smooth hands can both produce good design. The rough-hands method is practised in workshops and out of doors. It is the craftsman's way, the peasant's way, the ancient way. The smooth-hands method is to sit in an office working at measured drawings for implementation by others at remote sites. This is the modern way: the way of the engineer, the architect, the town planner and the landscape architect. Both methods have their strengths. In medieval times, the rough-hands method was universal. Today, it is the other way about. The change took place as part of a broad cultural trend, with the rise of modernism a significant factor. Planners can learn from designers.

PRE-MODERN DESIGN METHODS

Apprenticeship is a system of great antiquity. The Code of Hammurabi[1], a Babylonian king[2], required skilled craftsmen to teach the young. Books were not available. and technical knowledge was of great value. Those who possessed knowledge wished to keep it to themselves. In ancient Rome, most craftsmen were slaves. This was an effective means of retaining the ownership of knowledge. In the Middle Ages, craft guilds emerged in Western Europe, controlled by independent master craftsmen. Articles of apprenticeship bound trainees to their masters, often for seven years. to work for little or no pay. Some masons went on to become designers. This was the only way to become an 'architect'. The knowledge gained in apprenticeship was practical, not theoretical. In the great cathedrals. full-size drawings and large sets of dividers were used to set out masonrv. Shapes and forms developed gradually in the minds of master craftsmen. Small-scale drawings came into use at a later date.

选自 Tom tuner, City as Landscape: A Post-post modern view of Design and Planning

Part III Design Elements and Methods

Under the master and apprentice system, design decisions were taken on traditionalist grounds. Things were done in special ways because they had always been done in such ways. 'If twere right for Old Bill, twill be right for me'. Changes came about very gradually, if at all.

Most design was done in this way, in most countries in most historical periods. It was used for carts, buildings, ships, cars, towns, gardens and every other thing. Admiration for the products of traditional design methods continues to grow.

MODERN DESIGN METHODS

The modern approach, of design with smooth hands, has grown by degrees. It began in ancient times and resumed its advance with the Renaissance. Vitruvius wrote that the architect should be 'skilful with the pencil, instructed in geometry' (Vitruvius, 1914 edn). Since the translation of Euclid's *Elements*[3] into Latin, in 1482, the activity of making new places and products has become steadily re-entangled with the process of drawing. To *de-sign* is to make signs, originally on paper, increasingly on computer screens. To *plan* is to make a projection on a flat surface.

During the nineteenth century, the technical and aesthetic reasons for producing drawings grew apart, as did the architectural and engineering professions. The architect became a gentleman artist, reliant on experienced craftsmen and engineers to make buildings stand up and resist the elements. In the twentieth century, architects sought to gain control of the whole building process through their drawing skill. So much knowledge was available in books that it became feasible to produce drawings and specifications for every aspect of the building process. When waggon building was replaced by car building, a similar change afflicted vehicle production. Men in smart suits subjugated those in boiler suits.

During the early years of automobile manufacture, vehicles continued to be designed and built by craft methods. Components were machined, one at a time. Each part was honed to slightly different dimensions and often embodied minor design improvements. It was a very expensive way of making cars.

With his Model T, Henry Ford applied the techniques of mass production to automobiles. Each part was standardized. A gauging system was introduced. Parts were made in standard sizes to be attached in the simplest possible ways. Assemblers were given specialized tools and made to adopt a single task. Henry the First became king of the whole process. All design decisions were taken before the production line was started. Workers became operatives, not craftsmen. Uneducated immigrants to the New World could learn the job in a day. Each had responsibility for one tiny step in the production process and for an endlessly repeated operation, as satirized by Charlie Chaplin in *Modern Times*. Fordist production methods created the modern world. Not since the invention of gunpowder had smooth hands won such dominion over rough hands. Bronze defeated the peasant; the longbow defeated the knight; gunpowder defeated the castle; Fordism defeated the worker, temporarily.

POST-FORDIST DESIGN

By 1980, the Ford Motor Company itself was losing huge sums of money and market share, especially to Japanese competitors. Selected Ford managers were sent to Japan with sharp pencils and notebooks. They discovered that the Fordist system of mass production, named after their founder, had been overtaken by a new system, which came to be known as lean production. Compared with mass production, it required 40% less effort and resulted in products of superior quality. The Ford Motor Company adopted as many lean production principles as it could. Since then, people have been talking about post-Fordism in the same breath as postmodernism, Reflecting on how the company changed between 1980 and 1990, Ford's director of strategy observed that:

We had to stop designing cars we liked and start designing cars the customers liked. The Japanese had teamwork. We had macho designers who found it difficult to sublimate their own ideas to the new realities. (*Sunday Times*. 1994)

The design teams brought rough and smooth hands together.

Lean design and planning are more knowledge-intensive, less hierarchical and less demarcated. Everyone's experience and judgement is brought into the planning and design process. This includes customers, garage workers, production workers with experience of decision-making and decision-makers with experience on the production line. Despite the profusion of knowledge in books, lack of knowledge is the greatest drawback to the smooth-hands approach. You can learn much about the behaviour of steel, timber, brick and stone from books, but there is a great deal more that can be learned only by touching and using materials. You can also learn much about indoor and outdoor space in books, but there is a great deal more that can be learned only by knowing and using real places. Edwin Lutyens' ability to make good gardens was limited by his lack of interest in using gardens. First-hand knowledge comes from living in a place, driving a car or making a car.

Lean design has similarities to the way in which medieval cathedrals were made. A powerful master-craftsman controlled the whole project, while specialists had power to decide upon and regulate their own work. This is one of the things that Ruskin and Morris admired about medieval architecture. They hated industrialization, but as factories become *more* automated, the whole production process may become more like cathedral building. When the ultimate black-box factory is built, the lights will be switched off, the machinery switched on and the plant left to churn out products so long as they are wanted.

FORDISM AND THE BUILT ENVIRONMENT

Current design and planning practice in the built environment professions retains a disastrous similarity to Fordist production arrangements. The knowledge employed is abstract knowledge, gained in colleges. Professionals are 'advisers', not managers. The public are 'consultees', not planners. The design process begins with a big idea, tradi-

Part III   Design Elements and Methods

tionally scribbled on the back of an envelope. It is then passed down the design team, with more and more junior people checking the final details. At the 'coalface', on construction sites, workers are treated as indifferent automatons. They must obey written specifications, drawings and regulations, often drafted by people without practical experience of doing the job. Management contracting, and design-and-build, are bringing about changes, but component designers and clients still have little prospect of becoming involved. Nor do users of places and buildings have anything but a marginal role in the design process, even if they are the owners, which is never the case for bridges, public parks, mass housing, or speculative office developments. As with design for mass production, design teams for built environment projects tend to start small and expand. Once formulated, the plans are submitted to municipal authorities, modified and agreed. When such plans are implemented, they often run into stiff opposition. Why weren't we consulted? everyone wants to know. The technically correct reply, that 'You elected the people who hired the people who took the decisions', gives little comfort. It is Fordist autocracy. Henry took all the decisions himself. Lean design thrusts as many decisions as possible onto the shoulders of the workforce and the users. It deconstructs the Fordist hierarchy. It is knowledge-intensive instead of resource-intensive.

KNOWLEDGE-INTENSIVE PLANNING

Planners have responded to the public outcry against road building and other plans with offers of 'public participation in planning'. The idea is excellent. The practice is usually deficient. At worst, planners give an impression of treating the public according to the disdainful motto: 'They say. What do they say? Let them say. At best, planners have shown skill in drawing fresh ideas from the public and putting them to work. Public participation can operate in several ways: advisory committees, written comment, public debate and design workshops. Each has value. Each can be criticized.

Advisory committees can work in parallel with public committees, as in Germany and Holland. Authorities generally have subsidiary committees, of elected members, dealing with planning, parks, housing etc. Each is paralleled with an advisory committee. It is a good way of expanding the knowledge base for decision making. The difficulty lies in choosing the advisors. If they are professionally qualified in the subject, they will be an interest group. If they are volunteers, they will be unrepresentative. If they are elected, they will come under the sway of political parties. Normally, they will lack knowledge, and the decision-making process can become very lengthy.

Written comments can be invited on draft plans. A leaflet can be circulated or an exhibition mounted. The public can be invited to write letters and complete questionnaires. Sometimes, they receive written answers. Letters produce a good opportunity for individuals to let off steam but, generally, do not lead to constructive improvements. Too often, the minorities oppose one another. This leaves planners with the satisfying delusion that they have 'conducted the orchestra'

LESSON 10

and reached a balanced compromise.

Public debate can take place after the planners have given an account of their proposals. This allows people who are happier talking than writing to make a contribution, but the results are similar to exercises in written consultation. It too often seems that planners listen to what is said, as a formality, and then do what they intended in the first place. This is not necessarily the planners' intention, but it is the impression received by the public.

Design workshops can be enjoyable and productive. Public meetings are held. The planners come with open minds, largescale models, white paper and fat pens. Members of the public put forward ideas, which are drawn on paper and then countered with other ideas. Such sessions can be very creative yet unrealistic. With idealism in the air, it is too easy to ignore economic realities and entrenched interests.

So what should be done? Use all the methods? Reject all the methods? Devise new methods? Each solution is workable, provided it brings together those with both rough and smooth hands: clients, owners, builders, component-makers, designers, planners and maintenance workers. For architecture, Hassan Fathy wrote of re-establishing 'the Trinity':

Client, architect, and craftsman, each in his province, must make decisions, and if any one of them abdicates his responsibility, the design will suffer and the role of architecture in the cultural growth and development of the whole people will be diminished. (Fathy, 1973)

But for the environment, who is 'the client'? This is a central problem. For a private house, the client is the building owner. For speculative housing, shops and offices, the client is hydra-headed: financiers, insurance companies, property managers and, at the far end of a long list, those who merely spend their lives using the places. For transport schemes, too, there are many clients with divergent interests. When cycling, I want a vastly better provision of segregated cycle tracks. When driving, I can be heard muttering 'Bloody cyclists'. When walking, I feel threatened by cyclists on footpaths, and hostile to smug car drivers in comfortable seats pumping noxious fumes into my face. So what happens during public participation in planning? I am torn in three directions and have little to contributs.

A resort development can be used to illustrate Fordist and knowledge-intensive approaches to planning and design(Landscape Institute, 1990). The Hyatt Waikaloa is a typical American resort development, in Hawii. It cost $ 350 million and has 1200 rooms. The project was designed in California. The Hawaii coastline was reshaped. Different transport systems were made to offer 'ways to your room via monorail, grand canal boats, coronation carriages pulled by Clydesdale horses, or a moving sidewalk which offers the visitor a trip through Polynesian history'. It was a Fordist project. Also in Hawaii, a Japanese company is developing a post-Fordist resort. Two years were spent on community participation before design work began. A further year was spent preparing and modifying design concepts. In consequence of this effort, the resort was planned to revitalize a depressed economy, to support local agriculture, to build affordable new housing, to improve local healthcare facilities, to improve public access to the environment, to conserve the local heritage, to establish forest preserves, to develop local industry. The resort itself was developed as a series of small buildings in a style that was inspired by 'the traditional regional style of Kohale characterized by courtyards, verandas, open rooms with gracious overhangs'. I have not been to Hawaii, but I know which resort I would book into.

Effective public participation depends upon recognizing that there are many clients and many problems. Instead of *a plan*, we need *many plans*. This is the planning equivalent of lean production. Each specialist planning team should be for a component system. Each should have a *shusa*, charged with integrating all the financial, technical and aesthetic considerations. Assuredly, such plans will reflect the diverse economic and social character of different buildings, resorts, towns and regions.

When specialist plans have been prepared, it would be possible to go back to work on general plans. But what areas of land should they cover? Places are not automobiles. Specialist interests have their own geographies(Fig. 1). Few coincide with municipal boundaries. and few are represented within municipal committee structures. To cater for my personal transport needs, there needs to be a pedestrian plan, drawn up by pedestrians, a cycling plan, drawn up by cyclists, and a road plan, drawn up by drivers. Divergent interests cannot be fully resolved, but compromises are possible, if and when the component plans exist. Should there be only one plan, it will excessively favour one group, usually the group with the big bucks. Instead of an agreed city plan, societies require sets of 'landscape' plans, each produced for a special region from a special perspective.

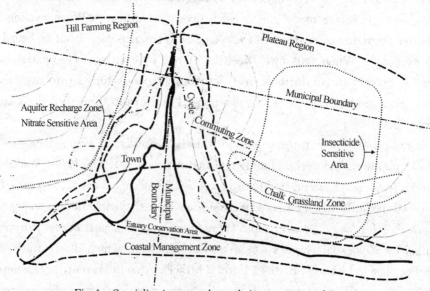

Fig. 1 Specialist interests have their own geographies

LESSON 10

Take the case of London's rivers. Neither town planners nor river engineers have sufficient knowledge, sufficient power or sufficient wisdom to produce the necessary plans. Most rivers have therefore been culverted, channelized and degraded into open sewers by those with the big budgets. Watercourses now need massive reclamation programmes, to bring them back to the dignity of rivers. Some work is being done on making them into nature reserves, which is not enough. River planning requires cooperation between many bureaucracies and voluntary bodies. Britain's National Rivers Authority cannot do its job without the help of community groups and planners. A time must come when Barton's heart-rending book, *The Lost Rivers of London* (Barton, 1962), will be followed by its necessary sequel: *How We Won The Rivers Back*. The River Thames must be rejuvenated. As in days of yore, and Canaletto, it should be crowded with animals, small boats, traders, floating restaurants, flowerships and ferries. There should be beaches and habitats on the banks. This requires multi-purpose planning and non-statutory planning, extending well beyond the margins of the river. The Pool of London, once the greatest port in the world, now almost dead, should be declared a waterpark and nature reserve. Open spaces need not be dry.

Specialist planning and design teams can be led by artists, planners, businessmen, architects, poets, landscape architects, politicians and surveyors. Alternative planning and design methods should be employed, according to circumstances. Extensive community, private and voluntary planning should take place, not mere 'public participation in planning'. Wise plans, which may conflict, will be required: some for rivers, some for greenspace, some for pedestrians, some for boroughs, some for groups of boroughs, some for street corners, some for London, some for the Dover to Bristol Edge City, some for the Calais-Folkestone Economic Zone, some for the areas around suburban stations in Washington DC. Planning competitions and exhibitions should be held, with prizes. Assistance from professional planners will be required. All the plans should be stored in geographical information systems.

Planners have felt themselves to be under attack since 'one way, one truth' modernism became questioned. My hope is that by producing varied plans that are better, more useful, more client-oriented, and more knowledge-intensive, it will be possible to raise the popularity of planning and, incidentally, to improve employment prospects for planners. As car firms throughout the world adopt the principles of lean planning and lean production, they are producing better products at lower prices with happier staff. Planners and designers need to follow these paths.

WORDS AND EXPRESSIONS

subjugate ['sʌbdʒugeit]   *vt.* 使屈服，征服，使服从，克制，抑制
embody [im'bɔdi]   *vt.* 具体表达，使具体化，包含，收录

Part Ⅲ Design Elements and Methods

gauge [gedʒ]	n. 标准尺，规格，量规，量表
	v. 测量
craftsman [ˈkrɑːftsmən]	n. 工匠，手艺精巧的人，艺术家
peasant [ˈpezənt]	n. 农夫，乡下人
medieval [ˌmediˈiːvəl]	adj. 中世纪，仿中世纪的，老式的
apprenticeship [əˈprentisˌʃip]	n. 学徒制
Hammurabi [ˌhæməˈrɑːbiː]	汉摩拉比，巴比伦王国国王（公元前 1792～前 1750）
the Code of Hammurabi	汉摩拉比法典
Babylonian [ˌbæbɪˈləʊnjən]	n.（古代）巴比伦王国
guild [gild]	n.（中世纪的）行会，同业公会，协分，行业协会
trainee [treiˈniː]	n. 练习生，新兵，受训者
mason [ˈmeisən]	n. 泥瓦匠，共济会
Euclid [ˈjuːklid]	欧几里德（约公元前 3 世纪的古希腊数学家）
specification [ˌspesifiˈkeiʃən]	n. 详述，规格，说明书，规范
postmodernism [poustˈmɔdənizəm]	n. 后现代主义
courtyard [ˈkɔːtjɑːd]	n. 庭院，院子
veranda [vəˈrændə]	n. 阳台，走廊
overhang [ˈəuvəˈhæŋ]	v. 悬于…之上，悬垂
	n. 挑出屋顶；悬挑

KEY CONCEPTS

landscape architect
lean design and planning
resource-intensive planning
knowledge-intensive planning
non-statutory planning
multi-purpose planning

NOTES

1. **Hammurabi**：Babylonian king (B. C1792～B. C1750) who made Babylon the chief Mesopotamian kingdom and codified the laws of Mesopotamia and Sumeria.

    汉摩拉比：巴比伦王国国王（公元前 1792～前 1750 年），他使得巴比伦王国称霸美索不达米亚地区，并且把美索不达米亚和苏美人的法律编集成法典。

2. **Babylonia**：The capital of ancient Babylonia in Mesopotamia on the Euphrates River. Established as capital c. 1750 B. C. and rebuilt in regal splendor by Nebuchadnezzar Ⅱ

after its destruction (c. 689 B. C) by the Assyrians, Babylon was the site of the Hanging Gardens, one of the Seven Wonders of the World.

巴比伦：古巴比伦王国的首都，位于幼发拉底河沿岸的美索不达米亚境内，作为首都大约建于公元前 1750 年，在它被亚述人毁灭后（公元前 689 年），它又被尼布甲尼撒二世重建于王室显赫之时，巴比伦是世界七大奇观之一的空中花园所在地。

3. **Euclid**: Greek mathematician who applied the deductive principles of logic to geometry, thereby deriving statements from clearly defined axioms.

欧几里德古希腊数学家，他把逻辑学中的演绎原理应用到几何学中，藉以由定义明确的公理导出语句。

QUESTIONS FOR REVIEW AND DISCUSSION

1. What are advantages and disadvantages of the apprenticeship?
2. Will you give some examples of the mass production in urban planning, landscape design and architecture?
3. Do you think that lean production is better than mass production? Why?
4. Which resort would you like to book into if you have a travel in Hawaii? Why?
5. What do you think about "one way, one true" modernism in landscape planning?

Part Ⅲ Design Elements and Methods

Reading Material

Design Thinking

The responsive, creative designer must be an ambidextrous thinker. Such a person, capable of dealing effectively with both intuition and logic, is centered and able to think holistically and integratively. To help the student become more centered, creative, capable at perceiving relationships, and insightful is one of the primary tasks of design education.

1 CONCEPTUAL BLOCKBUSTING

The college design student has spent more than a decade in a formal education system that has taught self-limiting behavior and has constructed behavioral filters. These filters are subliminal survival mechanisms that promote "appropriate" behaviors that, in some cases, serve as roadblocks to creativity. Design education can dismantle these roadblocks to help the student become more centered and creative. It can provide students with a knowledge of thinking forms, roadblocks to fluency and flexibility in thinking, and techniques for dismantling blocks In Conceptual Blockbusting (1979), James L. Adams identifies three primary types of thinking: visual, verbal, and mathematical. He helps readers discover which type(s) of thinking they use and which they avoid and how flexibly they think, as well as techniques for improved thinking effectiveness. Designers are encouraged to read this delightful book.

In Conceptual Blockbusting, readers discover that some situations are understood easily by visual thinking, and that others are difficult to understand visually but lend themselves to verbal or mathematical solution. Each thinking form is effective for certain situation types. For example, landform manipulation causes many designers trouble because it requires visualization of existing and designed landform (visual thinking) and computation of slopes and elevations (mathematical thinking). A tendency to avoid either type of thought can make the task quite difficult. The key to successful landform manipulation is the timely use of appropriate thinking forms.

In a given situation, the flexible thinker quickly and intuitively explores various forms of thinking and selects the most feasible form. while the search is probably unconscious, education can develop the ability to think flexibly, so that if the selected form proves nonproductive, the thinker can consciously shift to alternative thinking forms. Without such flexibility, the thinker can flounder.

2 PROBLEM-SOLVING

According to James L. Adams, creative thinking blocks are "mental walls that block the problem solver from correctly perceiving a problem or conceiving its solution." We all experience these blocks. Adams identifies four major types: perceptual blocks, emotional

LESSON 10

blocks, cultural and environmental blocks, and intellectual and expressive blocks. Perceptual blocks prevent the designer from clearly perceiving the problem or information necessary to solve the problem. One perceptual block is stereo typing, that is, placing inappropriately narrow boundaries upon conceptualization. Such boundaries prematurely limit the range of alternatives the designer considers. To dissuade stereotyping in the academic design studio, projects are often written in connotatively neutral language-for example, to design a human container rather than a chair. The intent is that the designed container will respond more to specifics of the situation(materials, user, and so on)and the task will not be short-circuited by introducing irrelevant stereotypical information, such as chair arms, four legs, and the like.

Another perceptual block Adams identifies is the inability to isolate a problem. If it cannot be isolated and defined, the problem cannot be solved. The problem can also be defined too narrowly. The textbook example was the attempt to invent a machine sensitive enough to pick tomatoes, thereby automating this labor-intensive industry. After years of pursuing a mechanical solution, the problem was redefined more broadly, and a tougher-skinned tomato was developed and harvested using conventional equipment. An inability to see the problem from different perspectives results in solving only parts of the problem, or even in creating more problems than those solved. This block relates to our tendency to see the world through narrow windows and our inability to look through other windows. Role playing, in which individuals identify and articulate specific roles, is an effective and stimulating technique commonly used in design education to develop the ability to overcome this block.

Another perceptual block, familiarity occurs as the mind filters out the common place as a means for coping with the multiplicity of stimuli. It is why we cannot, for example, place the appropriate letters with their corresponding numbers on a telephone dial even though we dial letters and numbers daily. It is also why crab-walking through a space helps us see it better: as perspective changes, the place becomes less familiar and, therefore, more noticeable.

Failure to use all our sensory stimuli is also a perceptual block. For example, when we move blind folded through a familiar area, we find ourselves suddenly hearing what was previously unheard, thereby perceiving the place differently. Generally, we emphasize the visual to the exclusion of other sensory stimuli. But the perception of place can be much richer if the place is designed so that all senses contribute to, and intensify, the experience.

According to Adams, emotional blocks are perhaps the most inhibitive of all thinking blocks. People have an instinctive urge to create, as expressed in the excellent movie Why Man Creates(1968). However, Freud revealed the other dimensions of self that can serve as blocks: the ego, or socially aware self, and the superego, or moralistic self. The ego rejects(often prematurely)ideas that it feels cannot be implemented; the superego rejects on the basis of "self-image."

Together, the ego and superego introduce an insidious set of emotional blocks. Fear of failure is often the most devastating emotional block. In academia, fear of risk-taking results in a greatly compromised learning experience. A closely related block in academia is overemphasis on grades. This block becomes quite destructive when grades are marginal and the student becomes more concerned with a grade than with exploration. Under these circumstances, the student often avoids taking risks, and learning and the grade both suffer. Being overly concerned with the opinion of others can result in trying to please rather than trying to learn. While feedback is important, it must be internalized and must become part of the synergistic process in which the designer remains true to self and design direction while also responding to feedback. A lack of appetite for chaos is a distrust of left-handed thinking that can result in premature judgment. Complex problems, on the other hand, of ten require a gestation period of tolerated chaos so that the subconscious mind can intuitively weigh variables and discover relevant patterns. Shortening this period can result in poorly conceived solutions.

Closely related to an intolerance for chaos is a tendency to judge rather than generate ideas. An idea generated but not judged can incubate and cultivate other ideas- Premature judging can eliminate the idea and its seeding tendency. Lack of curiosity results in too little conceptualizing. Lack of access to imaglnatlon, or an undeveloped ability to form and manipulate vivid images, and a failure to distinguish between reality and fantasy, although less common, are equally devastating emotional blocks.

Adams also discusses blocks caused by the cultural or environmental context. He regards cultural blocks as those established to implement rules of social conduct and to eliminate inappropriate behavior. Types of behavior often unfortunately labeled as inappropriate for adults include fantasy, reflection, playfulness, humor, intuition, feeling, pleasure, qualitative judgment, and desire for change. There are also many cultural taboos that society imparts or the designer fears society will impose. Such taboos discourage the consideration of many alternatives.

Adams identifies environmental blocks imposed by the immediate physical or human context. These include stressful interpersonal dynamics like distrust, lack of communication, and lack of earned rewards. They also include physical disruptions like noise, glare, and so on.

Adams also identifies intellectual and expressive blocks. Intellectual blocks include the use of ineffective thinking forms, the inability to move freely between forms, and the generation of incorrect data. Expressive blocks are the result of inadequate graphic or verbal communication skills, or an inability to apply these skills.

Any of the preceding blocks can function as impediments to effective decision-making. Removing or avoiding these blocks facilitates the consideration of appropriate stimuli, the pursuit of thought processes conducive to creative conceptualization, and the emergence of rich and relevant patterns in the mind's eye.

3 DESIGN MEANING AND LANGUAGE

Though only one aspect of design, problem-solving dominated modern architecture's pursuit of "form follows function." During the 1960s and early 1970s, design was reduced to a functional statement; deeper meanings were avoided. In the late 1970s and 1980s architects rejected modernism for many reasons, including its reduction of meaning to functional terms; its tendency to take shapes from other disciplines, such as machine technology or cubist aesthetics; and its perceived inability to develop a coherent visual language. Subsequent theories, such as postmodernism, have largely abandoned problem-solving as a design languages, typologies of form, and meanings. This text takes the position that both viewpoints are relevant. Rational and problemsolving concerns are essential in the functional arts; language and meaning are essential to design and civilization.

Semiotics, the science of language and logic, develops and understanding of symbols and their use to communicate meaning. Seminal works in development of design semiotics include Christopher Alexander's tandem books *A Pattern Language* (1977) and *A Timeless Way of Building* (1979). The first identifies some reoccurring symbols as examples of a vocabulary of physical expression. The second presents the concept of a language of physical expression. The second presents the concept of a language of physical expression, recognition of symbols, and encoding and decoding of meaning. While not the first or most recent works in semiotics, these remain two of the best; because they do not discuss a language of buildings or site developments but rather a language of patterns and genera of places that have recurred through history in various cultures. These books speak in a descriptive rather than prescriptive language. They address contexts within which a symbol, such as an alcove, emerges while allowing the expression to address place-specific issues. The language communicates the patterns of expression that recur at various scales and in various contexts.

Two strategies have emerged for managing the broad range and complexity of postmodern design meanings. The first, evidenced by Alexander and *Venturi's Learning from Las Vegas* (1972), embraces an eclectic language that permits the attribution of different meanings to the same gesture. This strategy relishes complexity and pluralistic meanings and does not seek to limit language, structure, or interpretation. A second, more recent approach focuses on forms, linguistic structures, and rules by which forms are generated, and seeks to prescribe acceptable rules. An example of this later approach is Peter Eisenmann's work, based on Noam Chomsky's Cartesian Linguistics: A Chapter in the History of Rational Thought (1966).

4 LANDSCAPE SEMIOTICS

The search for language and meaning in the designed landscape; the structure of this language; and its forms, symbols, and typologies is a worthy pursuit for landscape design. In the classical and Renaissance worlds, a relatively homogenous society changed

Part Ⅲ Design Elements and Methods

slowly, enabling the built-environment vocabulary and syntax to become established, and designed elements to be symbols with relatively fixed meanings. Modernism, occurring in a rapidly changing heterogenous culture and changing technology, was unable to achieve clear meaning. Taking a different approach, postmodernism has tried to clarify symbol and meaning when the condition itself is unclear. Whether postmodern semiotics can promote psychological health and well-being will depend on whether it can effectively reconcile design intent, the nature of complex systems, environmental perception, and user psychological needs into meaningful coherent places, as well as whether its advocates can effectively manage complexity for urban placeness and psychological healthy.

5 LANDSCAPE DESIGN AS MEMETICS

Landscape design education should embrace the search for language, meaning, complexity, and pluralism, and develop the student's ability to generate open-ended expressions sensitive to systems, complexity, and the essence of nature as change. This approach should educate students to solve problems, concentrate meaning, embrace pluralistic interpretation, express a range of influences, educate others, and lead society to a more positive future.

Memes are the value-laden messages a culture creates to communicate to its members how to see and attribute meaning to the world. Design education should develop understanding of design as *memetics*. It should teach students to recognize the memes of their culture and other culture and other cultures. It should also teach students to appreciate memetic complexity, envision desirable futures, and design to influence others to pursue these futures. From a systems view, it should educate students to recognize and respond to condition, integrate with system dynamics, apply principles, and pursue directions that simultaneously respond to ecological, physical, psychological, technological, political, and socioeconomic systems. Further, it should educate students in the integrated management of diverse systems to promote natural and human physiological and psychological health. It should also teach students to pursue landscape management, planning and design that integrates into systems in dynamic equilibrium. Finally, this approach should educate students to facilitate the emergence of more relevant management structures, planning strategies, and designs when systems are in dissipation.

6 GENERATIONS OF DESIGN PROCESSES

When one discusses design education, it is helpful to review the recent history of process, as covered by Broadbent (1984). *First-generation design processes* were a reaction against preconceived, intuitive design. They were linear, systematic, and "expert-driven" problem-solving approaches that were quantified and strongly based on a belief that expertise is distributed among the range of process participants, and that design should grow out of a dialogue between designer and user. *Third-generation design processes* saw planners as expert in making design conjectures, but not in determining how people should live.

While it is difficult to distinguish new directions while they are occurring, Motloch (1991) contends that *fourth-generation design processes* are emerging. He sees these as innovation-intervention type processes (Van Gigch, 1984) that manage dialogue, integrate expertise, and create decision environments within which responsive decisions can emerge. Fourth-generation designers dissolve the barriers between people's lives, formal planning, and design. These designers translate diverse value systems into planning and design.

WORDS AND EXPRESSIONS

ambidextrous [ˈæmbiˈdekstrəs]	adj. 怀有二心的，非常灵巧的
blockbusting [ˈblɔkˌbʌstiŋ]	n. 〈美〉街区房地产跌涨牟利
computation [ˌkɔmpju(:)ˈteiʃ(ə)n]	n. 计算，估计
flounder [ˈflaundə]	vi. (在水中)挣扎，困难地往前走，踌躇，发慌
	n. 挣扎，辗转，比目鱼
prematurely [ˌpreməˈtjuə]	adv. 过早地，早熟地
articulate [ɑːˈtikjulit]	adj. 有关节的，发音清晰的
	vt. 用关节连接，接合，清晰明白地说
dissuade [diˈsweid]	vt. 劝阻
neutral [ˈnjuːtrəl]	n. 中立者，中立国，非彩色，齿轮的空档
	adj. 中立的，中立国的，中性的，无确定性质的，(颜色等)不确定的
Freud [frɔid]	弗洛伊德(Sigmund, 1856~1939, 奥地利神经学家、精神病医学家、精神分析的创始人)
Ego [ˈiːgəu]	n. 自我，利己主义，自负
Moralistic [mɔrəˈlistik; (US) mɔːr-]	adj. 道学的，说教的，教训的
Insidious [inˈsidiəs]	adj. 阴险的
incubate [ˈinkjubeit]	vt. 孵卵

LESSON 11

THE PATTERNS OF DESIGN ELEMENTS

Complexity is one of the great problems in environmental design. Adequate information about the existing environment and about the types of place that it is desirable to make cannot be kept inside one brain. The invention of design-by-drawing made a significant contribution to the problem. Drawings help people to work out intricate relationships between parts. Mathematical calculations are facilitated. Many designers can cooperate on one project, each working on a part of the whole. This requires one person to Produce a Key Plan, or Master Plan. Which coordinates the phasing and drawings(Fig. 1). The people who produced these drawings became known as Master Planners, and, in environmental design, the art of producing overall layout drawings came to be known as Master Planning. If one is attracted to being a master, or having a master, this prospect may be alluring.

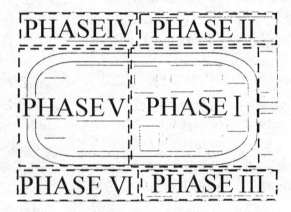

Fig. 1 Plans can master sites unfortunately

Christopher Alexander, an Austro-English-American mathematician who has been described as 'the world's leading design theorist'. proposed two radically different ways of dealing with complexity in design. Let us begin with a caricature. After leaving England to study architecture at Harvard, Alexander became a classical East Coast highbrow, applying cold reason and higher mathematics to design. His *Notes on the Synthesis Of Form* envisaged a modernist, computerized and wholly rational design method (Alexander, 1964). It did not work. After moving to the West Coast, Alexander grew his hair and applied group creativity and folk, wisdom to design. The *Pattern Language* was the result of this work. It was conceived as the archetypal core of all possible pattern languages, which can make people feel alive and human(Alexander, 1977).

THE EAST COAST SOLUTION

Alexander's East Coast solution to the problem of complexity in design dates from the 1960s, when electronic computers first became generally available. It seemed that well-programmed impersonal machines could take the place of fallible masters with a zest for tyranny. Maybe the computers could even become superior masters. Alexander's *Notes* suggested that large-scale forms could be synthesized after analysing large problems into small problems, so that they could be picked off one at a time. Appropriately. the first example was a vacuum cleaner. The design problem was divided into a series of binary relationships(for example, between 'jointing and simplicity' or 'performance and economy')so that they could be dealt with. The largest example was the determinants of form in an Indian village. They were broken down into 141 components and classified as religion, social forces, agriculture, water, etc. Here are seven of the 141 components:

1. Harijans regarded as ritually impure.

2. Wish for temples.

16. Women gossip extensively while bathing and fetching water.

18. Need to divide land among sons of successive generations.

79. Provision of cool breeze.

107. Soil conservation.

141. Prevent migration of young people and harijans to cities.

Before anyone takes offence at 'women gossip' as a 'design problem', it should be noted that the list contained both design objectives and design problems. The full sequence was described as a tree of diagrams(Fig. 2).

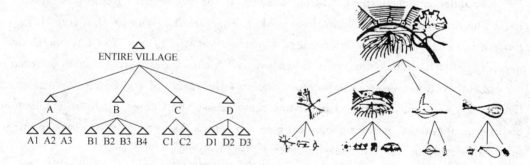

Fig. 2 The synthesis of form, for an Indian village

Two years later, Alexander had a change of heart and published his seminal essay 'A city is not a tree' (Alexander, 1966). By 'tree' he meant a hierarchy. Alexander emphasized that cities are not hierarchies, and that when planners believe they are, they produce the horrors of 'planned towns' with road hierarchies, business areas and useless open space. The example of a bus stop was used in 'A city is not a tree' to show that a bus stop is not merely a stage on a bus route. It also figures in patterns of shopping, walking. waiting, talking etc. These considerations led Alexander to argue against artificial cities and in favour of organic cities. He stated that cities are semilattice structures, not tree structures. As shown, the argument can be taken further(Fig. 3). A city is not a tree. It is not even an object. It is a set of landscapes. Every characteristic overlaps a host of other

Part III Design Elements and Methods

characteristics. Thinking about city structure led Alexander to recommend a second approach to the problem of complexity in design.

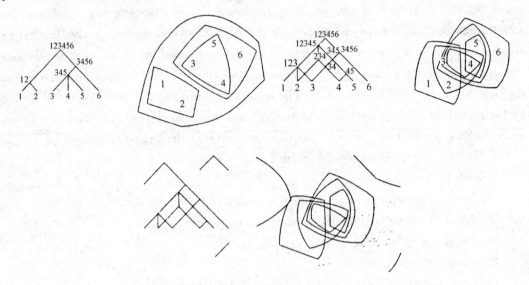

Fig. 3 'A city is not a tree'. It is a landscape

THE WEST COAST SOLUTION

Alexander launched the California answer to the problem of design complexity in 1977. The theory was explained in three books: *The Timeless Way of Building* (1979), *A Pattern Language: Towns, Buildings, Construction* (1977), and *The Oregon Experiment* (1975). Although colloquially described as 'Alexander's', the *Pattern Language* has six authors, numerous collaborators and was the result of eight years' work at the Center for Environmental Structure. If one came across the Center's title in a telephone book, one might take it for a geological research centre. As geologists also look for structures, one could learn from one's mistake.

The central argument of the *Pattern Language* is that, in the face of complexity, humans have evolved archetypal designs, which solve recurrent problems. These solutions are called patterns. In primitive societies, birds and humans had ways of using mud and grass to make dwellings. They remained constant from generation to generation. In modern societies, a greater range of patterns is available. Yet, the *Pattern Language* argues, there are still ways of doing things that, over an endless period of time, have satisfied complex human requirements. An ancient example is finding a choice location for an outdoor seat. Neglect of this pattern has led to a modern tragedy. Most outdoor seats in most towns are woefully sited: their locations are unprotected, isolated, noisy, windy, claustrophobic, too hot or too cold. The ancient pattern was to place a seat near a tree, with its back to a wall, in a sunny position with a good view (Fig. 4). The archetype for this solution balances prospect with refuge. Jay Appleton, in *The Experience of Landscape*, sees this as a fundamental human need: it satisfies human desires for safety, comfort and a good vantage point(Appleton, 1975). To avoid blunders. planners and designers must have this information.

Using the ancient patterns will, Alexander asserts, produce 'the quality without a name'. He explains:

The first place I think of, when I try to tell someone about this quality, is a corner of an English country garden, where a peach tree

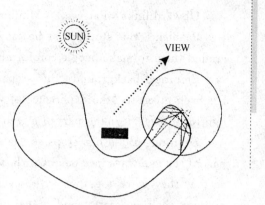

Fig. 4 An archetypal pattern for a seat place

grows against a wall. The wall runs from east to west. The sun shines on the tree and as it warms the bricks behind the tree, the warm bricks themselves warm the peaches on the tree. It has a slightly dozy quality. (Alexander, 1979)

In seeking to describe the quality, Alexander considers the following adjectives: alive, whole, comfortable, free, exact, egoless and eternal. But each is rejected. The *Pattern Language* is described as 'timeless'. Most of the book is devoted to accounts of the 253 patterns. As archetypes for good places, they have great theoretical importance for planners, architects and landscape designers. Tony Ward is quoted on the dust-jacket of the *Pattern Language* as saying 'I believe this to be perhaps the most important book on architectural design published this century. Every library, every school, and every first-year student should have a copy'. With regard to the social aspect of design, I wholeheartedly agree.

SOME EXAMPLES

I recommend scrutiny of the individual patterns. Each is set out according to an eight-part rule:

1. a number and a name;
2. a photograph, which shows an archetypal example of the pattern;
3. a paragraph on upward links, explaining how the pattern in question can help to complete larger patterns;
4. a statement of the problem, giving its essence;
5. a discussion of the empirical background to the pattern;
6. a statement of the solution, giving its essence;
7. a diagram, to show the main components of the solution;
8. a paragraph on downward links, explaining how it can provide the context for smaller patterns.

Let us take two examples, both of which I have abbreviated and labelled:

Name: Pattern 92 Bus stop

Part III Design Elements and Methods

Upward links: Pattern 20 Minibuses

Problem: Bus stops must be easy to recognize, and pleasant, with enough activity around them to make people comfortable and safe.

Empirical background: Bus stops are often dreary, shabby places where no thought has been given to 'the experience of waiting there'. They could be comfortable and delightful places, forming part of a web of relationships.

Solution: Build bus stops so that they form tiny centres of public life. Build them as part of the gateways into neighbourhoods, work communities, parts of town. Locate them so that they work together with several other activities, at least a news-stand, maps, outdoor shelter, seats, and in various combinations, corner groceries, smoke shops, coffee bar, tree places, special road crossings, public toilets and squares.

Diagram: Fig. 5.

Downward links: Pattern 53 Main gateway; Pattern 69 Public outdoor room; Pattern 121 Path shape; Pattern 150 A place to wait; Pattern 93 Food stand; Pattern 241 Seat spots.

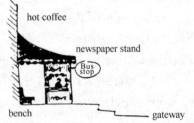

Fig. 5 Pattern 92, Bus stop

Pattern 92 is a delightful pattern. Multiple use is a necessity if bus stops are to provide personal security. With well-planned bus stops, cities would be better places. Here is a second example:

Name: Pattern 105 South-facing outdoors

Upward links: Pattern 104 Site repair

Problem: People use open space if it is sunny, and do not use it if it isn't, in all but desert climates.

Empirical background: If a building is placed right, the building and its gardens will be happy places, full of activity and laughter. If it is done wrong, then all the attention in the world, and the most beautiful details, will not prevent it from being a silent and gloomy place. Although the idea of south-facing open space is simple, it has great consequences, and there will have to be major changes in land use to make it come right. For example, residential neighbourhoods would have to be organized quite differently from the way they are laid out today.

Solution: Always place buildings to the north of the outdoor spaces that go with them, and keep the outdoor spaces to the south. Never leave a deep band of shade between the building and the sunny part of the outdoors.

Diagram: Fig. 6.

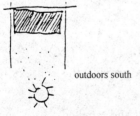

Fig. 6 Pattern 105. South-facing outdoors

Downward links: Pattern 111 Half-hidden garden; Pattern 106 Positive outdoor space; Pattern 107 Wings of light; Pattern 128 Indoor sunlight; Pattern 162 North face; Pattern 161 Sunny place.

A moment's reflection on the above two patterns will reveal that the 13-isms are paper tigers. Though a Taoist, a Christian, a Capitalist, a Communist, a Positivist and a Great Dictator may disagree about many things, they will surely agree that sitting in the sun is pleasant, while sitting in the cold or queuing for a bus on an exposed street corner are unpleasant.

As though to prove the point, Stalin, Roosevelt and Churchill are shown in the famous Yalta' photograph looking wrapped but miserable (Fig. 7). It is heartening to see three old men, with the fate of the world in their hands, lamenting the simplest of human pleasures. In a sunny place, they might have taken better decisions. If the Alexander patterns can attract broad support from diverse political and philosophical standpoints. they have sufficient truth to justify their use by environmental designers, without worrying too much about their epistemological and political status.

Fig. 7　The start of the Cold War

The Yalta photograph also illustrates that in one critical respect the patterns are relative truths, not absolute truths: they depend upon characteristics of the natural environment. Sitting out of doors is not always pleasant. Sunny places are loved in cool conditions. Shady places are necessary in hot arid conditions. Breezy places are desired in hot humid conditions. In the Arctic, shelter is essential and outweighs the need for sun. These climatic points can be broadened into the general proposition that the Alexander Patterns must be integrated with characteristics of the natural environment if they are to succeed. However well Pattern 52, Network of paths and cars, may be implemented, it will not succeed if it ignores the patterns of wind, rain, snow, floods and geological hazards. This consideration argues against the streak of absolutism that, it cannot be denied. exists in the Pattern Language. Many of the patterns seem to say: 'Do this. It is right. No other way exists.'

Another point arising from the individual patterns is that they cannot be divorced from aesthetics. Alexander writes that if an outdoor space is badly oriented then 'the most beautiful details will not prevent it from being a silent and gloomy place'. Nor will beauty sell many cars if they are unsafe, uncomfortable and unreliable. Yet who can doubt the importance of looks in marketing cars, houses, clothes, holidays and most consumer products? If the patterns in the Pattern Language are to reach their full potential, they must be integrated with aesthetic judgements. The high artistic standard of the photographs in the *Pattern Language* demonstrates the author's deep awareness of this point. Alexander's 1993 book on the colour and geometry of Turkish carpets provides further evidence on this point. The Pattern Language can gain considerable strength by linking arms with other types of pattern.

Part III Design Elements and Methods

A CLASSIFICATION OF PATTERNS

The above examples, selected from different fields of knowledge, can be conceived as structures. But for designers, 'pattern' is a more natural term than 'structure'. Patterns are of different ages and can be classified, like geological formations, using the terms Primary, Secondary, Tertiary and Quaternary(Fig. 8). The sequence of this classification is dictated by the following considerations: Primary patterns existed before man; secondary patterns, as traces of Stone Age[2] man, are the oldest signs of human life on earth; some tertiary patterns, like cave paintings, are very ancient; quaternary patterns are more recent. The foregoing types of pattern can therefore be grouped as follows.

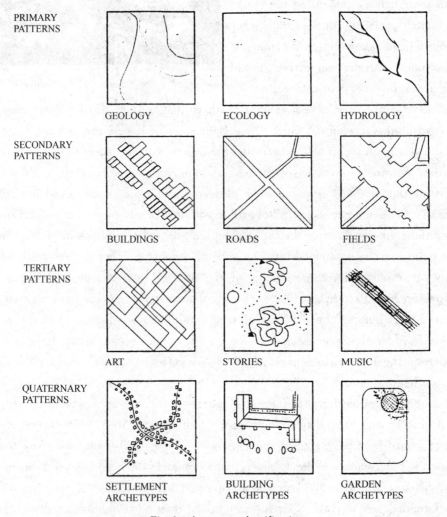

Fig. 8 A pattern classification

Primary/natural patterns are found in the existing landscape, resulting from flows of energy, from geology, from the nature of materials, from the processes of growth and decay. They might be represented in words and numbers, but maps and drawings are likely to be the most useful format. McHarg's map overlays represent the primary patterns of the existing landscape(McHarg, 1971). The emerging patterns of landscape ecology are of great importance(Forman and Godron, 1986). Dame Sylvia Crowe's book, *The Pattern of Landscape*(1988), considers natural patterns from both geomorphological and aesthetic points of view.

Secondary/human patterns are found in the urban and rural landscape. They result from the behaviour of humans, who adapt places to satisfy needs for food, shelter, transport, comfort and security.

Tertiary/aesthetic patterns result from the artist's imagination or the aesthetic appreciation of nature. They may derive from geometry, mathematics, decoration, representation, mythology, symbolism, allegory, metaphor, abstraction, philosophy, poetry, music and narrative. There are creative artists with expertise in all these areas. Environmental designers can work with them and learn from them.

Quaternary/archetypal patterns are tried and tested combinations of the other patterns. They are prototypes that have proved successful, like plant associations, house types, farm types and settlement types. Their place in outdoor design, which is a site-specific art, is as components. Like a sundial, no outdoor design can be exactly right for more than one point on the earth's surface.

Alexander's Pattern Language is made of quaternry patterns. The following examples draw upon primary and secondary patterns: Pattern 64, pools and streams, arises because 'We came from the water; our bodies are largely water; and water lays a fundamental role in our psychology'; Pattern 168, Connection to earth, arises because A house feels isolated from the nature around it. unless its floors are interleaved directly with the earth that is around the house'; Pattern 74, Animals, states that 'Animals are as important a part of nature as the trees and grass and flowers', and there is evidence that 'animals may play a vital role in a child's emotional development'.

The Pattern Language aims to avoid tertiary/aesthetic patterns, though some of them clearly to involve visual judgements. Pattern 249 states that 'All people have the instinct to decorate their surroundings'. Pattern 235, Small panes, recommends users to 'Divide each window into small panes' because 'the smaller panes are, the more intensely windows help connect us with what is on the other side'. The subject will be discussed in a forthcoming book on the *Nature of Order* and is previewed in a 1993 book on the colour and cometry of very early Turkish carpets: *A Foreshadowing of 21st Century Art*. He finds in carpets 'what the work of Bach and Monteverdi is in the world of music-a realm of pure structure, in which the deepest human emotions have their play' (Alexander, 1993). Yet carpets deal almost entirely with pattern and ornament. They are an exercise in colour and geometry.

The hidden strength of the Pattern Language lies in its imaginative appreciation of secondary patterns. They redirect designers attention away from style and back towards human behaviour. For example, Pattern 119 values arcades because they 'play a vital role in

Part III Design Elements and Methods

the way that people interact with buildings'; Pattern 164 recommends street windows because 'A street without windows is blind and frightening', and because 'it is equally uncomfortable to be in a house which bounds a public street with no window at all on the street'. Some of the patterns derive from what an earlier generation of psychologists would have called instincts: Pattern 181, Fire, observes that 'The need for fire is almost as fundamental as the need for water'. Pattern 129, Common areas at the heart, states that 'No social group-whether a family, a work group, or a school group-can survive without constant informal contact among its members'. The converse of this proposition is (Pattern 141. A room of one's own): 'No one can be close to others, without also having frequent opportunities to be alone'. The proposal for a teenager's cottage, in Pattern 154, seems part of an initiation rite: 'To mark a child's coming of age, transform his place in the home into a kind of cottage that expresses in a physical way the beginnings of independence'.

CONCLUSION

The full set of patterns required for outdoor planning and design depends on the nature of the proposals that are to be made. There is no finite set of 'survey information' that can be assembled before starting work, and there is no one inescapable starting point for a design project. When making a new place, planners and designers must know what factors made the existing place, how places can be changed, and what makes people judge places as 'good' or 'bad'. Specialized vocabulary is required. Patterns can use words. diagrams, models and drawings to describe complex processes and qualities. The language will not be symbolic, like computer code, but nor will it be a predominantly spoken language. For planning and design, it is most likely to be diagrams supported by words.

Many patterns will be appreciated by the general population; others will be particular to special groups; others will be unique to individuals. Words provide a common currency with which to interrelate the different structural approaches to the design and analysis of place. Diagrams can have a similar role, and are more readily transformed into designs. Structures reside in the environment but they are visible only to people and animals who have reasons to look for them. Each situation can be analysed within different structural frameworks. Ideas lead to surveys, to analyses and to designs. Patterns help designers to handle the complexity of environmental design.

WORDS AND EXPRESSIONS

highbrow ['haɪbraʊ]   n. 有高度文化修养的人，知识分子，卖弄知识的人
archetypal ['ɑːkitaipəl]   adj. 典型的
harijan ['hærɪdʒæn]   n. 神的子民（指印度社会最底层 "贱民"）
semilattice [ˌsemɪ'lætis]   n. 半网络，半网络结构

LESSON 11

Oregon [ˈɔːrigən]	n.	俄勒冈州
claustrophobic [ˌklɔːstrəˈfəʊbɪk]	adj.	令人不适地被关闭或被包围的
essence [ˈesns]	n.	精髓；要素
grocery [ˈgrəʊsərɪ]	n.	杂货店
Taoist [ˈtɑːəuist, ˈtauist]	n.	道士，道教信徒
positivist [ˈpɔzitivist]	n.	实证哲学家，实证主义者
epistemological [ˌepistiː(ː)məˈlɔdʒikəl]	adj.	认识论的
Arctic [ˈɑːktik]	n.	北极，北极圈
geomorphology [ˌdʒiːəuməːˈfɔlədʒi]	n.	地形学
symbolism [ˈsimbəlizəm]	n.	象征主义，象征手法
abstraction [æbˈstrækʃən]	n.	抽象，抽象观念
settlement [ˈsetlmənt]	n.	殖民(地)，租界，居留地，新建区，住宅区
sundial [ˈsʌndaiəl]	n.	(通过太阳知道时间的)日规，日晷
pane [pein]	n.	长方块，尤指窗格，窗格玻璃，边，面
arcade [ɑːˈkeid]	n.	连拱廊，(一侧或两侧有商店的)带拱顶街道
cottage [ˈkɔtidʒ]	n.	村舍，小别墅

KEY CONCEPTS

master plan
pattern language
archetypal designs
individual patterns
survey information

NOTES

1. Yalta: A city of southwest European U. S. S. R. in the southern Crimea on the Black Sea. A popular resort, it was the site of an Allied conference (attended by Franklin D. Roosevelt, Winston Churchill, and Joseph Stalin) in February 1945.

雅尔塔：原苏联西南欧部分一城市，位于黑海沿岸、克里米亚南部，是一个受欢迎的旅游胜地，它是1945年2月同盟国会议(由福兰克林·D·罗斯福，温斯顿·丘吉尔和约瑟夫·斯大林出席)的会址。

2. Stone Age: The earliest known period of human culture, characterized by the use of stone tools.

石器时代：人类文化可知的最早的时期，以使用石器为特征。

Part III   Design Elements and Methods

QUESTIONS FOR REVIEW AND DISCUSSION

1. Are you attracted to being a master or having a master? Why?

2. What's your opinion about dividing the design problem into a series of binary relationships?

3. Can you give the reasons for that the west coast solution is better than the east coast solution?

4. Why the author mention the Yalta photograph?

5. Do you agree that patterns can help designers to handle the complexity of environmental design? Give your reasons.

Reading Material

Planting Design

PLANTING DESIGN AS EXPRESSION OF FUNCTION

Throughout history the arrangement and cultivation of plantings has expressed human use of the land. This has been the case not only with the cultivation of food, timber and other crops, but also in planting which is not primarily for economic production. For example, the layouts of the earliest pleasure gardens in Persia were adapted from the functional agricultural landscape of the time with its irrigation canals and regularly spaced plantings of fruit trees. In eighteenth and nineteenth century England the hedges planted to enclose arable and pasture fields were carefully planned to improve farming efficiency. The ability of these hedges to shelter and protect and to give aesthetic pleasure helped to make the English pastoral landscape attractive as well as productive. These same qualities led to the extensive planting of hedges in gardens, ornamental parks and institutional grounds where human comfort and pleasure were essential for the function of the landscape.

Style and technique in planting are as varied as is the human use of the land. The environmental designer may be concerned with planning for almost any land use and for activities ranging from occasional visits to private or near inaccessible landscapes to the most intensive use in urban centres. These uses include domestic activities, play, work, study, and active or passive recreation. They all require an environment which fits the function, that is it must provide the right amount of space, the right microclimate, and the right aesthetic character as well as any specific facilities such as paving, seating and access which may be necessary. Planting can help create an environment which fits the function.

Many human activities require buildings, roads, car parks, waterways and other built structures. Planting design is much more than a cosmetic treatment to be applied to indifferent or insensitive architecture and engineering in order to "soften" the harsh edges or disguise an awkward layout. It can play a major role in integrating structures into the environment by reducing their visual intrusiveness, by repairing damage to existing vegetation and, more positively, by providing a setting which is attractive and welcoming. New planting, as well as the conservation of existing vegetation, is an essential element in good site planning for many types of land use.

If it is well designed, planting is an apt expression of function and of the needs of the users. Let us take a children's play area as an example. The basic provision of equipment such as swings and climbing structures will allow children to engage in certain play activities, but it does not create the best environment for play. This needs much more. It needs

---

选自 Nick Robinson, The planting Design Handbook

a defined and welcoming place, separation from traffic for safety, segregation of boisterous from quiet play, enclosure for shelter and to give older children a sense of independence, opportunities for discovery and adventure, and the raw materials for creative and fantasy play. Much of this can be provided by planting. A hedge or shrub belt can enclose and shelter and separate. But trees and shrubs also create a whole environment which can be explored, where dens and tree houses can be built, where there are trees to climb and swing from, and where plants and animals can be discovered. This kind of use requires an appropriate kind of planting. It must be robust, resistant to damage, varied and stimulating and it will be quite different from the kind of planting that would be right in a communal garden for the elderly or in a busy urban centre precinct.

One of the major challenges of environmental design is the need to accommodate several different functions within any single area. Modern forestry provides a good example of how recognition of multiple use requirements has led to more sophisticated design. Early plantations had narrow objectives. They were laid out and managed purely for commercial efficiency exploiting the maximum proportion of available land for timber production. Little attention was paid to visual amenity or to habitat conservation. But the increasing recognition of recreational uses, visual amenity and the need for wildlife conservation has led to forestry being more sensitively sited, the inclusion of a diversity of indigenous species along the more visible and accessible edges and the retention of the most valuable existing habitats within the forest area.

So good planting design endeavours to provide for all the uses of a place and to respect the needs of all the users.

PLANTING DESIGN FOR AESTHETIC PLEASURE

The importance of aesthetic pleasure as an objective of planting design should not be underestimated. The idea of pleasure is deliberately and often falsely associated with all manner of consumer products and lifestyles. It appears to be a persuasive and successful technique for stimulating demand, but the products and experiences rarely live up to their billing. In reality our culture is one which often frustrates genuine delight.

In landscape and planting design we are in the business of helping people to live fulfilling and enjoyable lives. The pleasure of a lovingly tended garden or of contact with wild plants and the creatures they support can contribute a great deal to our daily lives and foster a genuine recreation of the spirit.

WHAT IS SUCCESSFUL PLANTING DESIGN?

We have identified three major purposes of planting design: functional, ecological and aesthetic. The extent to which a design serves these purposes can be used to judge its success.

Of course, different planting schemes will have different priorities. These priorities

LESSON 11

will be reflected in the amount of thought that has been invested in meeting each of the functional, ecological and aesthetic requirements. For example, a shelter belt in a very exposed location will have the shelter function as its primary objective. The character of the indigenous vegetation and the aesthetic qualities of form, pattern and colour will need to be considered carefully but only after establishing the arrangements of species which are able to provide the optimum permeability and profile, and ensure the minimum damage to valuable existing habitats and take any opportunities there may be to create new habitats. A successful shelter belt will thus reduce wind speed and turbulence over the required distance, improve, or at least not damage, the ecology of the locality, and it will be attractive and in harmony with the local landscape character.

The criteria of functional performance and ecological fitness can be judged with a greater degree of objectivity than aesthetic value. That is, there is more likely to be disagreement on aesthetic criteria because opinions about what is visually appropriate and attractive vary enormously. This is the case not only when we consider different people's opinions, but one person's taste may vary markedly during their lifetime or even from day to day according to their mood. When assessing the aesthetic success of a planting scheme the designer should certainly ask "Do I like it?" and, if so, "Why?" or, if not, "Why not?" But if we are to give full and systematic answers to the questions of aesthetics we need to develop an understanding of the aesthetic characteristics of plants and the effects of these when they are combined in planting composition.

In addition to a personal analysis of the aesthetics of planting it is essential for the designer to ask "Does the client like it?" (that is, does it satisfy the person or persons commissioning the work?) and "Do the users like it?" The taste of the client and other users of a landscape may be different from that of a trained designer and it is essential to understand and provide for their various preferences and needs. As designers we may have a strongly individual style and firm opinions about aesthetics but if we do not achieve planting which is appreciated and enjoyed by the client and the users we are simply not doing our job.

WORDS AND EXPRESSIONS

arable ['ærəbl]	adj.	可耕的，适于耕种的
occasional [ə'keiʒnəl]	adj.	偶然的，非经常的，特殊场合的，临时的
cosmetic [kɔz'metik]	n.	化妆品
	adj.	化妆用的
domestic [də'mestik]	adj.	家庭的，国内的，与人共处的，驯服的
insensitive [in'sensitiv]	adj.	对…没有感觉的，感觉迟钝的
disguise [dis'gaiz]	v.	假装，伪装，掩饰
	n.	伪装

Part Ⅲ　Design Elements and Methods

intrusive [in'truːsiv]	*adj.* 打扰的，插入的
boisterous ['bɔistərəs]	*adj.* 狂暴的，喧闹的
fantasy ['fæntəsi, 'fæntəzi]	*n.* 幻想，梦幻
den [den]	*n.* 兽穴，洞穴，（舒适的）私室（作学习或办公用）
resistant [ri'zistənt]	*adj.* 抵抗的，有抵抗力的
communal ['kɔmjunl]	*adj.* 公共的，公社的
precinct ['priːsiŋkt]	*n.* 区域，围地，范围，界限，选区
accommodate [ə'kɔmədeit]	*vt.* 供应，供给，使适应，调节
	vi. 适应
persuasive [pə'sweisiv]	*n.* 说服者，劝诱
	adj. 善说服的
permeability [ˌpəːmiə'biliti]	*n.* 渗透性
turbulence ['təːbjuləns]	*n.* 骚乱，动荡，（液体或气体的）紊乱

Part IV

Site Planning and Landscape Design in Different Contexts

LESSON 12

SITE-STRUCTURE UNITY

We have discussed the importance of developing responsive site-project relationships. Let us now consider other means by which we may achieve site-structure unity.

We may design the structural elements so as to utilize and accentuate landforms. A lighthouse, for example, is an extension of jutting promontory. The ancient fort of castle extended, architecturally, the craggy top of a hill of mountain. Our modern municipal water tanks and transmission or relay towers rise from and extend the height of a topographical eminence. These applications are obvious. Not so obvious is the location of a community swimming pool to utilize and accentuate the natural bowl configuration of a landscape basin or valley. More subtle yet may be the conscious planning of a yacht club to utilize and emphasize the structural protective shoulders of a point or the soft receptive forms of a quiet bay.

A terraced restaurant stepping down the naturally terraced banks of a river, floating structures on water, light, airy structures fixed against the sky, massive structures rooted in rock-each draws from its site a native power and returns to the site this power magnified. Whole cities have been imbued with this dynamic quality-Saigon overhanging its dark river and slow-flowing tributaries, Lhasa[1] braced proudly against its mountain wall, Darjeeling[2] extending its timbered mountain peaks and towers into the clouds(Fig. 1)

A structure and its site may be strongly related by the architectural treatment of site areas or elements. Clipped allees and hedges, water panels, precise embankments and terrace, all extend the limits of design control.

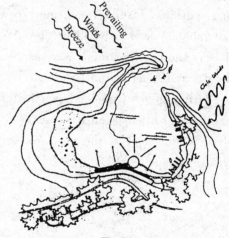

Fig. 1

Site-structure unity: yacht club, terrace, and restaurant have been planned to the natural ground forms, which overhang and command the bay. Boat slips are fitted to the protective ridge. The beach area extends the soft receptive wash of the harbor. Cabanas follow the natural bowl. The breakwater and light extend the existing rocky shoulders of the point. The parking areas are "hidden" in the shade of the existing grove. Such a *simpatico* feeling for the existing topography ensures a plan development of fitness and pleasant harmonies of aesthetics and function.

选自　John Ormsbee Simonds, Landscape Architecture, New York, Mcgraw-Hill Book Company

Part IV   *Site Planning and Landscape Design in Different Contexts*

Many of the French and Italian villas of the Renaissance were so architectural in their treatment that the entire property from wall to wall became one grand composition of palatial indoor and outdoor rooms. These grandiose garden halls were demarcated by great planes or arches of sheared beech, of masonry and mosaic, rows of plinths, and elaborate balustraded walls. They embraced monumental sculptured fountains and parterre gardens of rich pattern of mazes of sharply trimmed box hedges. The integration of architecture and site thus became complete.

Unfortunately, the results were often vacuous: a meaningless exercise in applied geometry—the control of nature for no more reason than for the sake of exerting control. Many such villas, on the other hand, were and still remain notable for their great symphonic beauty. In these, without exception, the highest inherent qualities of the natural elements of the site—plants, topography, water were fully appreciated by the planner and given design expression. Seldom, for instance, has water as a landscape element been treated with more imaginative control than at Villa d'Este[3] in Tivoli, where a mountain torrent was diverted to spill down the steep villa slopes through the gardens, rushing, pouring, gushing, foaming, spurting, spewing, surging, gurgling, dripping, riffling, and finally shining deep and still in the stone reflecting basins. Here at Villa d'Este water, slopes, and plant materials were handled architecturally to enhance both the structure and the site and superbly unite the two.

Alternatively, the landscape features of the site may be embraced by the dispersion of structural or other planned elements into the landscape. The satellite plan, the buckshot plan, the finger plan, the checker board plan, the ribbon plan, and the exploded plan are typical example(Fig. 2).

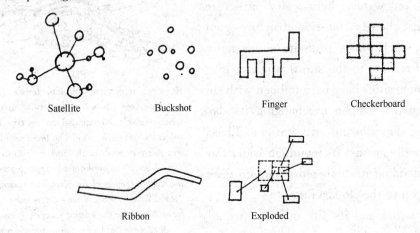

Fig. 2   Dispersion of plan elements

Just as the early French and English explorers in North American controlled vast tracts of land by the strategic placement of a few forts, so can the well-placed elements of a scheme control a given landscape. Such is true of our national parks with their trails, Lodges, and campgrounds so sited as to unfold to the user the most interesting features of the park. Such is true, in a linear plan expression, of any well-planned scenic drive or highway extended into the countryside. Our military installations are often, in plan, scattered over extensive land areas, each function be it rifle range, officer's quarters, tank proving ground, tent sites or artillery range—relating to those topographical features that seem most suitable. For this same purpose, many of our newer schools are exploded in plan. Unlike the old three-story monumental school set on the land, the newer schools of which we speak are planned to the landscape, embracing and revealing its more pleasant qualities with such success that school and landscape are one.

The site and the structure may be further related by the interlocking of common areas-patios, terraces, and courts, for example. A landscape feature displayed from or in such a court takes on a new aspect. It seems singled out. It becomes a specimen held up to close and frequent observation under varying conditions of position, weather, and light. A simple fragment of rock so featured acquires a modeling and a beauty of form and detail that would not be realized if it were seen in its natural state. As we watch it from day to days—streaming with rain, sparking with hoarfrost or soft snow, glistening in the sharp sun and incised with shadow, or glowing in subdued evening light—we come to a fuller understanding of this landscape object and thus of the nature of the landscape from which it came.

The landscape may be even more strongly related to structure by the orientation of a room or an area to some feature of the landscape, as by a vista or a view. A view or a garden may be treated as a mural, a mural of constant change and variety of interest, extending the room area visually to the limits of the garden(or to infinity for a distant view). It can be seen that, to be pleasant, the scale, mood, and character of the landscape feature viewed must be suited to the function of the area from which it is observed.

To the foreign visitor in a traditional Japanese home, one of the most appealing features of many is the use of smoothly sliding screens of wood and paper by which the entire side of a room may be opened at will to bring into the space a cloud like flowering plum tree, a vigorous composition of sand, stone, and sunlit pine, a view through tiered maple branches to the tiered roof of a distant pagoda, or quiet pool edged with moss and rippled by a lazying fanning goldfish. Each feature viewed is treated with impeccable artistry as part of the room, to extend and unite it with the garden or landscape, The Japanese would tell us that they have a deeper purpose, that what they are really trying to do is to relate people and nature completely and make nature appreciation a part of their daily lives.

To this end they introduce into their dwellings the best of those objects of nature that they can find or afford. The posts and lintels of their rooms, for instance, are not squared and finished lumber but rather a trunk or limb of a favorite wood shaped, tooled, and finished to bring out its inherent form and pattern of grain and knotting. Each foundation stone, each section of bamboo, each *tatami*(woven grass mat)is so fashioned by the artisan as to discover, and reveal in the finished object, the highest natural quality of the ma-

Part IV *Site Planning and Landscape Design in Different Contexts*

terial that is being used. In the Japanese home one finds plants and arrangements of twigs, leaves, and grasses that are startling in their beauty. Even in their art forms the Japanese consciously, almost reverently, bring nature into their homes.

In such ways we, too, may relate our projects and structures to their natural setting. We may use large areas of fenestration. We may so devise our approaches and paths of circulation as to achieve the most desirable relationships. We may recall and adapt the landscape colors, shapes, and materials. We may make further ties by projecting into the landscape certain areas of interior paving and by extending structural walls or overhead planes. We may break down or vignette our structures form high refinement to a more rustic quality as we move from the interior outward. This is a reverse application of the quality *wabi* mentioned before. This controlled transition from the refined to the natural is a matter of great design significance. It is a matter of such high art that only rarely can outstanding examples be found. One such example is the temple of Tofukuji in Kyoto.

If a building or plan area of any predetermined character is to be imposed on a landscape of another character, transition from the one to the other will play an important role. If, for example, a civic plaza and art museum are to be built at the edge of a city park, all plan elements will become more "civic" and sophisticated as one leaves the park to approach the plaza. Lines will become more precise. Forms will become refined and architectural. Materials, colors, textures, and details will become richer. The natural park character will give way gradually, subtly, to an intensified urban character consonant with the planned expression of the museum. Conversely, if a rolling, wooded public garden is to be built in a highly developed urban district, plan forms will relax and be freer and more "natural" as one approaches the garden preserve. Such controlled intensification, relaxation, or conversion of plan expression is the mark of skilled physical planning.

Yin and Yang The well-conceived plan involves far more than the application of a program to a plot of land; the fitting of the required use areas within the property boundaries. Planing that disregards the full array of landscape problem and possibilities can realize but a fraction of the site potential. Worse, it generates needless frictions. Often one or more of these frictions may become so insistent as to preclude the very uses for which the plans were made. Such a project fails.

Nor does a plan of excellence result often from the passive adaptation of designed components to the site as it exists. Such abject submission or attempt to blend into the scene usually produces an innocuous compromise.

The well-conceived project result instead from a design process of integration in which a new landscape is created. Components and site are consciously related and interrelated to yield the best that each can offer in dynamic interaction. Such unity is typified by the Chinese symbol yin and yang, evolved in the misty beginnings of time and representing the complete and balanced oneness of two opposing yet complementary elements—woman and man, earth and sea, and, in planing terms, the functions of the program and the functions of the site.

WORDS AND EXPRESSIONS

promotory ['prɔmpt]	n. 岬(角)，海角
jut [dʒʌt]	v. 突出，深出
fort [fɔ:t]	n. 保垒，要塞
municipal [mju(:)'nisipəl]	a. 市的，市政的
eminence ['eminəns]	n. 高地
magnify ['mægnifai]	vt. 放大，扩大
tributary ['tribjutəri]	n. (河)支流的
embankment [Im'bæŋkmənt]	n. 筑堤，堤岸
palatial [pə'leiʃəl]	a. 宫殿(似)的，宏伟的
grandiose ['grændiəus]	a. 雄伟的，壮观的
demarcate [di'mɑ:keit]	vt. 给…划界，勘定界线
beech [bi:tʃ]	n. 山毛榉
masonry ['meisnri]	n. 砖石建筑
plinth [plinθ]	n. 柱础
balustrade [ˌbæləs'treid]	n. 栏杆
vacuous ['vækjuəs]	a. 空的，空洞的
exert [ig'zə:t]	vt. 发挥(威力)
mountain torrent	山洪
spill [spil]	vt. 使溅出，使溢出
riffle ['rifl]	n. 浅滩，浅石滩；溪水作潺潺声
superbly [sju:'pə:bli]	adv. 雄丽地，壮丽地；可克服的
dispersion [dis'pə:ʃən]	n. 分散，散开
checkerboard ['tʃekəbɔ:d]	n. 棋盘
tract [trækt]	n. 一片土地
hoarfrost ['hɔ:'frɔst]	n. 白霜
subdued [sʌb'djud]	a. 柔和的，缓和的
vigorous ['vigərəs]	a. 朝气蓬勃的，精力旺盛的
tier [tiə]	n. (一)排，(一)层
impeccable [im'pekəbl]	a. 没有缺点的，无暇的
lintel ['lintl]	n. 楣，过梁
retroactivity [retrəu'æktIviti]	n. 倒行，反作用

Part IV Site Planning and Landscape Design in Different Contexts

KEY CONCEPTS

Site-structure unity
elements of the site
feature of the landscape
function of the area
functions of the site

NOTES

1. Lhasa

A city of southwest China, the capital of Xizang(Tibet). It is the center of Tibetan Buddhism.

拉萨，中国西南部的一个城市，是西藏的首府。它是藏传佛教的中心。

2. Darjeeling

A town of northeast India in the lower Himalaya Mountains on the Sikkim border. At an altitude of 2,287.5m(7,500 ft), it is a popular tourist center with commanding views of Mount Kanchenjunga and Mount Everest.

大吉岭，印度东北部一城镇，位于喜马拉雅山脉，地处锡金边界。位于 2,287.5m(7,500 英尺)的高度，因可以博览干城章嘉峰和珠穆朗玛峰而成为著名的旅游中心。

3. Villa d'Este

The Villa d'Este in Tivoli, with its palace and garden, is one of the most remarkable and comprehensive illustrations of Renaissance culture at its most refined. Its innovative design along with the architectural components in the garden (fountains, ornamental basins, etc.) make this a unique example of an Italian 16th-century garden. The Villa d'Este, one of the first giardini delle meraviglie, was an early model for the development of European gardens.

埃斯特庄园是文艺复兴时期的早期代表之一，它在花园设计中的创新使其在意大利 16 世纪花园中独树一帜。

QUESTIONS FOR REVIEW AND DISCUSSION

1. What can we learn from the example of the French and Italian villas of the Renaissance?
2. Can you cite some examples from the article to illustrate how to enhance both the structure and the site and superbly unite the two architecturally?
3. What are the ways Japanese really trying to relate people and nature completely and make nature appreciation a part of their daily lives?

LESSON 12

4. According to the article, can you give some examples about the landscape may be even more strongly related to structure?
5. In what ways we may relate our projects and structures to natural setting?
6. What the main idea of the concept of "Yin and Yang"?

Part IV Site Planning and Landscape Design in Different Contexts

Reading Material

Is Sustainable Attainable?

To smog-choked, drought-addled citizens of Southern California, the Ahmanson Ranch housing development may take some getting used to. To begin with, 90 percent of the 13,000-acre site-a former sheep ranch in Ventura County-won't be developed at all, but left as public open space with rolling hills and woodlands. And unlike most Californian communities, Ahmanson will eschew the auto, promoting electric shuttles, telecommuting and walking-biking paths to keep residents out of their cars.

What really sets Ahmanson apart, however, is its water strategy. Rather than shunting stormwater to the nearest sewer, bermed retention ponds will trap run-off, recharging depleted water tables. In place of lawns and exotic plants, native-or drought-tolerant species will be planted in public spaces. Even the centerpiece golf course will use hardy grasses. "This is definitely not what people around here are used to," agrees Mark Lorge, ASLA, with the Costa Mesa-based firm FORMA. Yet if successful, he predicts, within two decades, 8,000 people could be living and working in a town "that is self-contained, self-maintained and, ultimately, environmentally sustainable."

By then, more of us may be living in similar projects. With resurgent ecological awareness and rising anxieties over water and other resources, once radical design concepts are rapidly becoming mainstream. "We're seeing a tremendous interest in these ideas," notes Ahmanson Land Company Vice-President Guy Gniadek, who tracks green projects nationwide. Sustainable design, he says, "has momentum."

Where that momentum may lead isn't clear. To be sure, the ideal of a sustainable landscape-one that conserves or restores a site's natural processes-is an ancient one, revived with a modern twist in Ian McHarg's 1969 *opus*, *Design with Nature*. As well, many pieces of the green landscape-aboveground stormwater management or pedestrian-friendly layouts-have already been applied in places like McHarg's Woodlands project near Houston and in planned "towns" such as Seaside, Florida.

Yet with its current cache-even the White House grounds are slated for environmental retrofit-the idea has reached a crossroads that threatens to dilute its meaning. And even when earnestly pursued, efforts sometimes focus on single elements, like hydrology, while excluding others, like wildlife habitat and transit. McHarg himself, though heartened by the renewed interest in what he calls "regenerative design," worries that many so-called sustainable landscapes are "still being dealt with in terms of specific, discrete" systems without looking at the big picture.

It's precisely such concerns that make projects like Ahmanson Ranch so intriguing.

Roberts, Paul. (1994) "Is sustainable attainable," *Landscape Architecture Magazine*, vol 84: 1. pp. 57~61

LESSON 12

Ranging from housing communities to rural redevelopments, these are among the first endeavors to unify all elements of sustainability into coherent, replicable models.

Granted, many face technical and social challenges. Ahmanson Ranch, for example, is coping with nine lawsuits from environmental groups and others. Yet even as experiments, these projects can show what works and what doesn't. They can provide hard data on methods, materials and costs, and ultimately make this complex idea more accessible to clients, the public and design professionals themselves. "For years, we've been *talking* about sustainability," says Terry Minger, whose Denver-based Center for Resource Management is involved in efforts to help the Wal-Mart chain "go green." "Now, we're starting to see people *doing* it."

Among these is John Clark, a Washington-based developer who this summer plans to break ground on Haymount, a $100-million, 4,000-unit community in eastern Virginia. Slated for 1,700 acres of farmland along the Rappahannock River, Haymount will use only "eco" building materials, like permeable pavements and sustainably harvested lumber. Its energy plan was developed in part by conservation guru Amory Lovins' Rocky Mountain Institute. To encourage local employment and cut commuting, it calls for 750,000 square feet of office and retail space.

Yet it's Haymount's landscape-designed by a team that includes Warren Byrd, Associate, ASLA, with Florida architect-planners Andres Duany and Elizabeth Plater-Zyberk (DPZ)-where sustainable concepts seem most evident. All homes will be just a short walk from shops, playgrounds and services. Much of the site won't be developed, leaving large wildlife corridors. In developed areas, covenants restrict plantings to organically managed native or edible species. (Clark even foresees an organic farm and farmer's market.) Stormwater and wastewater will be cleaned on-site via constructed wetlands, at least six of which are anticipated for the first phase of 300 homes. Clark also plans numerous miniparks, many to be designed via competition. "It'll be a real grab bag for landscape architects", he said.

Some environmentalists worry over Haymount's proximity to the Rappahannock, one of Chesapeake Bay's most pristine tributaries. Yet Clark says his stormwater management system and organics will actually reduce toxic runoff to well below current levels. As well, Clark is lobbying Caroline County planning officials to raise environmental regulations on adjacent tracts to Haymount's standards. This protects both the riverfront ecosystem, Clark says, and his investment: "It keeps other, less sensitive developers from coming in and putting in anything tacky."

Haymount highlights several key issues. First, by melding the neotraditional community, advanced by DPZ and others, with innovative ecological techniques, like those of Lovins, Haymount depends on a team approach. To succeed, Clark says, such projects require cooperation among landscape architects, engineers, architects, hydrologists and planners. As important, by attempting to strengthen adjacent zoning standards, Clark ap-

Part IV *Site Planning and Landscape Design in Different Contexts*

plies McHarg's principle that sustainability cannot exist in discrete chunks. A landscape must not only integrate its own, internal systems, but mesh with the surrounding environment.

Integration also plays a major role for Pliny Fisk, an architect/landscape architect and director of the Center for Maximum Potential Building Systems in Austin, Texas. Fisk and landscape architect Lucia Athens began work last fall on the Advanced Greenbuilder Home(AGH). Planned for a 7,000 square-foot lot and scheduled for completion this spring, the AGH landscape will meld the systems of the home with those of the surrounding city.

Wastewater will flow into a settlement basin, then through a rock/reed filter, where roots of specially selected flowering plants, such as canna lily and rainbow iris, perform a natural treatment process. Outflow then irrigates a "living fence" of native thorn bush, a lawn(of native buffalo grass), an herb garden, an orchard and a bed of vines and other plants that, in turn, shade the house's southern face and funnels in breezes. The landscape "is designed to be a fully functional component of the building, as both a source and sink for materials," Fisk says. "That's how nature works and that's what we're trying to mimic."

Adaptable to any home size, region or climate, the AGH will intertwine with its surroundings in crucial ways. The thorn fence doubles as wildlife habitat. And by treating wastewater on-site, AGH helps recharge Austin's depleted aquifer and cuts demand on municipal treatment facilities. In fact, utility, health and water officials will monitor the project to determine whether AGH residents might earn credit for reducing their use of sewer and power services. "It gets back to the decentralized economics of sustainability," says Fisk. "It puts responsibility [for resource management] back onto the neighborhoods and individuals."

Fisk's concern with neighborhoods is telling. While sustainable landscapes will rely heavily on technology, social factors may prove as critical. As Carol Franklin, ASLA, of Philadelphia's Andropogon Associates, argues: "Sustainability isn't just about using the latest ecological gadgets."

In some cases, injecting social factors may be as simple as building walking trails to reduce auto trips. But designers must realize that they are sustaining more than natural systems. Just north of the mouth of Chesapeake Bay, inside a chain of 14 barrier islands, The Nature Conservancy(TNC) wants to protect a rare, pristine aquatic ecosystem. Yet the area also hosts thousands of longtime residents, many of whom make a living from the land and water. TNC's challenge is thus twofold: protecting an ecosystem without displacing its inhabitants.

TNC began by building community support for its plan, striving to show where local interests, like commercial fishing, dovetailed with conservation goals, like protecting unpolluted fishing areas. The objective, says Greg Low, TNC's vice-president for major program development, was to avoid imposing a solution. "You have to be a partner to get local support," Low said. "And if you don't have local support, you don't have sustainability."

Then, aided by the Ford Foundation, DPZ, Sasaki Associates and Vladimir Gavrilovic, a Reston, Virginia-based architect-planner, TNC produced an ambitious land-use plan that includes wastewater treatment, affordable housing and sensitive-lands protection. Key to that protection is a program of conservation easements: TNC buys parcels like coastal farms, then sells them, with density restrictions, to friendly investors.

Yet again, Gavrilovic says, social factors intruded. Using biological analysis, TNC initially determined that the easements' ecological "carrying capacity" could tolerate housing densities of one unit per eight acres. Such densities, Gavrilovic says, turned out to be "far too dense from a visual and design standpoint. What we were looking at was just rural sprawl." Changing course, TNC researched the area's colonial-era settlement and architectural patterns and analyzed the vistas. Ultimately, TNC concluded that the area's "visual carrying capacity," as Gavrilovic puts it, was closer to one house for every 20 to 40 acres.

The revised site plan now calls for a variety of traditional layouts, from "great houses" (one large home and two smaller ones on a 100-acre common area) to small villages. The overall lesson, Gavrilovic says, is that "biology alone can't sustain the character of a site. Landscape architects shouldn't play scientist. They need to be part of a team that has scientists, but they can't forget that everything has both a visual and a scientific component. For us, sustainability is maintaining the way a place functions and looks."

That finding is critical. Fisk and Andropogon's Franklin posit that aesthetic concerns keep many landscape architects from embracing green design. These holdouts fear that sustainable landscapes, guided by function, can't help but be drab and uniform-tough as nails but too ugly to sell.

Green design advocates, however, say such fears stem from a lack of creativity. Ahmanson's Lorge admits that using native and drought-tolerant plant species will, in fact, lend much of the ranch project "more of a shaggy, gray-green, informal landscape." But to balance that effect, Ahmanson's residential landscapes will be tended with lawns and ornamental shrubs. This compromise protects most of the site. It provides a transition between natural open areas and private spaces. Finally, it reflects market realism. "This is still an investment," says Lorge. "It has to appeal to investors," many of whom "expect certain conventional landscape imagery."

"I'm sick of hearing designers tell me why they can't do this or they can't do that," growls Clark at such reasoning. "My answer is, 'Quit whining!'" He insists that Haymount's huge list of allowable native and edible plants gives designers a more-than-adequate palette.

Landscape architects, argues Carol Franklin, must lead public tastes, not simply

Part IV Site Planning and Landscape Design in Different Contexts

follow them. That means educating clients as to the folly of many traditional, "ornamental" designs. Clinging to the art-driven, "horticultural-based landscape aesthetic, while the environment falls apart around them," she says, "is like rearranging the deck chairs on the Titanic."

Rob Thayer, FASLA, chair of the UC-Davis landscape architecture program, goes a step further. He'd like to see a new style derived from the profession's growing understanding of ecological processes.

He calls this the aesthetic of "transparency", describing it as the figurative "ripping off the landscape 'cover,'" of "letting people see what is going inside. We're so used to making facades, of covering up, of mimicking nature. Landscapes need to be arranged so they begin to function in the capacity of a natural ecosystem, not merely as symbols of natural ecosystems."

Easier said than done. Some designers may find the promotion of this new aesthetic uncomfortably close to activism. As well, not all landscape architects can work on the scale of large projects like Ahmanson Ranch or in design thinktanks like Fisk's.

Yet Lee Cooke-Childs, ASLA, of Brookline, Massachusetts, sees both the need and the opportunity for designer activism: in short, to lead. In 1992, she joined a community effort to redevelop Fort Devons, a 9,000-acre surplus military site 35 miles west of Boston. She eventually helped organize a design charette. Initially, however, Cooke-Childs found a group of earnest, hard-working community leaders with little grasp of such critical issues as soils or hydrology-issues that landscape architects are trained to consider from the start. Says Cooke-Childs: "There are plenty of planning commissions without a single design professional, who simply don't know to ask these kinds of questions."

Ultimately, such a small-scale approach may be the ideal complement to more visible projects. The Haymounts will take years to prove themselves. "We need to have projects up and running," agrees **architect Bob Berkebile, founding** chair of the AIA's environmental committee. "So architects and landscape architects can understand what's going on, so they can explain to their clients what's going on, show them the options."

The final ingredient is perseverance. Under conventional models, designers and planners create solutions, then move on to the next project. But a longer view is required. It calls for commitment-from clients and designers-to keep tabs on projects and, if necessary, make adjustments. "What we have to keep in mind," Gavrilovic says, "is that real sustainability isn't some kind of quick fix."

WORDS AND EXPRESSIONS

resident ['rezidənt]   n. 居民，住户
stormwater   n. 雨水
sewer ['sjuə]   n. 下水道，排水沟

LESSON 12

pond [pɔnd]	n. 池塘
native-or drought-tolerant species	本土的或耐旱的物种
self-contained [′selfkən′teind]	adj. 完备的，设施独立的
self-maintained [′selfmeɪn′teɪn]	adj. 自我维持的
process [prə′ses]	n.（大自然的）作用，活动
pedestrian [pe′destriən]	n. 步行者
layout [′leiˌaut]	n. 规划，设计
discrete [dis′kri:t]	adj. 不连续的，离散的
regenerative [ri′dʒenərətiv]	adj. 再生的，新生的
wetland [′wetˌlænd]	n. 湿地，沼泽地
minipark [′mɪnɪpɑ:k]	n. 小游园
ecosystem [i:kə′sistəm]	n. 生态系统
integrate [′intigreit]	n. 使成整体，结合
aquifer [′ækwifə]	n. 含水土层，蓄水层
aquatic [ə′kwætik]	adj. 水的，水上的，水生的，水栖的
vista [′vistə]	n. 狭长的景色，街景
shrub [ʃrʌb]	n. 灌木，灌木丛
transparency [træns′pɛərənsi]	n. 透明，透明度
activism [′æktivizəm]	n. 行动（第一）主义，激进主义

PARK AND BOUNDLESS SPACE

To impark an area of land is to enclose it with a barrier, which may be permeable or semipermeable (Fig. 1). When *homo sapiens* first erected a fence to protect an area of land, the world's first park was made. Outside was danger; inside was safety: for children, crops and domesticated animals. Later, when communities erected more extensive barriers to protect groups of families, the first settlements came into existence. Kings then began to think about private parks for their families. When grand cities came to be planned, spatial ideas were often developed in the rulers' parks and passed through to the streets and spaces of the cities in which their dictat ran. This practice no longer operates because, in modern states, rulers are shy of conspicuous consumption. Park planning, however, remains a crucial aspect of city planning.

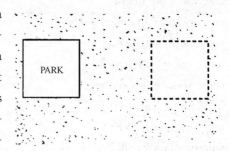

Fig. 1 Imparkments create parks

Fig. 2 The public park was once an oasis in the City of Dreadful Night

First in seventeenth century France and later in eighteenth century England, the rulers' parks burst from their imparkments. Louis XIV projected the avenues of Versailles ever outwards, and opened the park to his subjects. His 'park' became an unbounded space. Capability Brown's imagination, leaping the fence, saw that all nature was a garden. Many of England's royal and aristocratic parks were opened to the public. In the nineteenth century, special new spaces, known as 'public parks', were provided for the poor. To begin with, these parks were bounded: locked at night and strictly controlled, as oases in the City of Dreadful Night[1] (Fig. 2). Later, they were linked together by parkways. This idea came from Frederick Law Olmsted. He interlaced cities with parks.

选自 Tom Turner, City as Landscape: A Post-post modern View of Design and Planning, London, E&FN SPON, 1995, page 179~188

But the 'parkland' was no longer imparked. Greenspace leaked out and almost destroyed the ancient idea of a compact protected city (Fig. 3). New cities are not like old cities.

Fig. 3   Greenspace leaked out and almost destroyed the City

PARKS FOR EDGE CITY?

Now, the City of Tomorrow may not contain public parks. Joel Garreau has identified a new type of city: Edge City(Garreau, 1991)[2]. Its face is set against Le Corbusier's *City of Tomorrow*[3]. Edge City is that loose agglomeration of express roads, semi-isolated buildings, free car parking and sprawling urbanization that one finds the world over. Outside financial centres, they are the most economically active regions of the postmodern world. Garreau looks at Edge City with the dispassionate gaze of a journalist. To him, Edge City is 'what the consumer wants': safety, comfort, and convenience. Accessibility for the rich, inaccessibility for the poor. The high walls of Edge City are time and distance. Within these walls, there is no public open space, which bothers the professionals:

Designers who wish to make Edge City more humane frequently advocate that public parks and public places be added to match the piazzas of the cities of old. That sounds great. But as George Sternlieb points out… 'They don't want the strangers, If it is a choice between parks and strangers, the people there would sooner do without the parks'. (Garreau, 1991)

Safety comes first, so they don't want parks. But safety was the whole reason for making parks! With its defining characteristic removed, no wonder the modern park is about to die. Louis XIV started the process; Capability Brown carried it further. Municipal authorities, in many countries, have completed the process. No boundary means no park. Therefore all the imparked space in Edge City will be privately owned: as golf course, garden or theme park.

Kevin Lynch[4], a great urban planner, once observed that 'our city parks occupy only one small niche of the universe of open-space forms'. His plea for greater diversity was well made, but Lynch surely erred when he included parks within the 'universe of open space forms'. Parks should *not* be open spaces. They should *not* be places where people are

Part IV Site Planning and Landscape Design in Different Contexts

allowed to do anything. The very essence of a park is safety. Bounded space must not be confased with boundless space, though both are necessary. History is a good starting point for reconsidering park functions.

PARK HISTORY

At the dawn of European history, on the eastern shores of the Mediterranean, land was imparked for four non-agricultural uses. The Egyptians made domestic gardens and temple gardens. The Assyrians[5] also made hunting parks. The Greeks added **public** gardens, as meeting and market places protected within city walls. The Romans continued to make public meeting places, but the other three types of park became fused in the imperial villa and its progeny. Roman palace gardens, such as those made by Hadrian and Diocletian, merged the historic objectives of park-making. Parks were made for domestic pleasure, for exercise, for hunting, for the fine arts and for celebration of the emperor's godlike status. As such, they became models for Renaissance villas, in Italy and then throughout Europe, from the fifteenth to the eighteenth century.

North European park and garden designers paid their respects to this ancestry when they included Greek and Roman statuary in their designs. So do all those gardeners who place concrete casts of Diana, Flora and Aphrodite amongst the roses of their suburban 'villas'.

Fragments of classical park prototypes can be found in modern parks, but they are decayed and confused, like the statuary. Most urban parkspace is non-domestic garden, non-temple garden, non-hunting park. Those broad acres of green that look so fine on planner's plans and tourist brochures offer remarkably scant value to the public. They provide little to see and very little to do. A few years ago, at lunchtime on a hot Sunday, I visited Sheffield Botanical Gardens[6]. a well-known public park in one of England's older industrial cities. There were about 30 people lazing on the grass or giving their dogs an opportunity to relieve themselves. I then drove 15km over the hills to Chatswortn[7]. a famous old landscape park, still owned by the Duke of Devonshire. There, ten times as many people were queuing to pay money and enter the grounds. Why can't modern cities provide the outdoor space that people want? Partly, it is because too many are owned by municipalities. theoretically devoted to the 'greatest happiness of the greatest number', but in practice over-willing to entrust parkspace to operatives whose training is in the use of machinery and chemicals for ornamental horticulture.

To those who fear or mourn the death of 'the public park', I offer a simple solution: distinguish parkspace from greenspace; bounded space from boundless space; 'the public' from 'the park'. Use walls and fences to protect imparked land from unimparked land. Cities need both. But the two should never be confused. As with public space and private space, both are desirable. Each square metre of those Olmstedian green necklaces, which push their way through the cities of the world, should be systematically re-evaluated. Some of the land should be properly imparked, to make it safe and to make it special

(Fig. 4). The remainder should be properly disimparked, to set it free. Only thus will the people's needs be met.

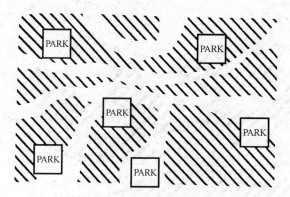

Fig. 4 Parks and boundless space

BOUNDED SPACE

There always were good reasons for bounding space and there always will be. Broadly, they may be classified as human, rather than natural. The ancient reasons for imparking land were both domestic and religious. Modern parks can have a variety of humanoriented themes. At present, even in the greatest cities, park space is insufficiently diversified. Most is under municipal ownership. Most is paved, gardened or managed to death. Orwell's Ministry of Peace made war. With equal perversity, municipal managers have made green deserts and grey deserts, using mown grass and concrete. It is time to set about the enjoyable task of differentiating urban space according to considerations of mood, age, ownership, history, culture, religion, ethnicity, politics, landform, habitat, climate and, yes, function. Diversification is the subject of my next essay, but Fig. 5 illustrates the argument so far.

BOUNDED YET UNBOUND

There is one very special type of urban space that is park yet not-park, bounded yet unbound. It depends on an osmotic membrane, which draws people in instead of keeping them out. As urban designers are seriously infatuated with this type of space, there have been endless tiffs and tribulations. So little has their essence been appreciated, they are named simply as The Place, Plaz, Plaza, or Piazza, depending upon which European language you are speaking. Where a Place just grows, it often succeeds. Where urban planners make a forced marriage between a people and a Place, they usually fail. The Places they plan do not attract those gay crowds of smartly dressed fun-loving folk who appear in the slick sketches that persuade clients to implement such schemes. This has led to great anguish, to a little research, and to a few worthwhile conclusions.

Camillo Sitte[8] launched our modern debate on Places(Sitte, 1938). As an architect,

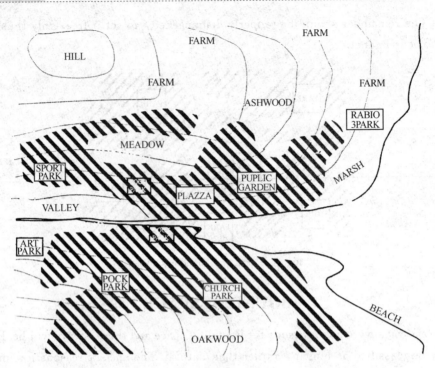

Fig. 5 Space for the hunter and space for the nester

he took the problem to be geometrical. Systematic studies of the old squares of Europe led him to conclude that the main factors behind a good place were plan, section and layout. Plans, he believed, should be irregular but enclosed. The typical size of 'the great squares of the old cities' was found to be 142m by 58m(465ft by 190ft). Christopher Alexander[9] accepted that such large spaces could work in great cities but argued that most squares should have a diameter of about 18m(60ft). Otherwise 'they look good on drawings; but in real life they end up desolate and dead'(Alexander, 1977). In cross-section, Sitte believed the width should be equal to the height of the principal building, while the length should be no more than twice this dimension. In layout, Sitte took it as a cardinal principle that statues should be placed on the edges of Places, never in the centres which, as Virtuvius[10] said, should be left for gladiators.

Americans have long admired the squares of old Europe. In making comparable spaces they have had a few great successes, like New York's Paley Park[11], and many great disappointments. Jane Jacobs[12] considered four squares in Philadelphia, with similar dimensions and at similar distances from the City Hall(Jacobs, 1962). Yet only one of them was 'beloved and successful'. Why? If urban designers do not have an answer to this question, they should be debarred from the design of urban squares. Jacobs' explanation was that the one popular space, Rittenhouse Square[13], was surrounded by diverse land uses, which generate a diversity of open space uses. Of the others, she saw one as a traffic island, one as a Skid Row[14] Park and one as a Pervert Park. While respecting her judgement, I believe that urban outcasts also need space.

LESSON 13

Willian H. Whyte[15] made an extremely thorough study of Plaza use in New York City, using time lapse photography (Whyte, 1980). Like Jacobs, he saw that some Plazas were very popular and most were empty. Why? He found that 'what attracts people most... is other people'. If a Plaza has a good relationship with a busy street, people will sit there to watch other people. There should be at least 1000 people per hour walking by at noon. Once they are in the Plaza, 'people sit most where there are most places to sit'. They like a wide choice of benches, steps, chairs, low walls, pool edges and planters. They also like a fringe of shops and fast-food outlets. None of these factors, it should be noted, bears any relation to dimensions, cross-sections or the placing of statues. Plaza planning is more difficult than Plaza design, yet both are important. The space must be bounded yet unbound. Success depends on the exact character of the bounding membrane.

COLOURED SPACE

This essay can be summarized with a colourful exercise. Please buy a plan of the town where you live. If it is a coloured plan, the 'parks' will almost certainly be a uniform shade of yellow-green. Urban squares, pedestrian streets, footpaths and surrounding farmland will probably be white. Lay a piece of tracing paper over the plan and reach for your marker pens. All the space to which pedestrians have free access should be shaded with a grey tone. This is the effective public realm. It does not include vehicular space, from which pedestrians are excluded by the danger of losing their limbs or lives. Now examine the grey pattern you have drawn. Those grey lines and blobs need to be enlivened. Which space should be boundless? Which should be bounded? A marker pen can be used to show your proposed boundaries. Within these boundaries, you can have special types of garden for plants, people and things that require protection from the harshness of the city. Outside those boundaries, you can let the people free. It is a good idea to find a map showing what the town was like a hundred years ago. Did it have heaths, woods, meadows, marshes, beautiful rivers or unspoilt beaches? They can be re-created. Bright colours should now be applied to the various categories of bounded and boundless space.

I hope this exercise will make you enthusiastic about the potential for developing the public realm and enriching public life. As most of the world's people will soon live in towns, the need for good public space will become a paramount concern in urban planning. When all the plans and data are stored in a GIS, specialized maps will be available for cyclists, swimmers, shoppers, ornithologists, campers, walkers, nut gatherers and others too.

WORDS AND EXPRESSIONS

homo sapiens [ˈhəuməuˈsæpiənz]	智人
avenue [ˈævinjuː]	n. 林荫道,大街,方法,途径,路
sprawl [sprɔːl]	v. 四肢伸开地坐(或卧),爬行,蔓生,蔓延

Part IV Site Planning and Landscape Design in Different Contexts

sprawling	n. & adj. 无计划地占用山林农田建造厂房(的)
urbanization [ˌəːbənaiˈzeiʃən]	n. 城市化
accessibility [ˌækəsesiˈbiliti]	n. 易接近性，可达性
piazza [piˈætsə]	n. 广场，走廊，露天市场
Hadrian [ˈheidriːən]	哈德良，罗马皇帝(117~138年在位)。
Diocletian	戴克理先，罗马皇帝(243~313年在位)。
Venus [ˈviːnəs]	n. 维纳斯，美神
Diana [daiˈænə]	n. 黛安娜，月亮和守猎女神
Flora [ˈflɔːrə]	n. 芙罗拉，花神
Aphrodite [ˌæfrəˈdaitiː]	n. 阿佛洛狄忒，爱与美的女神
Devonshire [ˈdevənʃə(r)]	n. 英格兰西南部的郡
diversification [daivəːsifiˈkeiʃən]	n. 变化，多样化
osmotic membrane	渗透隔膜
dimension [diˈmenʃən]	n. 尺寸，尺度，维(数)，度(数)，元
layout [ˈleiˌaut]	n. 规划，设计，（书刊等）编排，版面，配线，企划，设计图案，（工厂等的）布局图
marsh [maːʃ]	n. 湿地，沼泽，沼泽地
unspoilt [ˈʌnspoilt]	adj. 未被破坏的，原始的
GIS	Geographic Information Systems 地理信息系统
ornithologist [ˌɔːniˈθɔlədʒist]	n. 鸟类学者

KEY CONCEPTS

park planning
city planning
Edge City
City of Tomorrow
unbounded space
public parks
Paley Park
Olmstedian green necklaces

NOTES

1. *The City of Dreadful Night*

   《恐怖之夜的城市》(1874)，苏格兰籍英国诗人詹姆斯·汤姆逊(James Thomson, 1834~1882)的悲观主义作品。

2. *Edge City*

《边沿城市》是美国《华盛顿邮报》专题报道员乔尔·加诺(Joel Carreau)经过多年采访、研究，在1991年出版。这本书基本上是反规划的，很有影响力。加诺认为边沿城市是现代经济和社会中最自然不过的现象，教条式的规划只能妨碍和窒息这种自然发展。

3. Le Corbusier

勒·柯布西耶(1887～1965)，是现代建筑、现代设计、现代城市规划的最重要奠基人之一，对于现代建筑思想体系的形成，对于"机械美学"思想体系的形成都具有决定性的影响。*City of Tomorrow*《明日的城市》，由勒·柯布西耶所著，于1922年发表，书中提出"现代城市"设想，指导思想是彻底改造城市，改造社会，创造一种人类空间的新秩序。

4. Kevin Lynch

凯文·林奇(1918～1984)，著有《城市的形象》(The Image of the City)，认为规划师应该理解普通人认知他们周围环境的方法。

5. Assyria [əˈsiəiːə] An ancient empire and civilization of western Asia in the upper valley of the Tigris River. In its zenith between the ninth and seventh centuries b. c. the empire extended from the Mediterranean Sea across Arabia and Armenia.

亚述，亚洲西部底格里斯河流域北部一帝国和文明古国。公元前9世纪至7世纪，在它的强盛时期，亚述帝国的疆域从地中海跨越阿拉伯和亚美尼亚地区。

6. Sheffield Botanical Gardens

设菲尔德(英格兰北部城市)植物园。http：//www.sbg.org.uk/index.asp

7. Chatsworth

Chatsworth House and Gardens 英国首屈一指的豪华宅邸及庭园，巴洛克式宫殿是园区最美的景点。19世纪中叶经首席设计师帕克斯顿(Paxton, Sir Joseph)(1801～1865)拓展后成为著名典型的英国宅邸及庭园。http：//www.chatsworth-hʹouse.co.uk/

8. Camillo Sitte

卡米罗·西特(1843～1903)，19世纪末到20世纪初奥地利著名的建筑师和城市设计师。

9. Christopher Alexander

克里斯托弗·亚力山大(1936-)，当代建筑大师，著有《建筑模式语言》(*A Pattern Language*)，《建筑的永恒之道》(*The Timeless Way of Building*)等。

10. Vitruvius [iˈtruːviːəs] 维特鲁威，古罗马建筑师，《建筑十书》(*De Architectura Libri Decem*)作者。

11. Paley Park

佩里公园(1965～1968)，是位于纽约市中心曼哈顿的一个袋形公园，面积只有一栋建筑物那么大，被认为是20世纪最有人情味的空间之一。

12. Jane Jacobs

雅各布(1916-)，美国城市规划师、作家，著有《美国城市的死与生》(*The Death and Life of Great American Cities*)等书。

13. Rittenhouse Square

利顿豪斯广场公园(Rittenhouse Square Park)位于宾夕法尼亚州的费城，它是中心城

Part IV *Site Planning and Landscape Design in Different Contexts*

市的一道华美标志，也是一块备受人们珍爱的城市绿洲。

14. Skid Row

   穷街乐队，一支正式组成于1987年秋美国著名重金属乐队。

15. William H. Whyte

   威廉·怀特(1917～1999)，《组织人》(*The Organization Man*)、《最后的风景》(*The Last Landscape*)、《重新认识城市》(*City-Rediscovering the Center*)以及《小镇社交空间》(*The Social Life of Small Urban Spaces*)的作者。

QUESTIONS FOR REVIEW AND DISCUSSION

1. What do you know about Frederick Law Olmsted?
2. Do you think the Edge City is perfect for urban planning? Why?
3. Do you agree that the city of tomorrow may not contain public parks? Why?
4. Take a visit to the web site of Sheffield Botanical Gardens(http：//www. sbg. org. uk/index. asp)before class, and introduce the park in English?
5. How to bound space when you plan a park?
6. Which type of urban space is park yet not-park, bounded yet unbound? Try to give some examples.

Reading Material

Spatial Development

Perception is primarily visual, and visual perception is primarily spatial. We experience our world as a sequence of visual stimuli as we move through space. To the degree that the various stimuli we receive within any given space are related, we perceive coherence and a particular sense of place. We understand the place. To the degree that stimuli relate poorly, we perceive the place to be confused and incoherent. We do not understand the place and feel uncomfortable or disoriented.

Spatial development is the process of manipulating space, mass, and characteristics of the designed environment to intensify placeness. The process involves the management of visual perception, spatial relationships, and elements and principles of design using the exterior design palette of landform, water, plants, construction materials, and buildings.

1 SPATIAL PERCEPTION

Designing the built environment presents a paradox. on one hand, our culture is object-oriented, and design commissions usually involve the design of objects: furniture, sculpture, plazas, and buildings. On the other hand, our experience is spatial. At any time, our image of the world is directly influenced by perception of immediate space, its enclosed elements, and characteristics of its spatial edge. Awareness of reality beyond this edge consists only of mental images based upon past experience or imagination.

1.1 Relation of Space and Mass

We are encouraged by our culture to perceive objects. Therefore, in basic design terms, the beginning designer intuitively designs positive shapes (Fig. 1) and is less concerned with relationships between these shapes (Fig. 2). In designing 3-D form, the designer is usually concerned that the mass, including building facades, conveys unity and coherence. The inexperienced designer is usually less concerned that masses and facades unify and cohere with other masses and facades viewed concurrently, or that spaces communicate a unified sense of place.

While the novice designer is concerned with unity of the designed mass, the object is seldom seem in totality. We do not see at the same time, for example, opposite sides of a building. While the inexperienced designer is less concerned with relationships of the designed object to context, we usually perceive faces of designed masses, such as building facades in relation to other masses, building facades, and physical context (Fig. 3). When

---

选自 John L. Motloch., Introduction to Landscape Design, 2nded., America, Ball State University, 2001, page 184~196

Part IV Site Planning and Landscape Design in Different Contexts

facades relate to one another and context, spaces are coherent, integrated, and harmonious. When they fail to establish rapport, spaces lack coherence.

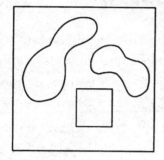

Fig. 1 Identifiable Positive Shapes

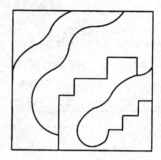

Fig. 2 Interrelated Shapes

Fig. 3 Building Facades and Spatial Perception

Whereas the inexperienced designer seeks to design meaningful objects, the artist

LESSON 13

seeks to create meaningful places. The novice designs masses according to some design attitude or form vocabulary; the experienced designer integratively explores mass and space and emphasizes spatial development. The novice designer allows different design vocabularies to confront one other in space (Fig. 4). The experienced designer makes design transitions within masses, allowing each space to express itself in a unified form vocabulary (Fig. 5).

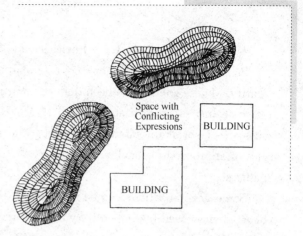

Fig. 4 Form Expressions Conflicting in Space

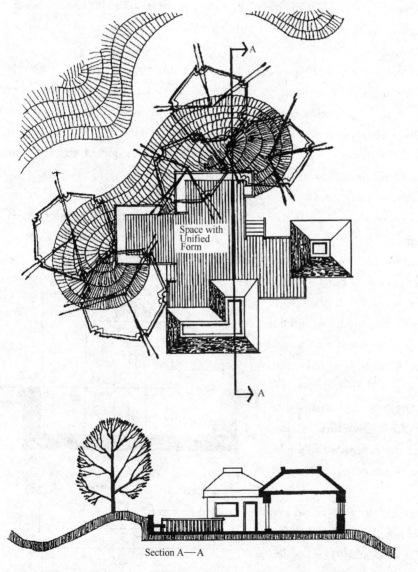

Section A—A

Fig. 5 Spaceas Unified Form

Part IV Site Planning and Landscape Design in Different Contexts

1.2 Enclosure and Spatial Perception

People are territorial: they cognize spatial envelopes or zones of differing perceived security. These zones have been defined as intimate space (0 to 18 inches), personal space (18 to 48 inches), social space (4 to 12 feet), and public space (12 or more feet). These zones affect social interaction. For each, the individual has a situational personality and rules of appropriate behavior.

Spatial size

Some generalizations can be made about the size of space and the feelings the space evokes when viewed by a stationary or slow-moving person. According to Lynch and Hack in *Site Planning* (1984), exterior spaces less than 10 feet in dimension seem distressingly small. Outdoor spaces 10 to 40 feet in size seem intimate; those 40 to 80 feet have a human scale. Exterior spaces 80 to 500 feet have a public human scale, and those larger than 500 feet, a superhuman scale.

Size of space and perceived territory also correlate. Small spaces provide a great sense of security, and the individual is prone to interact socially. Large spaces have a reduced sense of security, and the person is less prone to interact. In superhuman, scaled space, individuals usually feel unprotected and sometimes unsafe. They are drawn to human-scaled objects in these spaces, especially those at eye level. Inclusion of these objects allows the space to be more human in scale and humane in sense.

Degree of Enclosure

Spatial perception is also affected by edge character, percentage of edge closed, and height of enclosure in relation to angle of vision. According to Lynch and Hack, when the height of a continuous, opaque enclosure equals its distance from the viewer, the space is perceived as fully enclosed(Fig. 6) If the width-to-height ratio is 2:1, the space ceases to seem fully enclosed. At a ratio of 3:1, the space seems only minimally enclosed, and at a ratio of 4:1, the feeling of enclosure is almost lost.

Enclosure triggers our instinctive sense of territory and, therefore, security. As enclosure increases, we feel less exposed, and more protected, safe, and secure.

When objects are near or above eye level, we take refuge near the objects and sense the space to be smaller in scale. When objects block the view, we feel grea-

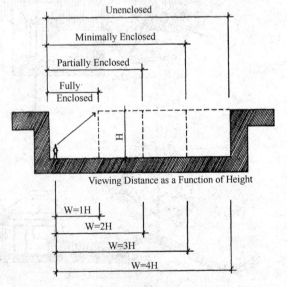

Fig. 6 Degree of Enclosure Based on W:H Ratio

ter protection and human scale (Fig. 7). Planes extending above eye level create spatial edge and provide enclosure. Intersecting planes or interior angles create edge on two sides and drastically change perceived size and enclosure. With the sky overhead, space is expansive. Introducing an overhead plane radically changes spatial perception. Enclosure overhead and on three sides gives the feeling of being within and of perusing the landscape from a point of refuge.

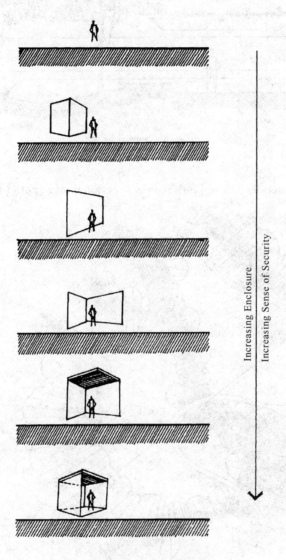

Fig. 7　Degree of Enclosure

1.3　Strata and Spatial Enclosure

Spatial definition and character, as well as the location (especially vertical) of enclosed elements, play a crucial role in perceived enclosure. Implications of vertical location can be best understood by exploring individually the base plane (and its vertical extensions near to the ground), the overhead plane, and the spatial edge, as shown in Fig. 8.

Part IV Site Planning and Landscape Design in Different Contexts

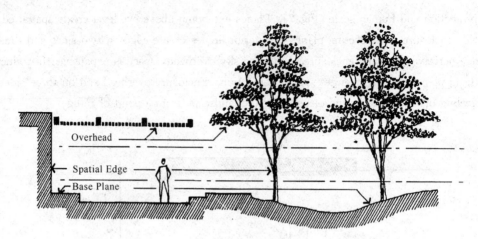

Fig. 8 Spatial Strata

Base Plane

The base plane serves as the landscape's functional and spatial floor. It is the surface

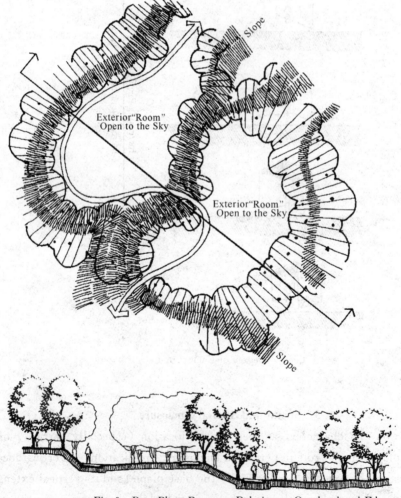

Fig. 9 Base-Plane Pattern: Relation to Overhead and Edge

on which we walk and drive; it forms the lowermost spatial limit. It also supports, structurally and biologically, elements that express themselves spatially in the overhead and the spatial edge.

The natural base plane, initially formed by environmental processes (uplift, erosion, sedimentation) is often reshaped by people. Its form usually expresses generative forces, local conditions, activities over time, and material. The base plane and its materials usually also convey information about land use. The sence of place is, there, in no small way, affected by the base plane.

As walking surface, the base plane also influences the route by which we experience the landscape. It structures our movement, choreographs the spatial story line, and affects our perception of place.

As the determinant of spatial story lines, and the structural and biological support for elements that express themselves in the overhead and edge strata, the base plane should bear strong spatial and pattern relationship to these other spatial strata (Fig. 9).

Base planes not approaching eye level might imply or articulate space, but they do not physically enclose it. On the other hand, landforms above eye level express themselves as base plane and as spatial edge to provide enclosure (Fig. 10).

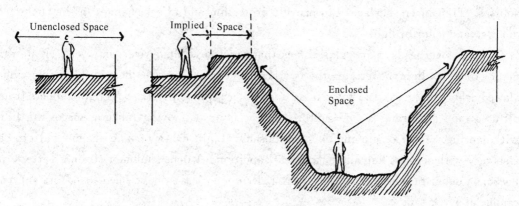

Fig. 10 Landform as Base Plane and Spatial Edge

Materials: Base-plane materials vary significantly. Each behaves uniquely with specific use and physical condition. Each affects perceived sense of place in its own inimitable way.

The base-plane material palette includes various types of soil (each with its own characteristic texture, slope stability, and behavior), plant materials (grasses, ground covers, and shrubs varying in size, texture, color, and so on), water (with power to convey mood), and human-made materials (cinder, brick, concrete, wood, and so on).

Overhead Plane

The overhead is the spatial ceiling. It can vary from ubiquitous sky, blue and expansive by day and sparkling at night, to hard exterior architectural ceilings. It can be a heavy, concrete slab oppressively perched above our heads, or a light and airy tracery of locust leaves fluttering in a gentle breeze.

Functionally and physiologically, the overhead protects us from the elements: solar radiation, rain, hail, sleet, and, to a degree, snow. Psychologically, it can provide a sense of shelter, protection, and unique placeness through the color and character it can impart to sunlight and the shading pattern it can create on walls and ground.

The feeling of "being under" is perceptually unique. It motivates us as children to explore under beds and tables, and later to venture into caves. An overhead plane increases this feeling and creates a dramatic sense of enclosure. Drama intensifies as the ceiling is brought ever closer to eye level.

Character of Overhead: As one who has hidden in a tree can tell you, the overhead is sensed more than seen. We seldom focus on the overhead. It is sensed primarily through movement, shadows it casts on other surfaces, and changes it imparts to the character, quality, and color of light. While it is sensed more than seen, the character imparted by the overhead can be important to perceived sense of place.

Solid, opaque, and static overheads can provide shelter from the elements, along with a sense of protection and repose. They can reduce the light level, and if deep can do so dramatically. They can also reserve as a surface upon which to mount artificial light sources. Translucent surfaces can provide protection and effect changes in the character, quality, and color of light.

Porous overheads, particularly ones that move or change over time, call create dramatic effects as light penetrates the overhead and paint surfaces below. Light piercing a slatted arbor can streak the space in an angular, rhythmic pattern. As light reflects from, diffuses, and penetrates a fine-textured lacy canopy of moving foliage, spaces are filled with dancing tracery or moving dappled mosaics. Light character and shadow pattern can also vary with season, sun angle, and leaf condition. A dense summer shading pattern can become a dendritic one in the winter after deciduous leaves have been lost from the tree canopy above.

Spatial Edge

Although relatively small in our cone of vision, the spatial edge near eye level is crucial in visual perception. while overhead and base planes affect spatial organization, use, and character and might imply space, closure at eye level is usually required to provide a sense of enclosure (Fig. 11).

Spatial edge is desirable when one seeks privacy, suspense, mystery, screening unpleasant views or accentuating (through framing and the like) desirable ones, defining spatial units, or other spatial effects. Successful spaces usually have edges that screen external elements that would otherwise destroy desired sense of place and that enframe views to promote this sense. Unsuccessful spaces tend to have poorly defined or improperly formed spatial edge. Spatial edge is important in helping people discover space in an appropriate manner.

LESSON 13

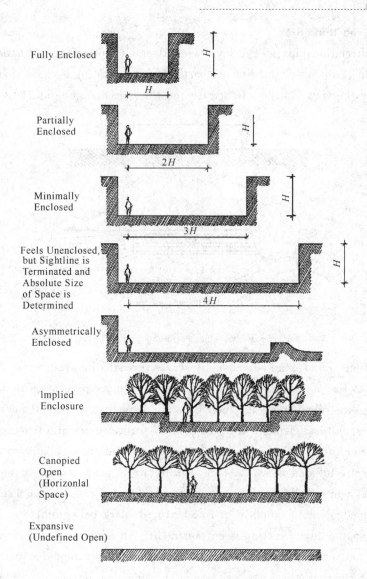

Fig. 11 Degree and Nature of Enclosure

Spatial edge encloses space, terminates sight line, and defines viewshed. Distance from edge to opposite edge determines absolute size of the space and contributes greatly to perceived scale (Fig. 12). The proportion of edge height-to-distance determines the degree of enclosure provided by an opaque edge.

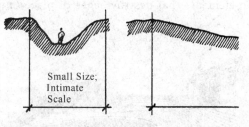

Fig. 12 Spatial Edge, Size, and Perceived Scale

Sightline Considerations: Eye level is the horizontal line of greatest visual attention. Elements, such as pictures on a wall or Landscaped derail, organized in relationship to this line can capture attention and provide a pleasurable sensation. As natural landform rises to eye level, "natural-ness" of the land-

Part IV *Site Planning and Landscape Design in Different Contexts*

scape increases substantially.

Unresolved relationships at eye level are extremely bothersome. Spatial edges that terminate within 12 inches of this line are particularly frustrating because spatial definition is indecisive and the viewer strains to see beyond the spatial edge (Fig. 13).

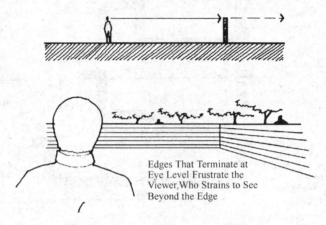

Fig. 13 Edges That Terminate at Eye Level

Edge Function: The spatial edge usually serves three distinct functions. As discussed, it encloses space. Second, it serves as a backdrop to enhance perception of sculptural elements within space. When doing so, the edge should enhance viewed elements, usually by contrasting the sculptural element in terms of line, form, color, and texture. A smooth, sinuous, white sculpture with subtle surface modulations might be displayed against a textured, deep-green, foliated mass. A lacy, wroughtiron sculpture might be displayed against a smooth, white wall. The coarse, white, peeling bark of a paper birch or an aspen might be displayed against a smooth- or fine-textured, dark background.

The third spatial-edge function is enframement. An edge can build to a crescendo to draw attention to openings. Elements outside a space can be enframed as part of the edge, thereby becoming part of the space. Effective enframement can greatly enhance sense of place (Fig. 14). Conversely, unintended enframement can incorporate and draw attention to elements that destroy sense of place (Fig. 15).

Fig. 14 Enframement and Sense of Place   Fig. 15 Unintended Enframement

Edge as Direction: As the most visually prominent spatial stratum, edge can effectively lead the eye to special features or elements of importance, such as otherwise hidden building entrances. It can also Lead the eye to visually important context (Fig. 16).

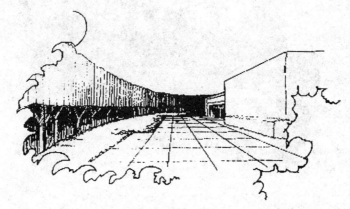

Fig. 16   Edge as Direction

Edge Character

As the dominant visual stratum, the edge is extremely important in determining spatial character.

If edge character relates to intended use and sense of place and if other spatial strata support this character, the place will seem coherent and the user will perceive a resolved quality. This feeling of resolve will establish a rapport within the user, and the space will feel comfortable.

The spatial edge can vary from a rugged cliff face to a smooth, polished aluminum or mirrored surface. The edge can be a dense, hard wall that conveys an architectonic sense (Fig. 17) or a porous vegetated edge (with dark shadows beyond), implying a deep, continuous, mysterious nature (Fig. 18). A vegetated edge can be closed like a vertical wall (Fig. 19), layered like a sunlit woodland edge with each vegetative stratum arching beyond the one above to capture sunlight (Fig. 20), or porous and open (Fig. 21) like the shaded north side of woodland canopies that have limited light for photosynthesis and leaf growth.

Fig. 17   Architectonic Edge

Part IV Site Planning and Landscape Design in Different Contexts

Fig. 18 Porous Vegetated Edge

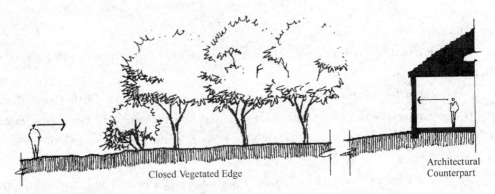

Fig. 19 Closed, Compressed Spatial Edge

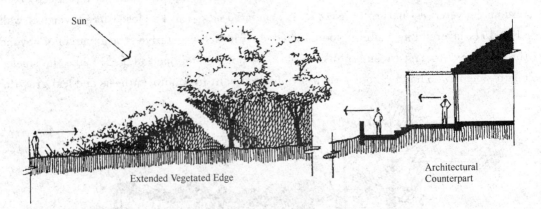

Fig. 20 Layered, Extended Spatial Edge

  The edge can have many layers, with diverse elements at various viewing distances, or be reduced to a single material and pure geometric form displayed at a consistent distance. Each edge condition conveys its unique character to the space.

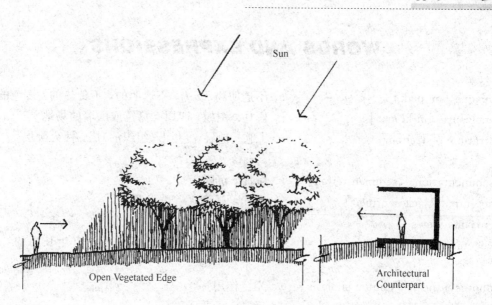

Fig. 21 Porous, Open Edge

2 SENSE OF PLACE

Spatial components, including base plane, overhead plane, spatial edge, and enclosed and enframed elements are part of the visual scene and, therefore, part of the place.

If the various stimuli relate to one another and support a common theme, the space has a strong meaningful sense. It will feel integrated; its elements will feel like they belong together. The space can be said to have a high degree of placeness.

If elements fail to relate one to another, the place feels discordant, chaotic, incoherent, and confused. Such a place can be said to lack placeness, or to exhibit placelessness.

Common Failures

When we design exterior space, a typical shortcoming is the inability to reconcile spatial edge with other strata and enclosed forms. It is common, for example, for the designer who seeks to create a sense of nature in the urban milieu to place naturalistic base and overhead planes and enclosed elements into a space whose edge is dominated by buildings. However, the dominant architectonic edge leads to conflicting stimuli, unintended contradictions, and an inability to evoke intended sense.

When we design into a space dominated by an architectonic edge, a more appropriate and realizable design concept might be that of "complement through contrast": yin-yang.

The chaotic visual nature of urban space in America today is evidence of the inability to address the perceptual dominance of the built edge, inadequate use of vegetation at eye level, and lack of designed relationships among spatial edge, other strata, and enclosed elements.

Part IV *Site Planning and Landscape Design in Different Contexts*

WORDS AND EXPRESSIONS

opaque [əuˈpeik]	n. 不透明物 adj. 不透明的, 不传热的, 迟钝的
enclosure [inˈkləuʒə]	n. 围住, 围栏, 四周有篱笆或围墙的场地
stratum [ˈstreitəm]	n. [地] 地层, [生] (组织的) 层, 社会阶层
	pl. strata
sedimentation [ˌsedimenˈteiʃən]	n. 沉淀, 沉降
accentuate [ækˈsentjueit]	v. 重读, 强调, 着重强调
enframe views	框景
vegetative [ˈvedʒitətiv]	adj. 有关植物生长的, 植物的, 有生长力的, 生活呆板单调
photosynthesis [ˌfəutəuˈsinθəsis]	n. 光合作用
contradiction [ˌkɔntrəˈdikʃən]	n. 反驳, 矛盾
intuitive [inˈtju(ː)itiv]	adj. 直觉的
sidewalk [ˈsaidwɔːk]	n. 人行道
frustration [frʌsˈtreiʃən]	n. 挫败, 挫折, 受挫
texture [ˈtekstʃə]	n. (织品的) 质地, (木材, 岩石等的) 纹理, (皮肤) 肌理, (文艺作品) 结构
contemplation [ˌkɔntemˈpleiʃən]	n. 注视, 沉思, 预期, 企图, 打算
rhythm [ˈriðəm, ˈriθəm]	n. 节奏, 韵律
sequence [ˈsiːkwəns]	n. 次序, 顺序, 序列

LESSON 14

LANDSCAPE DESIGN IN THE URBAN ENVIRONMENT

TREND TOWARD RECREATIONAL SYSTEMS

The urban dweller requires a complete, evenly distributed, and flexible *system* providing all types of recreation for persons of every age, interest, and sex. The skeletal outlines of such systems are emerging in many American cities—New York, Cleveland, Washington, New Orleans, Chicago—although usually in a fragmentary and uncoordinated form. Of these, the combined park systems of New York City, Westchester County and Long Island undoubtedly constitute the most advanced examples.

But, aside from their sheer inadequacy—no American city boasts even minimum standards of one-acre open space to each 100 population—these systems have many qualitative shortcomings. Public park systems are usually quite isolated: on the one hand, from the privately owned amusement and entertainment centers—theaters, dance halls, stadia, and arenas; and, on the other, from the school, library, and museum systems. This naturally makes a one-sided recreational environment. Even the largest elements—Lincoln Park in Chicago. Central Park in New York—are too remote from the densest population areas to service them adequately. And nearly all of these systems, or parts of systems, still labor under antiquated concepts of design, seldom coming up to the contemporary plane of formal expression. Nevertheless, the trend is more and more toward considering a well-balanced system essential, such a system including the following types:

1. *Play lot*—a small area within each block or group of dwellings for preschool children. One unit for every 30 to 60 families; 1,500 to 2,500 sq. ft. minimum. A few pieces of simple, safe but attractive apparatus—chair swings, low regular swings, low slide, sand box, simple play materials, jungle gym, playhouse. Open space for running. Enclosure by low fence or hedge, some shade. Pergola, benches for mothers, parking for baby carriages.

2. *Children's playground*—for children 6 to 15 years. At or near center of neighborhood, with safe and easy access. 1-acre playground for each 1,000 total population; 3 to 5 acres minimum area in one playground. Chief features: apparatus area; open space for informal play; fields and courts for games of older boys and girls; area for quiet games, crafts,

---

选自 John Dixon Hunt: Marc Treib, Modern Landscape Architecture: A Critical Review, MIT Press, 1993

dramatics, storytelling; wading pool.

3. *District playfield*—for young people and adults. ½-to 1-mile radius; 10 acres minimum size, 20 desirable. One playfield for every 20,000 population, one acre for each 800 people.

4. *Urban park*—larger area which may include any or all of above activities plus "beauty of landscape." Organized for intensive use by crowds—zoos, museums, amusement, and entertainment zones.

5. *Country park and green belts*—for "a day in the country"—larger area, less intensive use, merely nature trimmed up a bit. Foot and bridle paths, drives, picnic grills, comfort stations.

6. *Special areas*—golf coures, bathing beach, municipal camp, swimming pool, athletic field, stadium.

7. *Parkways and freeways*—increasingly used (1) to connect the units listed above into an integrated system and (2) to provide quick, easy, and pleasant access to rural and primeval areas.

BUT QUANTITY IS NOT ENOUGH...

But the types listed above constitute only the barest outlines of a recreational *system*; provision of all of them does not in any way guarantee a *successful recreational environment*. In other words, the problem is qualitative as well as quantitative—not only *how much* recreational facilities, but *what kind*. Here the element of design is vital, and success is dependent upon accurate analyses of the needs of the people to be environed. These needs are both individual and collective.

Every individual has a certain optimum space relation—that is, he requires a certain volume of space around him for the greatest contentment and development of body and soul. This space has to be organized three-dimensionally to become comprehensible and important to man. This need falls into the intangible group of invisible elements in humanlife which have been largely disregarded in the past. Privacy out-of-doors means relaxation, emotional release from contact, reunion with nature and the soil.

Collectively, urban populations show marked characteristics. Not only do their recreational needs vary widely with age, sex, and previous habits and customs (national groups are still an important item in planning); but they are also constantly shifting—influenced by immigration, work, and living conditions. Recent studies by Professor Frederick J. Adams of M. I. T. indicate constantly changing types of activity within definite age groups, and a gradual broadening of the ages during which persons participate most actively in sports. Organized recreation is spreading steadily downward (to include the very young in kindergarten and nursery) and upward (to provide the elderly with passive recreation and quiet sports).

In addition, the urban population uses a constantly increasing variety of recreation forms—active and passive sports, amusements, games, and hobbies. Old forms are being revived(folk dancing, marionettes); new forms are being introduced(radio, television, motoring, etc.); foreign forms imported(skiing, fencing, archery).

Consideration of the above factors imply certain design qualities for the recreational environment which are generally absent from all but the very best of current work. Design in the recreational environment of tomorrow must(1)integrate landscape and building, (2)be flexible, (3)be multiutile, (4)exploit mechanization, (5)be social, not individual, in its approach.

1. *Integration.* The most urgent need is for the establishment of a biologic relationship between outdoor and indoor volumes which will automatically control density. This implies the integration of indoors and outdoors, of living space, working space, play space, of whole social units whose size is determined by the accessibility of its parts. Thus landscape cannot exist as an isolated phenomenon, but must become an integral part of a complex environmental control. It is quite possible, with contemporary knowledge and technics, to produce environments of sufficient plasticity as to make them constantly renewable, reflecting the organic social development. It is possible to integrate landscape again with building—*on a newer and higher plane*—and thus achieve that sense of being environed in great and pleasantly organized space which characterized the great landscapes of the past.

2. *Multiple-use.* Most types of recreation are seasonal and, within the season, can be participated in only during certain hours of the day or evening. In addition, different age and occupational groups have free time at different hours, and a great variety of recreational interests exists within the same groups. The trend toward multiple-use planning reflects needs which permeate all forms of contemporary design: decreased maintenance, increased utility, and saving of time in unnecessary travel.

3. *Greater flexibility* in building design—to provide for wider varieties of use and greater adaptability to changing conditions—can be extended into the landscape. The construction creates a skeleton of volumes which are perforated enough to permit air and sunlight for plant growth. Plants now replace the interior partitions, and divide space for outdoor use. When building and landscape achieve this flexibility, we discover that the only difference between indoor and outdoor design is in the materials and the technical problems involved. Indoors and outdoors become one—interchangeable and indistinguishable except in the degree of protection from the elements.

Flexibility in design expresses in a graphic way the internal growth and development of society. For this reason, the great tree-lined avenues and memorial parks terminating the axes are not satisfactory, though they may have twice the open area per person above that which might be called an optimum. Once such a scheme is built, it is a dead weight on the community because it is static and inflexible. It is neither biologic nor organic, and neither serves nor expresses the lives of the people in its environs.

Part IV Site Planning and Landscape Design in Different Contexts

4. If scientific and technical advance has created the urban environment of today, it—and it alone—has also made possible the urban environment of tomorrow. This implies a frank recognition, on the part of landscape designers particularly, of the decisive importance of "the machine"; it must be met and mastered, not fled from. Indeed, the only way in which landscape design can be made flexible, multi-utile, and integral with building is by the widest use of modern materials, equipments, and methods.

As a matter of fact, this is already pretty generally recognized, though, again, in a fragmentary fashion. The great parkway systems of America are the best example of new landscape forms evolved to meet a purely contemporary demand. The sheer pressure of a mobile population forced their creation; and archaic design standards fell by the wayside almost unnoticed. The landscapings of the New York and San Francisco fairs are other examples, though perhaps more advanced in the construction methods employed than in the finished form. The use of modern lighting and sound systems, mobile theatrical units (WPA caravan theaters, Randall Island rubber-tired stages, St. Louis outdoor opera theater) is already widespread. Throughout America, advances in agriculture, silviculture, horticulture, and engineering are constantly being employed by the landscape designer.

But there are, as yet, few examples which exploit the full potentialities or achieve the finished form which truly expresses them. Nor does the use of the fluorescent light, microphone, or automobile alone guarantee a successful design. The real issue will be the use to which such developments are put. The parkway, for example, can either serve as a means of integrating living, working, and recreation into an organic whole; or it can be used in an effort to sustain their continued segregation. The theoretical 150-mile radius at the disposal of all urban dwellers for recreation is a dream of the drafting board, which, for the majority of people, is blocked at every turn by the inconvenience and cost of transportation. Only if the parkway reduces the time, money, and effort involved in getting from home to work to play, will it justify its original outlay[1].

In building the recreational environment of tomorrow even our most advanced forms must be extended and perfected. Man reorganizes materials consciously: their form effect is produced consciously: any effort to avoid the problem of form will produce an equally consciously developed form. Nothing in the world "just happens." A natural scene is the result of a very complicated and delicately balanced reaction of very numerous natural ecological forces. Man, himself a natural force, has power to control these environmental factors to a degree, and his reorganizations of them are directed by a conscious purpose toward a conscious objective. To endeavor to make the result of such a process "unconscious" or "natural" is to deny man's natural place in the biological scheme.

5. While the individual garden remains the ancestor of most landscape design, and while it will continue to be an important source of individual recreation, the fact remains that most urbanites do not nor cannot have access to one. And even when(or if)each dwelling unit has its private garden, the most important aspects of an urban recreational envi-

ronment will lie outside its boundaries. The recreation of the city, like its work and its life, remains essentially a social problem.

LANDSCAPE—LIKE BUILDING—MOVES FORWARD

Landscape design is going through the same reconstruction in ideology and method that has changed every other form of planning since the industrial revolution. The grand manner of axes, vistas, and facades has been found out for what it is—a decorative covering for, but no solution to, the real problem. Contemporary landscape design is finding its standards in relation to the new needs of urban society. The approach has shifted, as in building, from the grand manner of axes and facades to specific needs and specific forms to express those needs.

Plants have inherent quality, as do brick, wood, concrete, and other building materials, but their quality is infinitely more complex. To use plants intelligently, one must know, for every plant, its form, height at maturity, rate of growth, hardiness, soil requirements, deciduousness, color texture, and time of bloom. To express this complex of inherent quality, it is necessary to separate the individual from the mass, and arrange different types in organic relation to use, circulation, topography, and existing elements in the landscape. The technics are more complicated than in the Beaux Arts patterns, but we thereby achieve volumes of organized space in which people live and play, rather than stand and look.

WORDS AND EXPRESSIONS

skeletal [ˈskelitl]	adj.	骨骼的；轮廓的
fragmentary [ˈfrægmənteri]	adj.	由碎片组成的，不完整的，断断续续的
uncoordinated [ˈʌnkəuˈɔːdineitid]	adj.	不协调的，杂乱无章的，无组织的
sheer [ʃiə]	adj.	全然的，绝对的，彻底的
boast [bəust]	v.	拥有，包含
stadium [ˈsteidiəm]	n.	体育场，露天大型运动场
arena [əˈriːnə]	n.	竞技场，活动场所；圆形舞台
antiquated [ˈæntikweitId]	adj.	陈旧的，过时的
contemporary [kənˈtempərəri]	adj.	当代的，同时代的；当前的，现代(派)的
apparatus [ˌæpəˈreitəs]	n.	器械，设备
swing [swiŋ]	n.	秋千
slide [slaid]	n.	滑梯
jungle gym [ˈdʒʌŋgldʒim]		儿童游戏攀爬架
playhouse [ˈpleIhaus]	n.	，儿童游戏室，玩具小屋，剧场
hedge [hedʒ]	n.	树篱
pergola [ˈpəːgələ]	n.	(藤本植物的)棚架，藤架，绿廊，凉棚

Part IV Site Planning and Landscape Design in Different Contexts

carriage [ˈkæridʒ]	n. 婴儿车
wade [weid]	n. 趟水，涉水
playfield [ˈplerfi:ld]	n. 室外运动场；球场
radius [ˈreidjəs]	n. 半径
bridle [ˈbraid(ə)l]	n. 笼头；马缰
parkway [ˈpa:kwei]	n. 公园道路，驾车专用道路
freeway [ˈfri:wei]	n. (免费)高速公路
primeval [praiˈmi:vəl]	adj. 原始的
bare [bɛə]	adj. 仅够的，基本的
environ [inˈvaiərən]	vt. 包围，环绕
optimum [ˈɔptiməm]	adj. 最适宜的
contentment [kənˈtentmənt]	n. 满足，满意
intangible [inˈtændʒəbl]	adj. 难以明了的，无形的
disregard [ˌdisriˈga:d]	v. 忽视，漠视
reunion [ri:ˈju:njən]	n. 重聚；再统一
collectively [kəˈlektivli]	adv. 全体地，共同地
nursery [ˈnə:səri]	n. 托儿所
marionette [ˌmæriəˈnet]	n. 牵线木偶
mechanization [ˌmekənaiˈzeiʃən]	n. 机械化，机动化
plasticity [plæsˈtisiti]	n. 可塑性，塑性
permeate [ˈpə:mieit]	vt. 弥漫，渗透，透过，充满
skeleton [ˈskelitən]	n. 构架
perforated [ˈpe:fəreitid]	adj. 穿孔的，凿孔的
partition [pa:ˈtiʃən]	n. 隔离物，分割，划分
internal [inˈtə:nl]	adj. 内在的，内部的
terminate [ˈtə:mineit]	v. 停止，结束，终止
static [ˈstætik]	adj. 静态的
archaic [a:ˈkeiik]	adj. 古老的，古代的，陈旧的
theatrical [θiˈætrik(ə)l]	adj. 剧场的；戏院的
silviculture [ˈsilviˌkʌltʃə]	n. 造林术，森林学
segregation [ˌsegriˈgeiʃən]	n. 分离，隔离
outlay [ˈautlei]	n. 费用，开销
urbanite [ˈə:bənait]	n. 都市人
ideology [ˌaidiˈɔlədʒi, id-]	n. 意识形态，思想(体系)
facade [fəˈsa:d]	n. (建筑物的)正面
decorative [ˈdekərətiv]	adj. 装饰的
inherent [inˈhiərənt]	adj. 固有的，内在的
hardiness [ˈha:dinis]	n. 耐久力，顽强，强壮，坚强
deciduous [diˈsidʒuəs]	adj. 落叶的，非永久性的

LESSON 14

beaux [bəuz]   n. 喜修饰者，纨绔子弟

KEY CONCEPTS

Urban environment
Recreational system
Public park system
Play lot
Children's playground
District playfield
Urban park
Country park
Green belt
Parkway

NOTES

1. The theoretical 150-miles radius at the disposal of all urban dwellers for recreation is a dream of the drafting board, which, for the majority of people, is blocked at every turn by the inconvenience and cost of transportation. Only if the parkway reduces the time, money, and effort involved in getting from home to work to play, will it justify its original outlay.

在理论半径 150 英里内为城市所有居民安排娱乐是一种蓝图梦想，对于大多数人来说，可能会因为不便利或交通费用所限制。公园道路只有减少了时间、费用以及由家到工作（单位）到娱乐所费的周折，才能判断其真正的价值。

QUESTIONS FOR REVIEW AND DISCUSSION

1. What is the present situation of the American recreational systems?
2. According to the article, what types should a well-balanced recreational system include? What do you think about it?
3. What does the success of a recreational system design depend on?
4. What qualities should design in the recreational environment of tomorrow have? how do you understand and explain them?
5. What should one know to use plants as a building material well? How to express the inherent quality of these plants?

Reading Material

Eco-City Plans

Sustain derives from *sub-*[under] and *tenere* [hold]. It means to hold under, and thus keep up, as in 'a sustained musical note'. Environmentally, a sustainable city is one that can keep going because it uses resources economically, avoids waste, recycles where possible and adopts policies that bear fruit in the long term. Forestry is the oldest and best example of sustainable planning. Von Carlowitz, in 1713, explained that if forests were not planned on a sustainable basis, humanity would plunge into poverty and destitution, as was happening in Central Europe at that time(Speidel, 1984). Foresters aim at the highest timber yield that can be sustained. If the periodic harvest matches incremental growth, equilibrium will be maintained.

The Bruntland Commission[1], in 1987, defined sustainable development as 'development that meets the needs of the present without compromising the ability of future generations to meet their own needs' (Bruntland, 1987). This definition is often quoted verbatim, possibly because its meaning is so hazy. What is 'development'? Do the 'needs of the present'include two cars and two homes for each family? Who knows the needs of future generations? Even forestry is not sustainable development within the Bruntland definition, because new forests cannot be developed to meet 'the needs of the present'.

Then again, if future generations take our advice about recycling, new timber reserves will hardly be necessary. Nor will they be required if current moves towards the silicon office, the Internet book and the fibre optic data highway come to fruition. For all these reasons, I prefer Ecocity to Sustainable City. *Eco-*means home. *Eco-city* means 'home city', implying that a whole city can be looked after as wisely as a private house, economically and with cupboards for old pieces of string and empty jamjars. Modernist cities have high inputs and high outputs (Fig. 1). Eco-city planners should aim to produce cities with lower inputs of energy and materials, with lower outputs of waste and pollution.

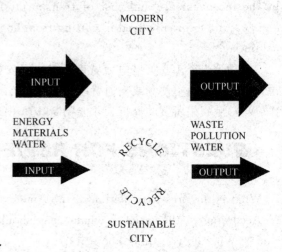

Fig. 1 Sustainable cities should have fewer inputs and fewer outputs, because they recycle

Despite the merits of the forester's conception of sustainability, it remains far from

选自 Tom Turner. City as Landscape: A Post Post-Modern View of Design and Planning London, E&FN Spon perfect. Modern scientific forestry, which originated in nineteenth century Germany, was aimed at producing a sustainable high yield of timber. But the technique depended on the exclusion of sporting and aesthetic interests from forest management. After 1919, British foresters followed the German example, as did Indian, American and other foresters. Factory methods came to dominate forest practice. In ancient times, forests had been maintained for timber, fuel, hunting, grazing and the gathering of wild food. It has been a great struggle to re-introduce other objectives back into forest management, and doing so has diminished the 'sustainable yield' of timber.

Cities, too, must be planned for multiple objectives. Sustainability is but one amongst many goals. We also want cities that are beautiful, convenient, comfortable and accessible. If sustainability were overemphasized, which is not very likely, cities would become miserable places. Residential densities would be high. Personal space would be restricted. Everyone would live in walk-up apartment blocks with flat roofs. Roofspace would be used to grow vegetables, irrigated by drip-fed sewage effluent. Most people would walk or cycle to work (Fig. 2). Definitely, there would be no golf courses. Walls would be thick, windows small, streets narrow, all to conserve energy. Much less food would be cooked and much less protein eaten. As Charles Correa puts it, in *The New Landscape: Urbanization in the Third World*:

Fig. 2   Sustainable cities could be joyless

If we look at all the fashionable concerns of environmentalists today-balanced ecosystems, recycling of waste products, appropriate lifestyles, indigenous technology-we find that the people of the Third World already have it all. (Correa, 1989)

There is a good case for making technology transfer a two-way process, but few inhabitants of the world's prosperous cities wish to be 'levelled down' to the condition of

Third World cities. This essay is about some of the things that can be done by physical planning to make cities more sustainable without losing sight of other urban objectives. If one were making a physical model of a city, the five chief elements would be: landform, water, vegetation, transport and buildings. Let us consider them in turn.

LANDFORM PLANS

Modern cities are on the move. The cycle of construction and reconstruction has become perpetual and may accelerate. Vast quantities of earth, rock and building rubble are shifted about. Waste material is excavated to make foundations. Tunnels are dug for transport and infrastructure. Sand and gravel deposits are quarried to make concrete and to obtain fill for embankments. Home improvements lead to skips in every street. Demolition of old buildings yields enormous quantities of rubble. Where should these wastes go? One solution is to place them in the clay, sand, gravel and rock quarries that are excavated when cities are built. Quarries and pits surround modern cities, but filling them has drawbacks. First, quarries are not likely to be near the city centres where most demolition and construction take place. Second, pits tend to be in low-lying land, where there is a danger of polluting groundwater reserves. Third, it seems a wretchedly unimaginative policy.

The eco-city solution is to prepare a landform plan, statutory or non-statutory, showing areas where new hills, valleys, plains and lakes are possible, desirable and undesirable (Fig. 3). The plan should also mark areas where waste materials can be stored for recycling. Most cities have large areas of land that, for one reason or another, are unused and await redevelopment. They should become temporary stockpiles of sand, gravel, clay, rock, demolition rubble, metal, timber, topsoil, garden waste and other materials, equivalent to the area behind your garden shed. At the town scale, areas for new hills, lakes and valleys should be marked. Often, they will be on the urban fringe, where the city is expanding. Such land can be made into wondrous new landscapes. All we need is imagination, and plans. Demolition material should not be removed from building sites unless it can be shown that it will be put to good use elsewhere.

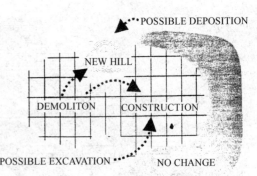

Fig. 3 Landform plans could show where change is possible, desirable and undesirable

WATER PLANS

Great cities should accumulate water, as they do knowledge and gold. This water should be recycled within city boundaries. In ancient Rome, fresh water was brought in by aqueduct and dirty water was discharged into streams, which became sewers, and then into the Tiber via the *cloaca maxima*. The Roman approach to water management remained the only possibility until modern times. Now, we can extract water from the foulest rivers and purify it for household use. We can also afford to lay different pipes for the supply and disposal of different types of water: roofwater, roadwater, sewage water (without solids). The water types can be described as bluewater, greywater and brownwater. Each should be used in a different way. Bluewater should be infiltrated where it falls. Greywater may have to be filtered to remove hydrocarbons. Brownwater should be treated in reedbeds or by conventional means.

The new approach to water management has profound consequences for physical planning. Roofs should be designed to detain and evaporate water. Parks should have reed beds, storm detention ponds and infiltration ponds. Gardens should have large tanks, as they used to in the old days, to store rainwater and to supply water features. Cities should have more trees. Pedestrian surfaces should be porous, so that they do not produce surface water runoff. Urban valleys should be designed so that they can flood. New buildings in flood plains should be floodable. All buildings should be designed with rainwater storage and infiltration capacity, on the roof or in the grounds.

VEGETATION PLANS

Medieval cities had little vegetation, because land within city walls was so scarce and so expensive. As artillery improved and the practice of siege warfare declined, private gardens and public parks became thinkable. In the nineteenth century they became popular, as did coal fires. The latter transformed rain into dilute sulphuric acid, which dissolved all but the toughest vegetation. There was also a shortage of firewood, which put trees at risk. It was only in the twentieth century that cities became richly vegetated. This process can be seen in the illustrations of Edinburgh. My guess is that if another photograph is taken in AD 2050, the process will have gone further.

As it was the public park and the private garden that created space for ornamental vegetation in cities, the vegetation was managed in a gardenesque way. It was not countryside. Park managers aimed for three categories of vegetation: clearstemmed trees, mown grass and ornamental beds. From a sustainability viewpoint, this was improvident. Heavy resource inputs are required for park maintenance, as fuel, fertilizer, pesticide, herbicide and irrigation. These inputs produce was: air pollution, soil pollution, water pollution and noise pollution. They also destroy wildlife habitats. Is it possible to strike a compromise between garden exotica and nature conservation? Yes. Small areas of garden, maintained by hand with loving care, are a delightful luxury. Large areas of seminatural habitat, maintained by adaptations of natural processes, provide a good environment for man. But it is time to do away with the middle landscape of 'amenity grass' and 'amenity shrubs', where the 'amenity' in question is gardenesque in the sense of 'like a garden'.

Instead, we should create networks of natural habitats extending from country to city. Holland, which is a densely populated land with little natural vegetation, is very advanced in this respect. They have four strategies for developing habitat networks in the Green Heart of the Ring City. Each is named after an animal that would benefit from the strategy. 'Godwit' is a plan for restoring variety to existing grassland ecosystems. 'Otter' is a plan for using corridors to improve the dispersal of habitats, especially open water and marshland. 'Elk' is a plan for segregated habitats, such as wooded marshes. 'Harrier' is a plan to create an optimal variety of ecosystems in reed, sedge and tidal areas (Lankhorst, 1994).

Food production in cities should also become the norm. This will enable life in the city to be sustained. Salad crops can be grown on flat roofs. Fruit and nuts can be collected from public orchards. Vegetables can be grown in the space around houses. Fish can be caught in reservoirs. Mushrooms can be grown in cellars. Producing these goods can be a leisure-time pursuit. It is known as permaculture, which is an abbreviation of *permanent agriculture* (Mollison, 1988). The idea has achieved cult status among environmental design students, if not yet among the general population. The aim is to model food production on self-sustaining natural ecosystems. Sunlight is the energy source, materials are recycled, synergy is encouraged. For example:

Chickens, as domesticated forest fowl, are at their best in forest-like environments, such as orchards. An orchard to them is a supermarket, where they can help themselves to basic needs such as water, shelter, shade, dust and grit, and moreover, they feed on pest insects and weed seeds and turn those into manure. (de Waard, 1994)

By these means, one plus one makes three. Permaculture can work in small urban gardens, where it sometimes goes under the name 'edible landscaping'. It makes cities more productive and therefore more sustainable, as the Russians found after the collapse of communism.

TRANSPORT PLANS

Red commuting takes its name from the red eyes, the blood and the environmental balance sheet which is reddened by commuting in private cars. Red commuters inflict many injuries on themselves and others, while the cities they inhabit are made less sustainable. Green commuters travel on foot, bicycle, roller skates, or whatever, without imposing social costs on cities. Such behaviour needs to be encouraged. It saves energy. It avoids pollution. It makes cities more sustainable. A 1 mile walk to work needs only the energy supplied by one slice of toast, without butter or marmalade. Travelling the same distance by car takes energy equivalent to 40 slices of toast for propulsion alone. By train, it takes 17 slices. Green soap powder is widely available. Green commuting is not. Red commuters hold all the trumps, at present. Each year they have more cars, more roadspace, more places to park their vehicles. Billions are spent on new bridges, tunnels, junctions and bypasses, which move bottlenecks but rarely cure them. Part of the reason for the reds' claim on the public purse is that roads are also used for the transport of essential goods. Car commuters are interlopers.

In most cities, green commuters are a neglected underclass grateful for the odd bean chucked in their direction, but always yearning for a wholesome meal. When pedestrian bridges are built, they usually remove an inconvenience from road users, and make the pedestrian walk further. When cycle routes are planned, they usually go beside busy oads, or through bumpy back streets which make the cyclist peddle further. Carrots and sticks should be used to encourage green commuting. Road pricing, restrictions on access and limitations on car parking can be used as sticks. But after years of chewing dry bones, green commuters dream of carrots.

The first Great Carrot would be a network of direct and environmentally pleasant routeways. It should be conceived as a second public realm. The first public realm, of vehicular roadspace, is as old as the wheel. Some roads are suitable for joint use by vehicles and pedestrians. Much depends on traffic flow. If a road has 500 vehicle movements per day, it can be reasonably pleasant for pedestrians. If there are 5000 movements per day, it is not pleasant. If there are 50000 movements per day, it is intolerable. For a really enjoyable walk to work, one does not want to be a second-class citizen on the edge of a road, subject to noise and fumes. Green commuters need a safe realm of pedestrianized public space. It should extend through parks, beside rivers, across urban squares and along pedestrian streets.

The second Great Carrot would be a network of cycle routes. Too many wives drive their husbands to the station and an earlier grave. Surely, ten minutes of useful exercise is better than ten wasted minutes on an exercise machine. Trains are more punctual than buses, and a cycle ride followed by a train journey and a short walk can be pleasanter than time spent in red commuting, and faster. If one has to catch a bus to catch a train to catch a bus, then over 30 minutes have to be allowed for missed connections. Depending on traffic volumes, cycle routes can be shared with pedestrians of motor vehicles or both. As few of us are willing to cycle or walk more than 30 minutes, green routes should be planned in conjunction with bus and train routes.

The bicycle works best as a feeder system for bus and rail transport systems, which are most economic in high-volume corridors. This requires excellent cycle storage facilities at bus and rail stations. Trains need high passenger volumes to be economic. Buses also need high passenger volumes, and are too slow if they snake about to collect passengers. It can make a bus journey take five times longer than the equivalent car journey. The solution is to plan commuter transport on a 'stars and stripes' basis (Fig. 4). The

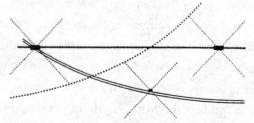

Fig. 4 Stars of cyclepaths should feed rail stations and bus stops

Part IV Site Planning and Landscape Design in Different Contexts

stars should be feeder paths for cyclists and pedestrians. The stripes should be linear bus and train routes. At the centre of each star there should be safe and secure cycle stores, cafes, shops, shelters and delightful gardens in which to sit to wait. Exotic forms of transport could also be interconnected. In Canada, some commuters travel by ice skate in winter and kayak in summer. In Britain, long-distance bridleways, and stables, would make it possible for some to commute on horseback. Others could use roller skates, as in Barcelona.

Eco-cities, with green transport systems, would meet the needs of the young, the old, the poor and the dispossessed. Lonely walks are dangerous. There is safety in numbers. Well-used walks and traffic interchange points enjoy the benefit of visual policing, and are safe from the danger of drunk drivers, joyriders and runaway trucks.

Provision for green transport costs money. It should not be done on the cheap. If the percentage of commuters who travel by bicycle is to rise towards 30%, as it has done in Freiburg(Vidal, 1994), then the allocated proportion of the transport budget should rise in the same ratio. Indeed, after years of neglect, there is an unchallengeable case for spending way above the 30% budget for a decade. We should allocate 100% in the first year. Some first-class examples of beautiful, safe, convenient green transport routes could revolutionize the received wisdom on transport planning and design. At some point we may be able to have a network of plastic tubes, with blown air assisting cyclists in their direction of travel.

ECO-BUILDINGS

In the past, great cities have been centres of government, military power, trade and manufacturing, which influenced their appearance. Future cities may have all these roles, but they will be predominantly residential. Fifty-years ago, 95% of the world's population was rural. In fifty years' time, 95% may be urban, certainly in terms of lifestyle, probably in terms of physical character. Man's home may become a low-density sprawl with high-density nodes. Life in the suburbs of great cities is becoming very similar to life in rural villages and isolated farmsteads. But the city of tomorrow may look very different from the city of today.

Buildings will be much more vegetated, for a variety of reasons. First, vegetation enables cities to hold more water. Second, it reduces glare. Third, vegetation takes in carbon dioxide and gives out oxygen. Fourth, it provides food and habitat for wildlife. Fifth, vegetation absorbs noise and prevents reflections from road to wall to window to roof. Sixth, dust collects on leaves and goes wherever the leaves go, so that particulate air pollution is reduced. Seventh. vegetation keeps buildings cooler in summer and warmer in winter. Eighth, vegetation on buildings contributes to the permaculture harvest of cities, as espalier apples have always done. Ninth, people love flowers and greenery. Tenth, the tide of history cannot be held back.

Clad with slates or tiles, roofs can support moss and lichens but not plants with invasive roots. That is why cities used to be made without vegetated roofs. Today it is comparatively easy to make flat and shallow-pitched roofs that are waterproof and can be vegetated. Concrete, steel and high-strength bricks also make it easy to build load-bearing structures that can carry the load. In high-density cities, vegetated roofs can provide the quiet and private spaces that people need for rest and relaxation. The city of tomorrow will certainly look green.

WORDS AND EXPRESSIONS

incremental [inkri'mentəl] adj. 增加的
equilibrium [ˌiːkwi'libriəm] n. 平衡，均衡
verbatim [vəː'beitim] adj. & adv. 逐字的（地）
hazy ['heizi] adj. 朦胧的，模糊的，没有清楚定义的
optic ['ɔptik] adj. 眼的，视觉的，光学上的
cupboard ['kʌbəd] n. 食橱，碗碟橱
effluent ['efluənt] n. 流出物；排水道，排水渠
rubble ['rʌbl] n. 碎石
quarry ['kwɔri] v. 采（石），挖出，挖掘 n. 采石场
drawback ['drɔːˌbæk] n. 缺点，障碍
low-lying ['ləu'laiiŋ] adj. 低的，低洼的，低地的，比平常高度低的
wretched ['retʃid] adj. 可怜的；恶劣的，质量差的
statutory ['stætjutəri] adj. 法定的，受法令约束的，依照法规的
stockpile ['stɔkpail] n. 积蓄，库存，原料储备
shed [ʃed] n. 棚，小屋
fringe [frindʒ] n. 边缘
aqueduct ['ækwiˌdʌkt] n. 沟渠，导水管
cloaca [kləu'eikə] n. 下水道，阴沟
hydrocarbon ['haidrəu'kaːbən] n. 烃，碳氢化合物
detain [di'tein] v. 留住，阻止
evaporate [i'væpəreit] v. （使）蒸发
detention [di'tenʃən] n. 阻止，滞留，阻留
porous ['pɔːrəs] adj. 多孔的，能渗透的，多孔渗水的
dilute [dai'ljuːt,di'l-] adj. 淡的，弱的，稀释的
sulphuric [sʌl'fjuərik] adj. 硫的，含硫的
Edinburgh n. 爱丁堡（英国苏格兰首府）
gardenesque [gaːdə'nesk] adj. 花园般的
mow [mau] v. 刈，割，收割
improvident [im'prɔvidənt] adj. 无远见的，目光短浅的

Part IV　Site Planning and Landscape Design in Different Contexts

herbicide [ˈhə:bisaid]	n. 除草剂
exotica [igˈzɔtikə]	n. 新奇事物
godwit [ˈgɔdwit]	n. 鹬科之长嘴涉水鸟
otter [ˈɔtə]	n. 水獭
elk [elk]	n. 麋鹿
segregate [ˈsegrigeit]	v. 分开，隔开；分离
harrier [ˈhæriə]	n. 猎兔犬
optimal [ˈɔptiməl]	adj. 最佳的，最理想的
sedge [sedʒ]	n. [植] 芦苇；莎草
cellar [ˈselə]	n. 地窖，地下室
abbreviation [əˌbri:viˈeiʃn]	n. 缩写，缩写词
cult [kʌlt]	n. 崇拜，风靡一时
synergy [ˈsinədʒi]	n. (=synergism) 协同（作用）
fowl [faul]	n. 家禽，禽，鸟禽类
grit [grit]	n. 砂砾，粗砂
manure [məˈnjuə]	n. 肥料
edible [ˈedibl]	adj. 可食用的
inflict [inˈflIkt]	v. （与 on 连用）予以（打击等）；使受（痛苦等）；造成
marmalade [ˈmɑ:məleid]	n. 橘子或柠檬等水果制成的果酱
propulsion [prəˈpʌlʃən]	n. 推进，推进力
trump [trʌmp]	n. （一套）王牌，法宝，最后大的手段
interloper [ˈintələupə(r)]	n. 闯入者，妨碍者，（为图私利）干涉他人事务者
yearn [jə:n]	vi. 渴望，想念，向往
bumpy [ˈbʌmpi]	adj. （道路等）颠簸的，崎岖不平的
peddle [ˈpedl]	vi. 挑卖，沿街叫卖 vt. 叫卖，散播
vehicular [viˈhikjulə]	adj. 车辆的，交通工具的，供车辆通过的
punctual [ˈpʌŋktjuəl]	adj. 按时的，准时的
feeder [ˈfi:də]	n. 支线；供应者
kayak [ˈkaiæk]	n. （爱斯基摩的）皮筏，皮艇
bridle [ˈbraidl]	n. 马勒
bridle-way	n. 马道（适宜骑马而不通行汽车的路）
stable [ˈsteibl]	n. 马厩，马房
joyrider [ˈdʒɔIˌraIdə(r)]	n. 驾车兜风的人
runaway [ˈrʌnəweI]	adj. 失控的
Freiburg [ˈfraibə:g]	n. 弗赖堡（德国西南部一城市）
allocate [ˈæləukeit]	vt. 分派，分配
predominant [priˈdɔminənt]	adj. 支配的，主要的

LESSON 14

sprawl [sprɔːl]	n. 不整齐的散布，杂乱的大片地方（尤指建筑物）
node [nəud]	n. 节点
farmstead [ˈfɑːmsted]	n. 农场及其建筑物
dioxide [daiˈɔksaid]	n. 二氧化物
particulate [pəˈtikjulit, -leit]	adj. 微粒的
espalier [isˈpæljə]	n. 树墙，墙式树木
greenery [ˈgriːnəri]	n. 草木
clad [klæd]	vt. 覆盖 adj. 被……覆盖的
slate [sleit]	n. 板岩，石板（瓦），石片
invasive [inˈveisiv]	adj. 侵入的
load bearing	承载，承重
waiver [ˈweivə]	n. [律] 自动放弃，弃权，弃权证书
mound [maund]	n. 堆，垛
verdant [ˈvəːdənt]	adj. 翠绿的，青翠的
undergrowth [ˈʌndəgrəuθ]	n. 矮树丛，灌木丛

NOTES

1. Bruntland

挪威首相布伦特兰夫人。1987年，以布伦特兰夫人为首的世界环境与发展委员会发表了题为《我们共同未来》(Our Common Future) 的研究报告。

LANDSCAPE DESIGN IN THE RURAL ENVIRONMENT

"There is a sentimentalism in America about 'the country' as a place to live," says Mr. Will W. Alexander in a report on rural housing, "Fresh air in the minds of many of our people—particularly city people—is thought of as a satisfactory substitute for a decent income, wholesome food, medical care, educational opportunities, and everything else which the city dwellers think of as necessary…" Such a romantic attitude is all too apparent among American designers, who fail to see that the "old swimming hole" needs lifeguards and pure water, that the baseball field needs illumination, or that the farm boy may be quite as interested in aviation or theatricals as his city cousin. On the other hand, there is the danger that—once recognizing these needs—the building or landscape designer(because of his own urban background and experience)will uncritically apply urban design standards to a rural problem.

The irreducible requisite of any successful planning is that the forms developed will direct the flow of energy in the most economic and productive pattern. This is the criterion in the design of the power dam, the automobile, and the modern cotton field; it should also hold in landscape and building design, where the energy and vitality directed is that of human beings. But to organize the rural areas into the most productive pattern requires an intimate knowledge of the characteristics, rhythm, and potentialities of rural life. For if it is true that people differ little in the fundamental living needs of food, shelter, work, and play(regardless of the locality in which they live), it is equally true that the physical aspects of that locality(its topography, fertility, accessibility, exploitation, and industrialization) influence and condition the extent to which, and the method by which, it can be adapted to the needs of its people.

Homesteading and the rugged individualism of the pioneers determined the general characteristics of the rural scene. This system necessitated staking out claims and living in relative isolation to defend and improve these claims. The family became the social and recreational unit, supplemented by the school and church in the village which grew up for trading purposes. But, as Mr. David Cushman Coyle has pointed out, with changing technology and local depletion of mine, forest, and soil, we find a new type of rural population

---

选自 John Dixon Hunt: Marc Treib, Modern Landscape Architecture: A Critical Review, Page 83~87

which no longer fits into the pattern of living developed by the pioneer. Recent surveys show:

1. Mechanization of agriculture has cut in half the man labor required per bushel of wheat in 1919. In one country of western Kansas, it is cut to one quarter.

2. The nation's supply of farmland is steadily decreasing. The National Resources Board reports that as a result of soil erosion, 35,000,000 acres of farm land have been made entirely unfit for cultivation. While another 125,000,000 acres have had topsoil largely removed. A good deal of land to be inherited by farm youth is practically worthless, and will be abandoned.

3. In spite of decreasing birth rate, we have a large surplus of rural youth in proportion to farms available, and our expanding farm population is squeezed within a shrinking area of farm land. In 1920, for example, 160,000 farmers died or reached the age of 65; and in the same year, 337,000 farm boys reached the age of 18. In 1930, the surplus of boys with no prospects was 201,000. Vital statistics indicate that with the decrease in infant mortality. This surplus will be increase.

4. The present and future farmer is also the victim of an accumulating drain of money from the farm to the city. He sells in a city market controlled by the seller. The farm youth is educated in rural districts, and then finds it necessary to migrate to the city to make a living. Dr. O. E. Baker, of the U. S. Department of Agriculture, estimates that this movement of population from 1920 to 1930 carried to the city human values that had cost over 12,000,000,000 dollars in private and public cash spent by rural districts.

5. The exhaustion of the farmland in some areas—such as Oklahoma or Kansas—and the simultaneous development of a highly mechanized agriculture in others—California, Texas, or Florida, for example—has meanwhile given birth to a new rural phemonenon— the migratory agricultural workers. This group constitutes a quite special and pressing problem over and above that of the rural population generally.

Special Characteristics of Rural Life

What do such trends as those listed above imply in the design of rural recreational systems? A recognition of the facts that first and foremost the country must be redesigned for country people—i. e., neither from the viewpoint of nor for the benefit of the urbanite. Second, in view of constantly changing social and economic conditions, that such systems should provide a plastic and flexible environment for both local and migratory farmers. Third, that such systems should be closely integrated with both urban and primeval areas, providing the greatest possible intercommunication between all three. Finally, that the following special and fairly constant factors of rural life be recognized:

1. The periods during which recreational facilities can be used by most rural inhabitants are more seasonal than daily. Whereas the city worker usually has a certain number of hours each day with a summer (or winter) vacation of free time during winter months. This implies an emphasis on enclosed and roofed facilities.

Part Ⅳ Site Planning and Landscape Design in Different Contexts

2. Since rural labor is largely physical, and requires the use of the larger muscular system, it is reasonable to supply facilities for recreation which afford experience which is physically, mentally, and psychologically different from the major labor experience, i.e., folk dancing, swimming, arts, and crafts, dramatic production, folk pageantry, etc.

3. The present relative isolation of farm families and dependence upon automotive transportation make it desirable for the entire family to seek recreation at one time. This places emphasis on the school, church, and country park as centers for recreation, and requires facilities for participation by all age and sex groups at one time.

4. Since the mobile fraternity has become such an important part of the rural scene, special facilities are necessary for the migratory laborers, the tourists, and the vacationists. It is necessary to provide for these groups, and integrate their activities with those of the more permanent residents without destroying the economic and social balance. The need here is for multiple use and flexibility in design with particular emphasis on a system integrated with the highway, shore front, waterways, and spots of scenic, natural, and historic as well as scientific interest.

Thus it can be seen that rural recreation is based on an entirely different set of conditions than urban, and it can be approached only by detailed study of specific local requirements in their relation to the region. In general, one can say that whereas in the cities more free space(decentralization), the rural need is for more intensive use of less space (concentration)to permit and provide for the social integration of a widely distributed population. But the latter does not imply mere urbanization of the country any more than the former means mere ruralization of the city.[1]

Roads Are First

The first and most essential element of any rural recreational environment will necessarily be an adequate highway system. Yet, despite the gigantic advances in construction in the past decade, the fact remains that most rural communities are without a road system adequate for their needs. Consciously or otherwise, the majority of federal and state construction is designed to facilitate communication between one city and the next. "With the by-pass or through-highway principle on the one hand, and the freeway or border control principle on the other, we have the tools to adapt our future network to meet recreational needs... but that is only part of the highway problem. There are still the problems of local access and touring... We must not only provide good trunk-highway access, but also good local-access roads. These local roads must serve directly the various cities, towns, and villages; and must open up recreational lands."[2]

Consolidated Communities Mean Better Recreation

Closely allied with the problem of transportation is that of rural housing. As long as the traditional pattern remains—thinly scattered houses. One to each farm—it is quite possible that a genuinely satisfactory recreational environment will not be evolved. In this connection, it is interesting to note how quickly social integration has followed *physical intercreation in the new towns by TVA, FSA, and in the greenbelt towns of the former Resettlement Administration.* As a matter of fact, leading agricultural economists are advocating a similar consolidation—the regrouping of farmers into villages from which they can work their land within a radius of 5 to 10 miles of them. (This type of village is of course prevalent in Europe and in isolated spots of America.) There is already a general trend toward consolidation and reorganization of schools and school districts. And the recent western projects of the Farm Security Administration—while of course designed for the landless migrants—clearly indicate the physical advantages of a similar concentration of housing facilities.

What types of Recreation Are Required?

WPA research reveals that the average rural community needs provision for the following types of recreation:

1. Crafts and visual arts, graphic and plastic. (These might well be organized around the rapidly developing science and manual arts curricula in most rural high schools.)

2. Recreational music, including outdoor concerts, popular orchestras, group singing, etc.

3. Dancing—ballroom, folk, social square, tap, ballet, etc.

4. Recreational drama, including marionettes and puppets, plays, motion pictures, pageants, festivals, etc. The outdoor theater is recommended as an ideal form; it also encourages children in their own improvisations.

5. Children's play center, including such equipment as slides, horizontal bars, swings, seesaws, trapezes, marble courts, sand box(preferably adjacent to the wading pool with an island where children can play and sail boats).

6. Sports and athletics(conditioned by the major labor), including baseball, softball, football, basketball, tennis, archery, horseshoe pitching, swimming and water sports, snow and ice sports, hiking, camping, and nature study.

7. Other activities and special events: picnics require an area of several acres with outdoor fireplaces, barbecue pits, wood supply, and provisions for waste disposal(can also serve as a wayside camp for motorist). Occasional field days, community nights, agricultural fairs, carnivals, traveling circuses can occupy the largest free area used for sports at different seasons.

What Sort of Facilities Are Implied?

All these activities require special equipment centering around the district school, rural park, or other location designed to serve the rural inhabitants rather than the urban overflow. The usefulness is multiplied by complete and well designed flood lighting, since most outdoor activities come in the summer—precisely when the majority of rural inhabitants are busiest during the day.

Part IV Site Planning and Landscape Design in Different Contexts

Although there is perhaps no single form which meets so well the various needs of the rural community, the outdoor theater has never been satisfactorily reinterpreted as a present day recreational form in its own right. Developed as an integral part of the rural park, and in a dynamic, three-dimensional pattern, it provides for almost constant use by all age groups. Actual productions require the assistance of practically, mentally, and psychologically different from the major labor experience. With stages at different levels, following the natural contours, and seats ingeniously arranged to accommodate both large and small audiences; with the present perfection of sound amplification; and with "scene-shifting" by spotlights instead of curtains, a type as flexible as the auditorium without its expense or intricacy is achieved. Its utility is as flexible as its organization, since it accommodates both large and small productions, festivals, pageantry, improvisations, summer-theater groups, exhibitions, meetings, picnics, and talks.

Many opportunities are overlooked by sticking too closely to arbitrary and static concepts of recreational planning. For example, the local airport is a form which deserves attention because of the interest and activity which surrounds it. Already a center of Sunday afternoon interest for many an American farm family, it orients the rural population to a larger social concept of the world outside, as well as satisfying the characteristic American interest in the technical. The same thing might be said about the old canal, the abandoned railroad engine, and the automobile junk pile—all of which hold an endless fascination for small children.[3]

Toward Scientific Landscape Design

With the exception of urban infringement in the form of summer colonies, tourist camps and hotels, and commercialized amusements, billboards, suburbanization, and the "naturalism" of "preserving rural beauty" by screening out rural slums with a parkway—prevents an indigenous and biological development of rural beauty. It is thus that we handicap ourselves with a static and inflexible environment, and lose the opportunity of developing forms which express the needs of the people and the qualities of the region.

This is particularly unfortunate as concerns landscape design. The country is thought of as a restorative for the exhausted city dweller, and a land of plenty for the farmer. When help is offered by well-meaning urban societies it is, as often as not, "for the preservation of rural beauties" which look well on a post card. Another group is afraid of destroying the "delightful informality" by intelligent and straightforward reorganization of nature for the use of man. They resort to "rustic" bridges, and "colonial" cottages which will "blend" with nature. Obviously this point of view can be held only by those who do not live on the land.

We may as well accept the fact that man's activities change and dominate the landscape; it does not follow that they should spoil it. Writing on the redesign of the American landscape, Paul B. Sears has said: "Not only must the scientist of the future work in awareness of social and economic processes, but he must clear a further hurdle….

The scientist must be aware of the relation of his task to the field of aesthetics. What is right and economical and in balance is in general satisfying. Not the least important symptom of the present decay of the American landscape of the Unitied States, with its two billions of acres for a potential population of one hundred and fifty million, or even two hundred million, can be made a place of plenty, permanence, without the aid of science. Nor can such aid be rendered by men of science unaware of the task which confronts them."[4]

WORDS AND EXPRESSIONS

swimming hole	n. 溪流和小河中可供游泳的深水潭
Life guard	n. 救生员
rural [′ʊər(ə)l]	adj. 乡下的，田园的，乡村风味的，生活在农村的
sentimentalism [ˌsenti′mentəlizəm]	n. 感情主义，沉于情感
criterion [krai′tiəriən]	n. (批评判断的)标准，准则，规范
shelter [′ʃeltə]	n. 掩蔽处，避身处，掩蔽，保护，庇护所，掩体 v. 掩蔽，躲避
recreational [ˌrekrɪ′eɪʃənəl, -kriː-]	adj. 休养的，娱乐的
consolidated [kən′sɔlideitid]	加固的；整理过的；统一的
regroup [′riː′gruːp]	v. 重组，重编
spotlight [′spɔtlait]	n. 聚光灯
billboard [′bilbɔːd]	n. (户外)布告板，揭示栏，广告牌 vt. 宣传
seesaw [′siːsɔː]	n. 秋千
arts and crafts	n. 工艺
fraternity [frə′təːniti]	n. 兄弟关系，友爱，互助会，兄弟会
puppet [′pʌpit]	n. 傀儡，木偶
motion picture	n. 电影
pageant [′pædʒənt]	n. 盛会，庆典，游行，虚饰，露天表演
slide [slaid]	v. (使)滑动，(使)滑行 n. 滑，滑动，幻灯片
trapeze [trə′piːz; (US)træ-]	n. (健身或杂技表演用的)吊架，秋千
archery [′aːtʃəri]	n. 射箭；射箭术
carnival [′kaːnivəl]	n. 狂欢节，饮宴狂欢

KEY CONCEPTS

Rural environment
rural scene
rural recreation
rural inhabitant

Part IV *Site Planning and Landscape Design in Different Contexts*

country park
mechanized agriculture
vacationist
soil erosion
road system
parkway

NOTES

1. See Garrett Eckbo, Daniel U. Kiley, and James C. Rose, "Landscape Design in the Urban environment," Architectural Record(May 1939), 70~71. (Reprinted in this volume)

参考加勒特·埃克伯,丹尼尔·凯利,詹姆斯·罗斯. 城市环境的景观设计. 建筑学报告,1939(5):70~71.

2. From a paper by Roland B. Greeley read at the Outdoor Recreation Conference, Amherst, Massachusetts, March 11, 1939.

来自 Roland B. Greeley 学习户外娱乐讨论会. 马萨诸塞州,1939.3.11.

3. Recently, a recreational expert, showing some distinguished visitors in Washington the advanced planning of children's play areas in one of the greenbelt towns, was somewhat chagrined to find them quite deserted. But, as they started back to Washington, they passed the town's children playing on a dump used for fill along the roadway. One of the ladies of the party turned to the expert and inquired brightly: "And I suppose you will plan something for these children, too?"

近来一位娱乐方面的专家为一些名流展示位于华盛顿周边城镇的儿童游乐场的先进规划时,有点懊恼地发现这些游乐场已经彻底地荒废。但是,在他们返回华盛顿的途中却看见镇里的孩子们在沿着公路的垃圾堆存处玩耍。一名党派女士于是向专家询问:"我想你是不是也该为这些孩子们设计一些游乐场?"

4. Paul B. Sears. "Science and the New Landscape." *Harper's Magazine* (July 1939). 207. Paul B. Sears.

科学和新景观. 哈珀杂志,1939(7):207.

QUESTIONS FOR REVIEW AND DISCUSSION

1. What's the characteristics of rural life?
2. What's the differences between urban life and rural life?
3. What kinds of recreations are required in rural environment?

LESSON 15

Reading Material

Axioms for Reading the Landscape
Some Guides to the American Scene (Part one)

Peirce F. Lewis

About the axioms and about cultural landscape

For most Americans, ordinary man-made landscape is something to be looked at, but seldom thought about. I am not talking here about "natural landscape," but about the landscape made by humans-what geographers call cultural landscape. Sometimes Americans may notice cultural landscapes because they think it is pretty, or perhaps ugly; mostly they ignore the common vernacular scene. For most Americans, cultural landscape just is.

Usage of the word tells a good deal. As a common verb, to "landscape" means to "prettify." If a suburban lot is advertised as "landscaped," it is generally understood that somebody has fussed with the shrubbery on a small bit of ground, perhaps planted a few trees, and has manicured the bushes-more or less artfully. It rarely occurs to most Americans to think of landscape as including everything from city skylines to farmers' silos, from golf courses to garbage dumps, from ski slopes to manure piles, from millionaires' mansions to the tract houses of Levittown, from famous historical landmarks to flashing electric signs that boast the creation of the 20 billionth hamburger, from mossy cemeteries to sleazy shops that sell pornography next door to big city bus stations-in fact, whole countrysides, and whole cities, whether ugly or beautiful makes no difference. Although the word is seldom so used, it is proper and important to think of cultural landscape as nearly everything that we can see when we go outdoors. Such common workaday landscape has very little to do with the skilled work of landscape architects, but it has a great deal to say about the United States as a country and Americans as people.

At first, that idea sounds odd. The noun "landscape" evokes images of snow-capped mountains and waves beating on a rock-bound coast. But the fact remains that nearly every square millimeter of the United States has been altered by humankind somehow, at some time. "Natural landscapes" are as rare as unclimbed mountains, and for similar reasons. Mallory expressed a very American sentiment when he said he wanted to climb Everest because it was there. Americans tinker with landscape as if pursued by some inner demon, and they have been doing so ever since their ancestors landed at Jamestown and Plymouth and began chopping down trees. They continue today, and the sound of the power lawn-mower is heard throughout the land.

All of this is obvious, but the implications are less obvious, though very simple,

---

选自 D. W. Meining, The Interpretation of Ordinary Landscapes, New York, Oxford Vniversity Press, 1979, Page 14~32

Part IV Site Planning and Landscape Design in Different Contexts

and very important to our understanding of the United States. The basic principle is this: *that all human landscape has cultural meaning*, no matter how ordinary that Landscape may be. It follows, as Mae Thielgaard Watts has remarked, that we can "read the landscape" as we might read a book. Our human landscape is our unwitting autobiography, reflecting our tastes, our values, our aspirations, and even our fears, in tangible, visible form. We rarely think of landscape that way, and so the cultural record we have "written" in the landscape is liable to be more truthful than most autobiographies because we are less self-conscious about how we describe ourselves. Grady Clay has said it well: "There are no secrets in the landscape." All our cultural warts and blemishes are there, and our glories too; but above all, our ordinary day-to-day qualities are exhibited for anybody who wants to find them and knows how to look for them.

To be sure, reading landscapes is not as easy as reading books, and for two reasons. First, ordinary landscape seems messy and disorganized, like a book with pages missing, torn, and smudged; a book whose copy has been edited and re-edited by people with illegible handwriting. Like books, landscapes *can* be read, but unlike books, they were not *meant* to be read.

In the second place, most Americans are unaccustomed to reading landscape. It has never occurred to them that it *can* be done, that there is reason to do so, much less that there is pleasure to be gained from it. That is one reason why so many Americans prefer driving on freeways with their bland highway-department roadsides, to driving on old-fashioned roads with their curves and crossroads and billboards and towns and irresponsible pedestrians and cyclists and straying livestock and roadside houses that spew forth children chasing balls-in short, all the things that make driving backroads interesting and hazardous. Very few academic disciplines teach their students how to read landscapes, or encourage them to try. Traditional geomorphology and traditional plant ecology (and one must, alas, stress "traditional" here) were two happy exceptions: these were disciplines which insisted that their practitioners use their eyes and *think* about what they saw, and it is no accident that some of America's most accomplished landscape-readers, such as J. Hoover Mackin, Pierre Dansereau, and Mae Thielgaard Watts, derive from those fields. A few cultural geographers are also noteworthy. In America, much of the inspiration derived from Carl Sauer, who built the remarkable and influential "Berkeley School" in geography at the University of California, and whose students number some of the most accomplished landscape-readers in American professional geography. Fred Kniffen comes immediately to mind, as do Wilbur Zelinsky, David Lowenthal and James Parsons. One thinks, too, of the Minnesota geographers, John Fraser Hart, Cotton Mather, and Harry Swain. But the list of geographers is not long. More often, you run across accomplished landscape-readers in unexpected places. J. B. Jackson, founder and longtime editor of *Landscape* magazine, diffidently disclaims association with any particular discipline; his work is dazzling and his influence (inside and outside academe) has been profound.

Henry Glassie, the folklorist and student of Kniffen, is another. George Stewart, one of the best, hung his academic hat in the English Department at Berkeley, and we are all the richer for it. Some journalists are among the most perceptive, perhaps because they spend their lives looking and writing about what they see, no matter how trivial the subject may seem. Tom Wolfe argues that police reporters of the old school are among our most potent social analysts-the old fellows in battered felt hats who walked through life with the wide eyes of cynical children, noting everything in a curiously innocent way, and writing about what they saw. But it remains a sad fact that most academics in those fields where we might expect to find expert landscape-reading are egregiously inept. To be sure, there are glorious exceptions-people like Alan Gowans, Reyner Banham, and Grady Clay-but they remain exceptions nonetheless.

So unless one is lucky enough to have studied with a plant ecologist like Dansereau, a geomorphologist like Mackin, a folklorist like Glassie, or simply a Renaissance man like Jackson, one is likely to need guidance. To "read landscape," to make cultural sense of the ordinary things that constitute the workaday world of things we see, most of us need help.

I took a long time learning that fact. Years ago, when I started teaching about cultural landscapes of the United States, I was puzzled and annoyed that students seemed so obtuse. They seemed blind to all that marvelous material around them, and even worse, some of them seemed insulted when they were told to go outdoors and use their eyes and think about what they saw. Gradually, I realized that the students were not obtuse; I was. The students were simply aping the great majority of their faculty mentors, who by their inattention to ordinary landscape were teaching the students very effectively that landscape didn't matter: that serious students did not deal with trivial questions about ordinary everyday things, such as what Howard Johnsons's cupolas were meant to symbolize, or why people put pink plastic flamingos in their front yards.

What we needed, I concluded, were some guides to help us read the landscape, just as the rules of grammar sometimes help guide us through some particularly convoluted bit of syntax. Little by little, I began to write down some of the rules that I discovered over the years of looking and learning and teaching about American landscapes and which I found helped me understand what I saw. I call these rules "axioms," because they now seem basic and self-evident, as any proper axiom must be. I may be wrong in using the word "axiom": what seems self-evident now was not obvious to me a few years ago. But call them what you will: They are nevertheless essential ideas that underlie the reading of America's cultural landscape.

LESSON 16

LANDSCAPE DESIGN IN THE PRIMEVAL ENVIRONMENT

The American people had and largely still have a natural environment which is unsurpassed in both scale and Variety. But only within the last decade or so have they began to view it as anything other than an inexhaustible storehouse of material wealth—of minerals, timbers, and furs. Farsighted Americans long ago realized the cultural, social, and scientific potentialities of the wilderness. In 1812 John James Audubon[1], patiently recording American wildlife while his contemporaries staked out new claims, lamented that he was not rich again, "so strong is my enthusiasm to enlarge the ornithological knowledge of my country." And later, Thoreau urged "that every community in America should have, as part of its permanent domain, a portion of the wilderness."

But such observers merely anticipated the time when the American people would awake to the fact that they faced, on the one hand, a land from which the primeval was rapidly disappearing and, on the other, a greater need for such environments than ever before. Now—with a population largely concentrated in or near an urban environment—the problem becomes one of *establishing and then controlling an environmental equilibrium*—urban, rural, primeval.

The environmental distinction implied in the word primeval is largely one of time: as such, it denotes that which came first. All habitats and life itself have their origins in the primeval. But the adaptation of the earth and its natural forces to the needs of various types of organic life has constantly developed new types of habitat, of which the human is only one. The dominance of man is predicated on his having exploited the more primitive forms of life and materials until he has developed what Benton Mackaye defines as "the habitats of fundamental human relations" —urban and rural environments.

The importance of the primeval—its integral relation and the extent to which we are dependent upon it in modern life—is apparent in both a physical (or material) and emotional (or recreational) sense. For instance, trees and other plant forms originate in the wilderness, are developed by science, and are then used in the organization of city streets, playgrounds, gardens, and for the production of fruits and vegetables. Poultry, livestock, and beasts of burden are all products of the wilderness which have been adapted

---

选自 John Dixon Hunt: Marc Treib Modern Landscape Architecture: A Critical Review, page 88~91

and exploited by man. On the other hand, various forms of life that are not completely domesticated, such as fish, game, and different plants and insects are often controlled to the extent necessary and desirable for the type of exploitation intended (sport, study, etc.).

The geographical distinction which separates man from the wilderness is produced by the cultural, social, and economic needs of his own advancement. i. e., complicated trade relations, group activity in recreation and work, industrialization, mobility. These activities fall natural into geographical centers of easy communication and distribution (water ports, trade posts, etc.), where the rural environment develops. The main factor which distinguishes both the urban and rural from the primeval is that, although the primeval may be exploited by him, it is not inhabited by man. This does not mean that it is an "untouchable" wilderness with an arbitrary fence around it. On the contrary, its intimate and tangible relation to both man and the environments which he does inhabit is apparent in the ease with which human habitats return to the primeval (Mayan[2] cities, Stonehenge[3], archaeological ruins, etc.).

Design for Primeval Inhabitants

As all design of the urban environment is based primarily on the needs of the city dweller, and that of the rural environment on the inhabitants of the country, any intelligent planning of the primeval must be based on the *needs of its native "population"* —either by man or nature or both—that provides its chief recreational value to man. Thus, when he controls the survival and selection of the primeval "population," he is at the same time providing for his own.

A primeval system must first establish and then control a dynamic equilibrium between man and nature. This means that we must build up the primeval itself, creating the best conditions which science can provide for the native inhabitants, and protecting them against ruthless invasion and destruction from any form or source (human, animal or insect, fire, flood, etc.).

Science Shows the Way

Recent technological advances at once reveal the complexity of the problem and indicate a trend toward more scientific control of the wilderness. For instance, scientific methods of determining food, feeding, and other wildlife habits, together with a technic for the production and distribution of forage, have in some instances completely reversed the wildlife depletion. At the same time, more than fifty million acres of swamp land, which formerly provided habitat for wild life, have been converted to farm land by advanced methods of drainage. In other sections, zoning of primeval areas has reduced the amount of arable land (particularly in lumbered and burned sections of northern Wisconsin, Minnesota, and Michigan) which can be sold for farm use. This cuts the cost of maintenance on toads to isolated and unproductive farms, and the money is used in reforestation and fire control.

Part IV Site Planning and Landscape Design in Different Contexts

The U. S. Forest Service includes silviculture, nursery and planting methods to insure forest reproduction, selection and breeding of individual trees and tree species to increase future forest values and current forest inventories, as well as sustained-yield forest management. This is undoubtedly one of the most striking examples of a technical service whose planning for primeval inhabitants simultaneously develops the recreational value of the wilderness for man, and concretely benefits both the rural (control of floods and erosion) and urban environments (development of new plant forms). A corollary is the development of new industrial technics using raw materials, one time abandoned as "waste," on a productive basis in excess of that found in their original use. For instance, 50%~60% of the actual lumber grown, or available on the stump, was at one time "waste," but has lately become an important source of building materials such as wall board and plywood.

The problem of designing a primeval environment, however, is far larger than the mere development of new methods for utilizing the "leftovers," or the "economic" exploitation of raw materials with potential commercial value (salt and borax products from desert areas, for example). For, in planning the primeval, we must consider also its *interplay with the urban* (almost every stream of importance in New Hampshire has been impaired for recreational use by industrial sewage) and the rural (destruction of the western grass lands equals dust storms in the Mississippi[4] Valley).

Clearly, it is not enough to "establish monuments and reservations" and "preserve the natural scenery." As already pointed out, it is neither possible nor desirable to put a fence around an environment that is a result of complicated and delicately balanced reactions of natural, ecological, and biological forces. Since the primeval is really a distinction of time, what is satisfactory for today may disturb the environmental equilibrium of tomorrow, unless it is shifted and modified to meet new elements in the balance. Even a thoroughly scientific and rational technic can destroy the balance if it considers only one objective.

Man in the Primeval

Even the fragmentary coordination of technics in the attempt to establish an equilibrium for the plant, animal, and insect life fulfills its purpose, in a qualitative sense, to a greater degree than the specific planning for human enjoyment of the primeval. The majority of our "resort" areas and too many of our parks, although planned to provide man with access to the primeval, actually defeat their own purpose—the primeval retreats before this advance.

As Lewis Mumford points out, the purpose is "to make the region ready to sustain the richest types of human culture and the fullest span of human life—offering a home to every type of character and disposition and human mood, creating and preserving objective fields of response for man's deeper subjective needs. It is precisely those of us who recognize the value of mechanization and standardization and universalization who must be most alert to the need for providing an equal place for the complementary set of activities…the natural as opposed to the human… the lonely as opposed to the collective. A habitat planned so as to form a continuous background to a delicately graded scale of human feelinge and values is the genuine requisite of a cultivated life."

As a start toward this end, the Recreation Committee of the National Resources Board has divided the primeval into four classes to meet the varying needs of the population. The following types of activity are recommended to go with the classification:

DEVELOPED—specific areas especially equipped for concentrated human use. This is the link which integrates urban and rural with the primeval wilderness. It is the last point designed exclusively for the needs of human activity(and the point from which man goes deeper into the areas designed to satisfy his own subjective and objective need for contact with nature). It includes such recreational types as:

1. camping and picnicking(with facilities provided for both day and vacation needs);

2. summer sports(Swimming, diving, boating, beach activities, etc.). including instruction and facilities;

3. winter sports(skiing, tobogganing, bobsledding, iceboating, etc.);

4. recreational drama, including music, play, and festival organization, amateur and professional productions, summer companies, etc.;

5. arts and crafts, including woodcraft skills such as fire lighting and lean-to building, as well as horseback riding, archery, pistol practice, etc.

SCIENTIFIC—areas which contain special zoological, botanical, geological, archaeological, or historic values especially developed as natural museums or collections for the enlightenment of interested groups or individuals or students of the natural sciences.

MODIFIED—areas where man has made alterations with emphasis on the needs of the native population, and some provisions for travel and communication. This includes such activity types as:

1. nature tours, group and individual;

2. camping with and without facilities provided;

3. practice of arts and crafts, with restrictions;

4. some sports, including hunting, fishing, hiking, cross-country skiing, etc.

PRIMITIVE—mainly unexplored or partially explored areas with conditions of transportation as well as vegetation or fauna unmodified by man. The main types of activity are scientific investigation; study and collection of natural species valuable in cross breeding for the development to new forms; exploration; and satisfaction of the last degree of subjective and emotional need for contact with the primitive.

Design Implications… Access

It is true that the primeval resources and their ultimate value to man depend upon scientific control, but the extent to which the recreational value thereby created can be used by man depends upon its accessibility. "This does not mean," says Lewis Mumford,

Part IV *Site Planning and Landscape Design in Different Contexts*

"that every type of environment should be equally available to every type of person, and that every part of the natural scene should be as open to dense occupation as the concert hall of a great metropolis. This vulgarization of activities, that are by their essential nature restricted and isolated, would blot out the natural varieties of the habitat, and make the whole world over into a single metropolitan image. In the end, it would mean that one must be content with only one type of environment—that of the metropolis…a degradation in both the geological and human sense."

There is, however, a discrepancy between the distribution of population and the accessibility of primeval recreation which cannot be overlooked. For instance, although 45% of the population in the United States lives within 55 miles of the sea and Great Lake shores, only 1% of this area is available for public use. Inland primeval areas are also insufficiently accessible to urban and rural populations—partly due to occupational shifts and the difficulty and cost of transportation. The situation has been somewhat alleviated by legal processes such as zoning and the right of eminent domain, donations from individuals, public subsidy of transportation, and programs of the state parks.

Toward "the Remodeling of the Earth"

But the problem is more qualitative than quantitative since wholesale invasion of the wilderness is by no means desirable. On the other hand, access which is necessary to make the primeval useful in satisfying the varying degrees of human needs can not be camouflaged out of existence by "styles" of architecture which are supposed to retain the "feeling" of a particular section, or by "rustification" which is supposed to "blend" with nature, and simulate the honest craftsmanship of the pioneers. There is no reason for abandoning the scientific and rational methods of building and construction simply because we come close to nature. The clean out, graceful forms of the T. V. A.[6] constructions are certainly less destructive of nature than the heavy, often purely ornamental forms used mainly for their association with primitive technics, rather than because they are the best solution of the problem. The result of such affectation is usually a mutilation of nature which has nothing in its method that is common to that of the pioneer. It cannot be justified even on the aesthetic basis of "harmonizing" with nature. Harmony is the result of contrast: opposites that complement one another.

Thus, we come back to the biological conception of environmental design as found in scientific agriculture, and as exemplified by the life cycle and group habits found in many of the lower organisms. Man's forms must be designed to meet his biologic needs. His social and scientific as well as cultural advancement have placed him in an evolutionary position where he can no longer survive without the protection from the natural elements which science has provided. He has also found that the so-called "fittest of the species" which survive in a struggle on an elementary plane are not always the most desirable, and that the "natural" environment is seldom the best for the optimum development of desirable human, plant, animal, or insect species. Through the application of science he has the means of developing those species which will benefit his own existence and controlling those which do not, and by that method he will retain dominance.

The design principles underlying the planning of the urban, rural, and primeval environments are identical: use of the best available means to provide for the specific needs of the specific inhabitants; this results in specific forms. None of these environments stands alone. Every factor in one has its definite influence on the inhabitants of the other, and the necessity of establishing an equilibrium emerges. To be in harmony with the natural forces of renewal and exhaustion, this equilibrium must be dynamic, constantly changing and balancing within the complete environment. It is this fact which makes arbitrary design sterile and meaningless a negation of science. The real problem is the redesign of man's environments, making them flexible in use, adaptable in form, economical in effort, and productive in bringing to individuals an enlarged horizon of cultural, scientific, and social integrity.

WORDS AND EXPRESSIONS

primeval [prai'mi:vəl]	adj.	原始的
storehouse ['stɔ:haus]	n.	仓库
ornithological [ˌɔ:niθə'lɔdʒikəl]	adj.	鸟类学的
domain [dəu'mein]	n.	领土,领地,(活动、学问等的)范围,领域
equilibrium [ˌi:kwi'libriəm]	n.	平衡,平静,均衡,保持平衡的能力,沉着,安静
habitat ['hæbitæt]	n.	(动植物的)生活环境,产地、栖息地,居留地,自生地,聚集处
livestock ['laivstɔk]	n.	家畜,牲畜
fence [fens]	n.	栅栏,围墙,剑术
forage ['fɔridʒ]	n.	草料
swamp [swɔmp]	n.	沼泽,湿地,煤层聚水
arable ['ærəbl]	adj.	可耕的,适于耕种的
bobsledding ['bɔbslediŋ]	n.	滑大雪橇运动(或比赛)
poultry ['pəultri]	n.	家禽
livestock ['laivstɔk]	n.	家畜,牲畜
arable ['ærəbl]	adj.	可耕的,适于耕种的
toad [təud]	n.	[动] 蟾蜍,癞蛤蟆,讨厌的家伙
reforestation	n.	重新造林
borax ['bɔ:ræks]	n.	硼砂
sewage ['sju(:)idʒ]	n.	下水道,污水
toboggan [tə'bɔgən]	n.	一种扁长平底的雪橇(作滑雪和比赛用)
zoological [ˌzəuə'lɔdʒikəl]	adj.	动物学的

Part Ⅳ *Site Planning and Landscape Design in Different Contexts*

geological [dʒiəˈlɔdʒikəl]   *adj.* 地质学的，地质的
archaeological [ˌaːkiəˈlɔdʒikəl] *adj.* 考古学的，考古学上的
metropolitan [metrəˈpɔlit(ə)n]   *adj.* 首都的，主要都市的，大城市
craftsmanship   *n.* 技术，技艺；创造技巧

KEY CONCEPTS

Primeval environment
Primeval Inhabitant
wildlife depletion
arable land
silviculture
botany
zoology

NOTES

1. John James Audubon Haitian-born American ornithologist and artist whose extensive observations of eastern North American avifauna led to the publication of The Birds of America(1827~1838), a collection of his engravings that is considered a classic work in ornithology and American art.

奥杜邦，约翰·詹姆斯，1785~1851，海地裔美国鸟类学家及艺术家，他对北美东部鸟类的广泛观察促成了后来的美洲鸟类图谱(1827~1938年)的出版，这部著作被认为是鸟类学及美国艺术中最优秀的作品。

2. Maya Amember of a Mesoamerican Indian people inhabiting southeast Mexico, Guatemala, and Belize, whose civilization reached its height around a. d. 300~900. The Maya are noted for their architecture and city planning, their mathematics and calendar, and their hieroglyphic writing system.

马雅人中美洲印第安人，居住在墨西哥的东南部、危地马拉和伯利兹，其文明在大约公元300~900年发展到最高点。马雅人以其建筑、城市规划、数学、历法和象形文字著称。

3. Stonehenge Stonehenge are basically Megaliths. Megaliths are single large stones, or a group of "standing stones" usually arranged in a circular or semi-circular formation, and that archaeologists believe were religious temples or monuments.

由一个或者多个排列成圆形或者半圆形的直立的巨石构成的景观，考古学家认为其是宗教上的寺庙或者纪念碑。

4. Mississippi A state of the southeast United States. It was admitted as the 20th state in

1817. The first settlers in the region (1699) were French, and the area became part of Louisiana. It passed to the British (1763~1779) and then to the Spanish before being ceded to the United States in 1783. The Mississippi Territory, organized in 1798 and enlarged in 1804 and 1813, also included the present state of Alabama. Jackson is the capital and the largest city. Population, 2,586,443.

密西西比,美国东南部的一个州。它于1817年被接受为第二十个州。此地区最早的定居者(1699年)是法国人,当时这一片地区是路易斯安那的一部分。后来又归英国(1763~1779年)和西班牙统治,最后于1783年割让与美国。1789年成立密西西比区,并于1804和1813年两次扩大,其中也包括今天的阿拉巴马州。杰克逊是州首府和最大的城市。人口,2,586,443。

5. T. V. A. Tennessee Valley Authority

田纳西河流域管理局

QUESTIONS FOR REVIEW AND DISCUSSION

1. Do you know what does the planning of primeval base on?
2. What does Lewis Smumford think about the purpose of landscape design in the primeval environment according to the text?
3. What's the problem of "the Remodeling of the Earth"?

Part IV Site Planning and Landscape Design in Different Contexts

Reading Material

Axioms for Reading the Landscape
Some Guides to the American Scene (Part two)

1. THE AXIOM OF LANDSCAPE AS CLUE TO CULTURE. *The man-made landscape-the ordinary run-of-the-mill things that humans have created and put upon the earth-provides strong evidence of the kind of people we are, and were, and are in process of becoming.* In other words, the culture of any nation is unintentionally reflected in its ordinary vernacular landscape.

THE COROLLARY OF CULTURAL CHANGE. Our human landscape-our houses, roads, cities, farms, and so on-represents an enormous investment of money, time, and emotions. People will not change that landscape unless they are under very heavy pressure to do so. We must conclude that if there is really major change in the *look* of the cultural landscape, then there is very likely a major change occurring in our national culture at the same time.

THE REGIONAL COROLLARY. If one part of the country (or even one part of a city) *looks* substantially different from some other part of the country (or city), then the chances are very good that the cultures of the two places are different also. Thus, much of the South looks different from the rest of the country, not only because the climate and vegetation are different, but also because some important parts of Southern culture really are different from the rest of the country, although not necessarily in the way that some propagandists would like us to think. So also, black ghettos in Northern cities look different from adjacent white slums, because the culture of such ghettos remains distinctive.

THE COROLLARY OF CONVERGENCE. To the degree that the look of two areas comes to be more and more alike, one may surmise that the cultures are also converging. Thus many small Southern towns look quite different from their Northern counterparts, while Atlanta looks more and more like the "standard" Northern city, and even something like Phoenix, which is perhaps American's most super-American city. One may properly conclude that the cultural rift between North and South is growing narrower, but the process of reunion is taking place faster in urban places than in rural ones, and fastest of all in the suburbs.

To take another example: black suburbs of Northern cities look increasingly like white suburbs, and the shacks of rural Southern blacks are simultaneously being replaced by replicas of the "ranchettes" of exurban Northern whites. It may be legitimate to speculate that such convergence of landscapes represents some real convergence of cultures

---

选自 D. W. Meinig, The Interpretation of Ordinary Landscapes, New York, Oxford University Press, 1979, page14～32

and perhaps some lessening of racial tensions.

THE COROLLARY OF DIFFUSION The look of a landscape often is changed by imitation. That is, people in one place see what is happening elsewhere, like it, and imitate it if possible. The timing and location of such imitative changes are governed by various forms of geographic and social diffusion, which are surprisingly predictable, and which tell us a good deal about the way that cultural ideas spread and change. For example, Greek Revival architecture spread from Virginia into upstate New York in the early nineteenth century and from there, in debased form, to other parts of the country. Both the spread and the debasement took nearly a century to complete. Now, in the 1970s, California landscape tastes are widely and wildly imitated in most parts of the country. The delay between California invention and Eastern imitation is extremely small-sometimes almost instantaneous.

THE COROLLARY OF TASTE. Different cultures possess different tastes in cultural landscape; to understand the roots of taste is to understand much of the culture itself.

While most people admit they have "taste" in landscape, and in fact would insist they do, they often claim that their tastes are based on "practical" grounds. That is ludicrously untrue in most instances. A huge amount of our day-to-day behavior and the landscapes created by that behavior is dictated by the vagaries of "fashion" or "taste" or "fad." And when we speak of "taste," we are talking about culture-not about practicality.

At first glance, some fads seem trivial, like hula-hooping or skateboarding: apparent eccentricities that sweep the country and then are gone. But what guides those fads? Are they really so different from the deep-seated cultural biases that anthropologists and cultural geographers take so seriously: dietary "laws" that encourage us to eat the meat of steers and chickens, and produce nausea at the thought of eating rats and snakes? Why do we build domes and spires on public buildings, but rarely on our houses? Why did lightning rods suddenly appear on the American scene, and then disappear except as antiques? Why do we plant our front yards to grass, water it to make it grow, mow it to keep it from growing too much, and impose fines on those who fail to mow often enough? (Why not let the dandelions grow, or pour concrete instead? Occasionally people do just that, and are ostracized by their neighbors.) At best, the answers to these questions are subtle, fascinating, and often very hard to get. At worst, we simply have no answers at all. But we know enough about taste to know that it is a powerful cultural force(avoiding rat-eating, for example), and those tastes do not come about by accident. Indeed, to trace the paths of taste through historic time and across geographical space tells us a good deal about the nature of American cultures: what it is, and how it got to be the way it is.

Thus, if we ask why America's human landscapes look the way they do, it may seem that we are asking simple-minded questions. In fact, we are also asking: Why do Americans possess certain tastes and not others? We are asking where those tastes came from and why they take hold in certain times and disappear at others.

Part IV *Site Planning and Landscape Design in Different Contexts*

2. THE AXIOM OF CULTURAL UNITY AND LANDSCAPE EQUALITY. *Nearly all items in human landscapes reflect culture in some way. There are almost no exceptions. Furthermore, most items in the human landscape are no more and no less important than other items-in terms of their role as clues to culture.*

Thus, the MacDonald's hamburger stand is just as important a cultural symbol (or clue) as the Empire State Building, and the change in design of MacDonald's buildings may signal an important change in cultural attitudes, just as the rash of Seagram's "shoebox skyscrapers" around exurban freeway interchanges heralds the arrival of a new kind of American city - and a new variant of American culture. So also the painted cement jockeyboy on the front lawn in lower middle-class suburbia is just as important as a symbol as the Brooklyn Bridge; the Coney Island roller rink is as important as the Washington Monument-no more, no less.

This axiom parallels an equally basic proposition: that culture is *whole-a unity-like* an iceberg with many tips protruding above the surface of the water. Each tip looks like a different iceberg, but each is in fact part of the same object. The moral is plain: no matter how ordinary it may seem, there's no such thing as a culturally uninteresting landscape.

But note these caveats:

a. If an item is really unique (like the only elephant-shaped hotel south of the 40th parallel, located in Margate, New Jersey), it may not seem to mean much, except that its creator was rich and crazy.

b. However, one should not be too hasty in judging something "unique." That elephant-shaped hotel has many close relatives: giant artichokes in Castroville, California; billboards that blow smoke rings in Times Square. In some circles such things are called "camp" or "pop" or "kitsch," and it is fashionable to snicker at them. But ridicule or deprecation cannot dismiss the persistent, nagging and fascinating question: what do these ordinary things tell us about American culture?

c. The fact that all items are equally important emphatically does *not* mean that they are equally easy to study and understand (cf. Axiom 7). Sometimes the commonest things are the hardest to study; which leads us to…

3. THE AXIOM OF COMMON THINGS. *Common landscapes - however important they may be - are by their nature hard to study by conventional academic means.* The reason is negligence, combined with snobbery. One has no trouble finding excellent books about famous buildings like Monticello or famous symbolic structures like the Brooklyn Bridge. Curious antique objects get a lot of attention too: "olde" spinning wheels and "Olde" Williamsburg. But it is hard to find intelligent writing which is neither polemical nor self-consciously cute on such subjects as mobile homes, motels, gas stations, shopping centers, billboards, suburban tract housing design, the look of fundamentalist churches, watertowers, city dumps, garages and carports. Yet such things are found nearly everywhere Americans have set foot, and they obviously reflect the way ordinary Americans think and behave most of the time. It is impossible to avoid the conclusion that we have perversely overlooked a huge body of evidence which-if approached carefully and studied without aesthetic or moral prejudice-can tell us a great deal about what kinds of people Americans are, were, and may become.

THE COROLLARY OF NONACADEMIC LITERATURE. Happily, not all American writers, nor foreign visitors, are as snooty as American scholars. Even though there is little written about motels and fast-foot eateries in the "standard" scholarly literature, the country is awash with fascinating and useful material about these common items. One merely has to look in the right place. Some of the "right places" include:

a. Writings of the "new journalists," like Tom Wolfe, who reflect with devastating accuracy on such things as the landscape of drag racing, Las Vegas billboards, the architecture of surfing (including surfers' arcane haircuts), and above all, the cultural contexts from which such landscapes spring.

b. Trade journals, written for people who make money from vernacular landscapes. if, for example, you want to know why your local franchised hamburger joint looks the way it does, try browsing through the pages of the journal *Fast Food*. The magazine is intended for and read by a very select audience of restaurateurs and investors, and it contains advice to help its readers get rich as fast as possible. Large sections of the journal deal with such matters as the workings of space-age ovens that fry quarter-pound hamburgers instantly, but nestled among the technical esoteria, the student of vernacular landscape can find a treasury of cultural information. There is remarkably candid advice on restaurant design that has been road rested to catch the traveler's eye: outdoor signs and landscaping formulas that are based on cool, even chilly appraisals of American popular taste, a matter that lies at the very roots of culture. Then too, trade journals often contain a page or two of "political news" (often called something like "Washington Hotline") which report on political and legal matters of importance to the industry in question. Thus, a trade journal for highway engineers and road contractors, *Rural and Urban Roads* (previously called *Better Roads*), reports on congressional hearings which may result in new laws which will in turn determine what our road systems and roadsides will look like for years to come. The journal often urges subscribers to support legislation that has not even been written yet, and it suggests ways to promote that legislation by influencing politicians, inserting "plugs" in the popular press, and generally engaging in what is politely termed "PR".

For the would-be landscape-reader-one who is neither restaurateur nor highway engineer-browsing through those trade journals can be disconcerting. It is rather like stumbling accidentally across a highly classified document that outlines detailed plans for a military invasion across home territory. Not only does one learn what our future landscapes may look like, one learns in advance about some of the methods by which they may

Part IV Site Planning and Landscape Design in Different Contexts

be created. It is not often that scholars in any field have such a chance to look into the future.

Trade journals, especially the old, established ones, can usually be trusted for their cultural judgments. (If their appraisals are wrong too often, they simply do not stay in business.) There are hundreds, indeed thousands, of such journals, and they are not hard to find.

c. Advertisements for commercial products. One need not speculate very long to identify the strain in the American psyche that the obviously successful ad-makers for Marlboro cigarettes are trying to touch. By whatever name it is called, Marlboro's wild-west country has a very real place in America's collective landscape tastes, and those tastes emerge in some very real places: fire departments that look like pueblos in the suburbs of Buffalo, New York; "Western stores" in eastern Louisiana; and "desert lawns" (replete with sand, cactus, bleached wood, and longhorn skulls) spread from and Tucson to the foggy shores of San Francisco Bay. Old advertisements are equally valuable, for they speak volumes about past technology, past taste, and past cultures. In the same way, old illustrations, picture postcards, or photographs may serve similar purposes.

d. Promotional travel literature, often in the form of slick brochures that tell you not very subtly what you are supposed to see when you visit certain places. Recent changes in the landscape of the Pocono Plateau, for example, are much easier to understand after one has seen the marginal eroticism in brochures that beckon newlyweds to any of several Pocono "honeymoon retreats." Indeed, travel literature can *act* as an agent of landscape change. Much of New Orleans's French Quarter, for example, has been "upgraded" and sanitized so that it would accord with tourists' expectations. Those expectations, of course, largely derive from advertising which has been directed at the tourist himself. The advertisement thus becomes a self-fulfilling prophesy.

e. The rare book by a perceptive person who has looked intently at a landscape and discovered what it means. If one really wants to understand what Americans are doing and thinking and aspiring to, sample the glories of George Stewart's U. S. 40: *Cross-section of the United States of America* (1953) or Grady Clay's superb *Close-up: How to Read the American City* (1973). Almost anything by J. B. Jackson will do the job nicely, although "The Stranger's Path" is especially perceptive.

4. THE HISTORIC AXIOM. *In trying to unravel the meaning of contemporary landscapes and what they have to "say" about us as Americans, history matters.* That is, we do what we do, and make what we make because our doings and our makings are inherited from the past. (We are a good deal more conservative than many of us would like to admit.) Furthermore, a large part of the common American landscape was built by people *in* the past, whose tastes, habits, technology, wealth, and ambitions were different than ours today. Thus, while we live among obsolete artifacts of past times-

LESSON 16

"old-fashioned houses" and "obsolete cities" and "inefficient transportation" or "bad plumbing" -those objects were not seen to be" inefficient "or silly by the people who made them, or caused them to be made. To understand those objects, we must try to understand the people who built them-our cultural ancestors-in *their* cultural context, not ours.

THE COROLLARY OF HISTORIC LUMPINESS. Most major cultural change does not occur gradually, but instead in great sudden historic leaps, commonly provoked by such great events as wars, depressions, and major inventions. After these leaps, landscape is likely to look very different than it did before. Inevitably, however, a lot of "pre-leap" landscape will be left lying around, even though its reason for being has disappeared. Thus, the Southern landscape is littered with sharecroppers' houses, even though the institution of sharecropping has nearly disappeared-a victim of the boll weevil and a concatenation of other forces that combined to destroy the old Cotton Belt of the early 1900s, and provoked a migration of black farmers northward, eventually to change the entire urban landscape of industrial America. Most small towns in America-at least of the Norman Rockwell ilk-are like the Cotton Belt: obsolete relicts of a different age. There are no more being built today, and, unless things in America change radically, there never will be.

THE MECHANICAL(OR TECHNOLOGICAL)COROLLARY. To understand the cultural significance of a landscape or an element of the landscape, it is helpful(and often essential)to know in *particular* about the *mechanics* of technology and communications that made the element possible.

For example, we can speculate endlessly(and often pointlessly)about the "symbolism" of, say, the American front lawn, made of mown green grass: perhaps it is a status symbol reflecting a borrowing from England, and thus a subliminal reflection of our admiration for things English. But much of that "symbolic speculation" is likely to be hot air unless we really know *how* a lawn works in a very mechanical way. The fact that most of us have direct experience with lawns, planting and mowing and fertilizing and irrigating and cursing them, obscures two important facts: 1. We do many mechanical things to establish and maintain a lawn that we take for granted(such as getting the lawnmower serviced), but which are nonetheless essential and that would baffle people from lawnless societies. Except for companies like the Scott Grass Seed Co., nobody bothers to write about such behavior, commonplace as it is. 2. We need to know who invented the machinery to make the lawn possible: who took that invention and engineered the machinery so that it came within the financial reach of Everyman(invention and engineering are emphatically not the same thing); who adopted the machinery; how the idea spread; and above all, *when* all this happened and in what order; and *where* these events took place and how they spread, often in direct defiance of environmental good sense. (Why are there green lawns all over Sun City, Arizona, for example? And why, only recently, the sudden efflorescence-if one may call it that-of those "desert lawns" throughout the West?)

Part IV Site Planning and Landscape Design in Different Contexts

All that, of course, is a big order for something so commonplace as the American lawn. Yet pause and consider what we are really discussing. Every step of the way we are investigating the evolution of American culture: where things started, when, and how. The key work is *how*, for unless one knows about the technology behind the landscape element we are concerned with, the fact remains that we really know very little about it. Speculation about symbolisms will remain unprofitable.

5. THE GEOGRAPHIC(OR ECOLOGIC)AXIOM. *Elements Of a cultural landscape make little cultural sense if they are studied outside their geographic (i. e., locational) context.*

To a large degree, cultures dictate that certain activities should occur in certain places, and only in those places. Thus, all modem American cities are segregated: streetwalkers are not found throughout the city, nor are green lawns, trees, high buildings, or black people. This axiom is so obvious that it should not have to be mentioned, except that so many scholars and "practical" people persistently flout it. Architectural historians publish books full of handsome photographs of "important buildings," artfully composed so that the viewer will not see the "less important" building next door, much less the telephone wires overhead or the gas station across the street. The "important building" is disembodied, as if on an architect's easel in a windowless studio somewhere. So also, planners make grand schemes to improve sections of existing cities, plans drawn on large blank sheets of paper, with adjacent areas shown in vague shades of gray or not shown at all, as if the planning district existed *in vacuo*. The planners are perplexed when residents of those gray areas rise up in anger, and perplexity turns to frustration when city councils send the elegant plans back to rest ignominiously in a file drawer, full of similar material, rejected from the past. Again and again, historic preservationists throw up white picket fences around "historic buildings," while adjacent neighborhoods go to ruin. Inside is "history"; outside, it isn't history. (Then we wonder why the general public equates historic preservation with Disneyland!)To study a building as if it were on an artist's easel, detached from its surrounding, is to remove some of the most important evidence explaining why the building looks the way it does, and what its appearance has to tell us about the culture in which it was built.

It is easy to understand why buildings(for example)are isolated for study outside their geographic surroundings. It is what scientists call a "simplifying assumption," and it makes things easier for the student. So, the epidemiologist studies a deadly microbe in an antiseptic pan of agar so that he can see how the bug behaves in isolation. Thus, he meets the bug. But he knows enough to realize that the microbe is important only *in context*, because it causes the disease in a larger body; in this instance, the environment of the human body. So it is with houses and barns and lawns and sidewalks and any other "item" in the landscape: to make sense of them, one must observe them in context.

6. THE AXIOM OF ENVIRONMENTAL CONTROL. *Most cultural landscapes are*

intimately related to physical environment. Thus, the reading of cultural landscape also presupposes some basic knowledge of physical landscape.

We often boast that we have "conquered geography," meaning that contemporary technology is so powerful that we can build anything, wherever we like, and effectively ignore climate, landforms, soils, and the like. To be sure, we grow tomatoes in greenhouses all winter long, and Pennsylvanians flee to Florida when their native winters grow excessively obnoxious. We send men to the moon, and we build superhighways almost anywhere we want.

But "conquering geography" is often very expensive business. Compare the price of tomatoes in January with the price in August(and compare the quality, too!), or contrast the cost per mile of a crosstown expressway in New York with one across North Dakota prairies. In earlier simpler times, with less money, less sophisticated tools, and less information, "conquering geography" was even more expensive, and people avoided such extravagance whenever they could. Thus, the South differed culturally from the North largely because it differed physically. Southern cities stopped looking Southern about the time that cheap air conditioning made it possible to ignore the debilitating heat of a super-tropical summer, which lasted sometimes for five months, a season in which nobody who could help it did any work between noon and 7 p. m. The "Southern way of life" was renamed "the Atlanta spirit" and began to take on Yankee ways, largely because of air conditioning. Then the Arabs tripled the price of oil, and suddenly air conditioning became "uneconomical." Sitting on verandahs came back into style, and glass-lined offices in high-rise skyscrapers with windows that wouldn't open were seen as something less than Paradise on an August afternoon. Environment continues to matter after all.

7. THE AXIOM OF LANDSCAPE OBSCURITY. *Most objects in the landscape although they convey all kinds of "messages" -do not convey those messages in any obvious way.* The landscape does not speak to us very clearly. At a very minimum, one must know what kinds of questions to ask:

As for asking questions, one can quickly get into the habit of asking them simply by doing so. What does it look like? How does it work? Who designed it? Why? When? What does it tell us about the way our society works? (It is remarkable how many intelligent perceptive people have never asked questions of the landscape, simply because nobody ever suggested they do it.)

As for the answers, and judging their validity, that is a trickier matter. Many historians, geographers, and others will ask the obvious question: "If you want to interpret American culture, why not simply read books about it? Why use landscape as evidence, especially when you have already admitted that the interpretation of cultural landscape is such a slippery uncertain enterprise?"

There are two answers to this not-so-simple question:

a. Many of the books are not yet written. For example, I know of no satisfactory book

Part IV *Site Planning and Landscape Design in Different Contexts*

about the landscape of recreation in America despite the fact that we spend billions of dollars on recreation every year, that in many places it is the chief source of revenue, and that most Americans spend huge chunks of time either having fun or thinking about it. To be sure, there is no dearth of books about "recreation planning" -solemn tomes about parks and playgrounds-but if one wants to know about how American tastes have changed through time, one finds the bookshelves nearly empty. Visible evidence is nearly all we have; however, the visible evidence is plentiful: everything from abandoned amusement parks to Little League baseball fields to the little signs stuck on telephone poles in Minnesota and upstate New York that admit that snowmobiles have priority in much of the Northland in winter and thereby admit existence of a subculture that did not exist a decade ago.

b. Many books about certain important subjects(e. g. ,why American houses look the way they do) disagree with each other, and not in minor ways, either. One must conclude that somebody is not telling the whole truth. The most immediate way to resolve such disagreement is to go back to the real thing(in this case, the house itself). The chances are excellent that part, if not all, of the difficulty can be cleared up by visible evidence(and we will begin to have a growing suspicion that many authors have never looked closely at what they write about).

One can, of course, claim too much for the virtues of landscape reading. It is not a panacea, not the master key to an understanding of culture. Indeed, it may be no more than a diverting game, because it is pleasant to go outdoors and let your eyes roam idly across some nice bit of scenery and tell yourself that you are engaged in research. (Landscape reading will not put libraries out of business.)

One can, however, quite literally teach oneself how to see and that is something that most Americans have not done and should do. To be sure, neither looking by itself, nor reading by itself is likely to give us very satisfactory answers to the basic cultural questions that landscape poses. But the alternation of looking, and reading, and thinking, and then looking and reading again, can yield remarkable results, if only to raise questions we had not asked before. Indeed, that alternation may also teach us more than we had ever dreamed: that there is order in the landscape where we had seen only bedlam before. That may not be the road to salvation, but it may be the road to sanity.

WORDS AND EXPRESSIONS

vernacular [vəˈnækjʊlə(r)]   *adj.* 本国的，本地的(语言)
fuss with   *v.* 过分讲究
shrubbery [ˈʃrʌbərɪ]   *n.* (庭院中的)灌木栽植地，灌木丛生处
silo [ˈsailəu]   *n.* 筒仓，地窖，[空] 竖井，(导弹)发射井
garbage dump   *n.* 垃圾堆
tract houses   *n.* 排屋建立在一片土地上有相似的或相互补充的设

LESSON 16

              计的许多房屋

cemetery [ˈsemətrɪ; (US) ˈsemətɪ]   n. 墓地，公墓
pornography [pɔːˈnɒgrəfɪ]   n. 色情文学，色情书刊，色情画，色情电影
Everest [ˈevərɪst]   n. 珠穆朗玛峰（世界最高峰）
autobiography [ˌɔːtəbaɪˈɒgrəfi]   n. 自传
pedestrian [peˈdestriən]   n. 行人，步行者
geomorphology [ˌdʒiːəʊmɔːˈfɒlədʒi]   n. 地形学
plant ecology   n. 植物生态学
folklorist [ˈfəʊkˌlɔːrɪst]   n. 民俗学者
mentor [ˈmentɔː]   n. [希神]门特（良师益友），贤明的顾问，导师，指导者
ghetto [ˈgetəʊ]   n. (城市中的)少数民族聚居区；犹太人聚居区；(某些阶层、集体的)聚居区
slum [slʌm]   n. (城市的)贫民区，贫民窟；非常肮脏的地方
suburb [ˈsʌbəːb]   n. 市郊，郊区
exurban [eksˈɜːbən]   adj. 城市远郊的
upstate [ˈʌpˈsteit]   adj. 远离大城市的，北部边远的（州内地区）
fad [fæd]   n. 时尚，一时流行的狂热，一时的爱好
dome [dəum]   n. 圆屋顶
spire [ˈspaɪə(r)]   n. 塔顶，尖顶
epidemiologist [ˈepɪˌdiːmɪˈɒlədʒist]   n. 流行病学家
expressway [ikˈspreswei]   n. 高速道路
prairie [ˈprɛəri]   n. 大草原，牧场，〈美方〉林间小空地

237

Part V

20th Century Landscape Architecture Practice

LESSON 17
AN ECOLOGY OF DESIGN

NOTE

The global landscape is at a turning point from an equilibrium to a dissipative state characterized by breakdown of global life-support systems. Although the human-dominated technosphere is experiencing what seems to be increased organization, output, and better quality of life, this incomplete view is at the heart of our dilemma. Global society must turn from its reductive thinking to an integrative thought pattern, from Cartesian[1] to systems science, and from anthropocentric(human-centered) to metabolic(lifecycle) thinking.

This chapter calls for the landscape design professions to lead society by shifting to an *ecology of design* with planning and design serving to regenerate system ecological, physiological, and psychological health and productivity. This chapter speaks to the role of an ecology of design in sustainable communities and global peace. It extends the discussion beyond immediate and local problems to larger scales of space and time. The chapter also reviews emerging design approaches, such as regional, biometric, and metabolic design, that manage life-cycle flows. It discusses performance measures, such as ecological baselining and ecological footprinting, and changing environmental performance standards.

TEXT

An ecology of design is an appreciative system sensitive to environmental and human needs, cultural diversity, and the broad range of perceived people-environment relations. It promotes ecological responsibility, social equity, long-term economic viability, and design that connects people to place(*placemaking*) and to other people(*community-building*). An ecology of design promotes management, planning, and design that regenerate the systems upon which we ultimately rely(*regenerative planning and design*).

An ecology of design replaces conventional resource flows that are linear(source-to-waste)with ones that are cyclical(regenerative). It seeks also to integrate and align the flows of material, energy, information, and dollars(Fig. 1)so that energy, Information, and dollars support resource regeneration rather than waste production.

1 TURNING POINT

More than two centuries ago, White wrote about diverse flora and fauna united in an interrelated system(Worster, 1994). In the mid-1930s, Secretary of Agriculture Henry

---

选自 John L. Motloch., Introduction to Landscape Design, 2nded, America, Ball State University, 2001, page 305~330

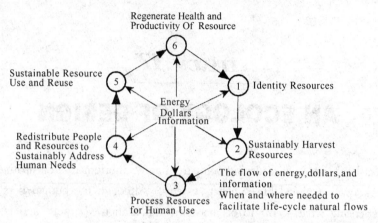

Fig. 1 Aligned Flows of Material, Energy, Information, and Dollars
(Extended from the work of the Center for Maximum
Potential Building Systems)

Wallace was asserting the need for a Declaration of inter-dependence, and in the 1950s, Aldo Leopold expressed concerns about assaults on global carrying capacity. In the 1960s and 1970s, physicists and others were calling attention to the growing number of crises occurring across diverse physical, ecological, and social dimensions (Fig. 2) and asserting that global society had reached a cognitive turning point. From a systems view, concurrence of crises across diverse dimensions indicate a deeper, more pervasive meta-crisis, in this case, human disconnection from the most basic life-sus-

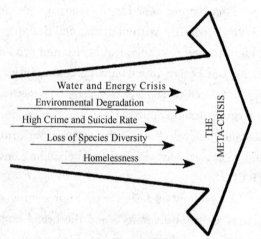

Fig. 2 Multidimensional Expression of the Meta-Crisis

taining relationships upon which the future depends. This self-reflective view was at first marginalized but has become widely embraced by those who deal with the reality the planet is about to face, and has become the basis of a redirection of our most fundamental beliefs and actions.

- shift in Societal Paradigm Life-Cycle Flows
- An Ecology of Design as Life-Cycle Flows and Organic Patterns

2 GLOBAL NEED FOR AN ECOLOGY OF DESIGN

Since human impacts have grown beyond system capacity to self-regulate, designers must integrate decisions with system dynamics and promote regeneration by enhancing life-cycle flows. Fortunately, the integrative sciences—landscape ecology, ecopsychology, memetics—have developed theories, methods (life—cycle assessment, ecological footprinting), and tools(input-output and system-dynamics software) capable of adaption and integration into design processes to facilitate an ecology of design, and a life-cycle design that promotes system health and regeneration.

2.1 Planning and Design for System Regeneration

To prevent system breakdown, designers must embrace an ecology of design that integrates decisions into system dynamics and embraces life-cycle methods, tools, and techniques. In doing so, they can benefit from the example of overlay methods. Unlike other tools not adopted into mainstream practice, overlay methods were widely embraced by landscape architects and planners because they were easily understood, defensible, and articulately and eloquently championed by spokespersons like McHarg (*Design With Nature*). System dynamics and life-cycle methods, tools, and techniques have similarly been developed with complexity and defensibility. Champions are needed to translate these into powerful and easily understood messages to be embraced by practitioners, clients, and the public.

2.2 Triggers Needed for an Ecology of Design

The following *change triggers* can initiate a main-stream professional shift to an ecology of design. They can help entry-level and seasoned practitioners and the public understand, appreciate, and demand regenerative design.
- In form ation-Flow Trigger
- Project-Dissemination trigger
- Assessment Trigger
- Case-Study-Application trigger
- Decision-Guidance-System Trigger
- Guidance-System-Technology Trigger
- Design-Education trigger
- K-12 Education trigger

3 RECONNECTING PEOPLE TO SYSTEMS

Value Systems Theory (VST) contends that individuals and cultures, motivated by cycles of relative focus on individual versus communal success (Cowan & Beck, 1996), have progressed through levels of biopsychosocial complexity (Fig. 3). Each is based on assumptions of how the world works through which people define problems, develop coping strategies, solve the problems they defined, and create new problems that cannot be envisioned or solved from that world view. VST includes six levels of complexity in one cycle and two levels of a profoundly different cycle.

3.1 VST Cycles as an Expression of the Turning Point

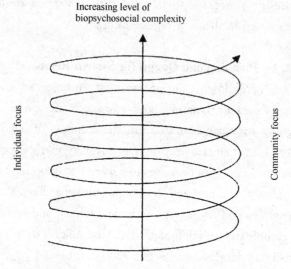

Fig. 3 Value Systems Theory(From Cowan & Beck)

Simplified, the six levels of the first VST cycle include individuals and cultures that perceive the problem of existence as: 1)addressing individual need to survive; 2)establishing norms for group survival; 3)asserting individual power to escape group norms; 4) implementing rules to limit the range of acceptable variance from group norms; 5) manipulating rules to optimize individual success within this limited range; and 6)managing allowable rule manipulation for the common good. Understanding the filter through which one views the world is important, especially when designers work with people(inner-city, Third-World, children)who see the world differently than they).

3.2 Shifting Human Role in Life-Cycle Flows: Mining and Harvesting

A systems view recognizes two types of people: *miners* take resources in a manner or amount that reduces system capacity, and *harvesters* take resources in a manner that sustains health and productivity. Quinn(1995)refers to the former as takers and the latter as leavers. Takers see themselves free from the need to obey natural laws; leavers operate within these laws. The first type operates in the throughput source-to-waste paradigm; the second, with a closed-loop life-cycle paradigm.

3.3 Reconnecting with Living Systems as Pathway to Ecological and Human Well-Being

New physics reconnected science and mysticism, rationality and chaos, and people and organic patterns. It ushered in the second cycle of biopsychosocial awarenesses that reconnects humankind with other species and the laws of the universe. People connect with, rather than assault, systems, addressing the meta-crisis of disconnect and guilt that comes from assaulting the environment and other life forms. Reconnecting with living systems enables people to move beyond the unhappiness of global cultures that see nature as an enemy to be conquered. An ecology of design will help society reconnect its management, planning, and design decisions with living systems. It will play a major role in helping society move beyond built environments that assault the environment and other life forms, and reconnect with the systems we rely upon, and with our own physiological and psychological wellness.

Ecopsychology stresses the urgency of reconnecting with living systems. It connects sanity, quality of life, and the natural world, and asserts that our disconnection from nature is in opposition to humankind's evolutionary imperative to survive.

4 TENETS OF AN ECOLOGY OF DESIGN

4.1 Design in Concert with Natural Principles

Ecological designers understand the failure of mainstream design: it takes excessively, and in a harmful way, from nature; it builds environments that require excessive energy and generate excessive toxins and pollutants(in construction and use); and it uses methods and environments that generate extraordinary wastes that adversely affect all current and future species. An ecology of design respects nature, conserves resources, and minimizes pollution. Ecological design sees fundamental principles of nature— "waste equals food", "nature runs off of current solar energy," and "nature depends on diversity, thrives on differences, and perishes in the imbalance of uniformity" —as the pathway to over come problems. In *Gaia2*, Thompson addresses the first principle, as he calls for buildings "not made on a ground, but out of the pollution that is the profound description of their deepest nature." Passive designers and soft technologists make decisions based on the second principle. Rapoport(1969)addresses the third principle, as he calls for design diversity grounded in place, technology, and culture.

4.2 Partner with Nature's Productive/Regenerative Capacity

An ecology of design partners with nature's *negentropic* ability, through life processes, to concentrate energy, create order, and increase complexity, productivity, and stability. It partners with nature to understand relationships among a number of people, lifestyle, and efficiency of operation; and it promotes solutions that do not exceed *appropriated carrying capacity* as the maximum sustainable rate of resource harvesting and waste generation. As partners, ecological designers dance with ecological dynamics, regenerate life-cycle flows, and define design success as symbiotic with the success of contextual systems and other life forms. An ecology of design also promotes communities partnering with nature. It seeks to improve community *social carrying capacity*, that is, the community's ability to identify and assess a range of criteria(social equity, diversity, and safety) and actions(projects, policies, and so on), and make decisions that lead to a sustainable, regenerative community.

4.3 Partner with Succession

Succession is nature's tendency to productivity. When sites are disturbed, through fire, erosion, or clearing, pioneering plants invade. These plants are adept in moving quickly and harvesting abundant resources but are generally short-lived, inefficient, and lacking in diversity. The early successional ecosystems they form improve the environment so more diverse, efficient, stable, and long-lived, late successional plants and ecosystems can survive. Through succession, natural systems regeneratively increase the productivity of the global system. An ecology of design partners with succession.

For decades, Howard Odum has mapped energy flows through early and late successional natural ecosystems, and their urban corollaries. He has shown early successional ecological and urban systems to be dependent on a surplus of available resources, and characterized by low degrees of organization, diversity, complexity, efficiency, productivity, and stability. In the 1970s, Odum asserted that early successional urban systems had outlived their validity, yet continued to grow(as resources dwindled) by unsustainably mining ecological capital, to the detriment of future generations. Hawken repeats this thesis and calls for decisions based on ecological models:

The American culture is still the bare field full of colonizing weeds... We've consistently chosen the resource-hungry path of least resistance.... demanding ever-increasing supplies of all resources, but especially energy.... Rather than argue about where to put our wastes, who will pay for it, and how long it will be before toxins leak into the groundwater, we should be trying to design systems that are elegantly imitative of climax ecosystems found in nature. Companies must re-envision and re-imagine themselves as cyclical corporations, whose products literally disappear into harmless components, or whose products are so specific and targeted to a specific function that there is no spillover effort, no waste, no random molecules dancing in the cells of wildlife, in other words, no forms of life must be adversely affected. If Dow, Ciba-Geigy, and Henckel think they are in the synthetic chemical production business, and cannot change this belief, they and we are in trouble. If they believe they are in the business to serve people, to help solve problems, to use and employ the ingenuity of their workers to improve the lives of people around them by learning from the nature that gives us life, we have a chance.

An ecology of design is grounded in a similar metamorphosis, shifting from the design of early successional buildings, sites, and cities to the design of late successional urban ecosystems.

4.4 Address a Range of Spatial and Temporal Scales

An ecology of design integrates broad scales of space and time. *Spatially*, it sees sustainability and landscape regeneration as global phenomena that must be locally implemented. It is scale-interdependent: decisions at one scale affect, and integrate with, those at other scales. Like Fuller's World Games decades ago, an ecology of design looks beyond political boundaries and national scales to understand ecological units and global productive potential. It continues a way of thinking with long-established, deep roots (Worster, 1994), and integrates a hierarchy of interdependent scales from global bioregion(natural-resource region) to building/site component, with each seeking to address natural principles internally before passing responsibility to another level above or below. It sees each biome as an ecological performance boundary, as well as a global library of the diverse solutions produced by different cultures and different attitudes about people-environment relationships within that biome as a resource region, and the implications of those solutions in that biome. An ecology of design is input-output based, with wastes at one scale serving as potential resources at that or other scales. *Temporally*, an ecology of design promotes sustainability, landscape regeneration, and increased future capacity by simultaneously addressing present and future needs, health and productivity.

4.5 Embrace Ecological Economics

Hawken sees the most detrimental aspect of current economics as the "expense of destroying the earth is largely absent from the prices set in the marketplace." Before the 1960s, design decisions were also focused on the present and based on first-cost economics that discounted the future. Resources were mined to address current needs, maximize shortterm economics, and "take the money and run." Focusing on the present enabled designers to ignore off-site, upstream, and downstream impacts, In the 1960 and 1970s, design shifted to address the near future, as well as operational and maintenance costs over the life of a project. Resources continued to be mined to address needs. We still took the money but tried to run efficiently and longer.

An ecology of design further extends the focus to full cost accounting(short-and long-term costs, local and distant impacts) and life-cycle economics based on harvesting resources, mitigating local and distant upstream and downstream impacts, and regenerating system health and productivity. It seeks to build *natural capital* (stock of productive and regenerative resources)in the ecological bank and to maintain healthy *natural flows* (life-cycle flows). An ecology of design sees components of natural capital as *renewable* (living organisms, ecosystems), *replen ishable* (oxygen, groundwater), or *nonrenewable*(fossil fuels, minerals). It seeks to sustainably harvest renewable resources, balance flows to replenish resources, and avoid the depletion of nonrenewable resources. An ecology of design addresses all five of Lyle's temporal scales of economics from short-term, degeneratively narrow economics that promote system breakdown, to long-term regeneratively broad economics.

4.6 Address Hierarchical Levels of Decision-Making

An ecology of design requires that designers promote professional and lay participation in system regeneration by making decisions at all three levels of the hierarchy of decision-making. Designers must make *meta-level decisions* to create environments that promote decisions based on life-cycle flows and information and dollar flows that promote regeneration. Meta-level decisions include the development of models(setting performance criteria, benchmarking quantity and quality targets, and so on), translating these into planning and design processes, and negotiating political issues(threats to existing industries, land rights, and so on)to avoid implementation roadblocks. At another level, designers must make *systems-level decisions*, including managing the environment at global, biome, regional, and local scales; and managing life-cycle flows (materials, information, dollars)at scales from global to site. Because of the primacy role of cities, systems-level decisions integrate urban planning and design, smart growth, livable and healthy city, and sustainable community initiatives. These decisions include long-term environmental monitoring, and feedback/feed-forward flows necessary for sustainable decisions. At the third level, *object-level decisions* include facilities design and operation that produce ecologically, physiologically, and psychologically healthy buildings and sites, and integrate into life cycles of contextual systems. They include project decisions that harvest (rather than mine)resources, limit ecological footprints, and build facilities from wastes and pollution. At this level, design harvests site and near-site resources(earth-, fiber-, and waste-based). Products are selected and facilities operated with sensitivity to upstream and downstream environmental impacts, as well as the health of local, regional, and global systems.

4.7 Implement Integrated Management

To regenerate the ecological and cultural landscape, designers must think through the integrative lens of the ecologist. Since the planet and future of humankind require knowledge of, and ethical commitment to, optimal people-environment relationships, designers must integrate systems knowledge, ecology, environmental ethics, and environmental economics, with an understanding of local value systems. Designers also must effectively manage planning and design decision-making environments, teams, tools, processes, and products to regenerate the ecological and cultural landscape, and raise lay understanding of necessary integrations. To achieve these ends, ecological designers must make meta-level decisions and integrate decisions made at systems and object levels.

4.8 Integrate with Life-Cycle Flows

An ecology of design replaces linear, source-to-waste flows with cyclical, regenerative ones. It integrates and aligns the flows of material, energy, information, and dollars. It embraces long-term economics and the mitigation of local and distant impacts, using information and dollars to promote regenerative decisions. Fortunately, in the decades since McHarg spoke of the imperative to obey nature's laws, science has provided new tools(inputoutput modeling, life-cycle assessment, and so on) and environmental performance measures(ecological footprinting, ISO standards, product labeling, and so on). An ecology of design integrates these into processes that move design from its current role of mining and consuming resources and disrupting regeneration, to one of resource harvesting and living regeneratively. Ecological designers and sustainable communities make decisions based on broadly defined current and future performance, using methods that weigh demands for new construction with the energy and material benefits of retrofitting, adaptive use, and flexible construction(tenets of open architecture). Issues of open architecture are being addressed, within the building, by Vivian Loftness and Volker Hartkopf at Carnegie-Mellon, but their work does not address the community-scale, life-cycle flows, or the effects of material extraction, transport, processing, distribution, use, and disposal on regional resources and landscape regenerative capacity. This broader work is urgently needed.

4.9 Pursue Eco-Balance

An activity achieves eco-balance when it balances upstream and downstream resource stocks. Integrated water/wastewater systems can achieve ecobalance. Human oxygen consumption and industrial carbon-dioxide discharge can be balanced by photosynthesis in living plants that produce oxygen and sequester(hold)carbon. These designers can specify construction materials so that the carbon-dioxide produced upstream in processing the material is balanced by the long-term sequestering of carbon within other construction materials, such as biocomposites, appropriately used wood materials, and so on.

Understanding that current populations, lifestyles, and technologies interfere with system regeneration, ecological designers and communities can seek to balance the life-cycle flows through which systems regenerate. They can use tools like the ecobalance game (Center for Maximum Potential Building Systems) to make planning and design decisions that balance flows, as well as to educate other designers and the public of needs for, and pathways to, eco-balance. Land labs(Center for Maximum Potential Building Systems, Center for Regenerative Studies, Center for Wetlands)Will continue to develop eco-balancing knowledge and tools for an ecology of design.

4.10 Integrate Life-Cycle Assessment, Planning, and Design

Balancing flows requires that designers(as decision-makers and facilitators of design teams and community groups)integrate life-cycle assessments into decision frameworks and planning and design methods. It also requires that designers assess existing conditions and flows, and whether interventions perform at desired levels. Balancing flows calls for designers to assess costs and guide decisions based on life-cycle dynamics, as well as implement decision frameworks as knowledge-based guidance systems that integrate conventional planning and design processes with life-cycle costing and with the life-cycle flows of materials, energy, information, and dollars.

Ecological designers integrate a range of environmental and performance assessments (ecological baselining, life-cycle assessment, impact assessment, site monitoring), at various scales, into planning and design processes. At the biome scale, they integrate *life-cycle assessments* to identify and locate resources and technologies, including where they are mined, harvested, transported, processed, distributed, used, reused, and returned to usable form; and to identify the potential for improving life-cycle performance. At the project scale, they make decisions based on assessments of project impacts on local and distant system health and productivity. Ecological designers create *life-cycle decision frameworks* to integrate the actions of diverse people over long periods of time into regenerative outcomes. These designers make *life-cycle planning and design decisions* that factor in where resources are mined or harvested, transported, processed, distributed, used, reused, and regenerated. They organize and interpret data to facilitate life-cycle decisions, pursue processes that promote regeneration, and make decisions based on local and distant impacts, such as environmental impacts on EPA non-attainment.

4.11 Address Current System State

The Introduction identifies two types of system conditions. The first, *systems in equilibrium*, are slowly changing and characterized by hign levels of integration, interaction, positive feedback, self-perpetuation, and regeneration. They are highly ordered in a way that integrates variables and optimizes health and productivity. Decisions informed by past system behavior generally produce positive and reinforcing feedback. These systems evolve slowly with increasing interrelatedness of parts and, with time, become finely tuned with highly interrelated components, high integration with context, and few internal or external conflicts. The systems sustain and regenerate themselves. The second type, *systems in dissipation*, are highly spontaneous, rapidly changing, and inherently unstable. Decisions informed by past behavior often produce negative feedback, as well as internal and external conflict and stress. These systems promote emergence of new, more relevant interrelationships.

Currently, planners and designers are taught to integrate design into equilibrium systems. They are ill-prepared to design appropriately as conditions degrade and dynamics become dissipative. Ecological designers, on the other hand, manage life-cycle flows with an understanding of system state. They function as managers when feedback from societal decisions is positive and as change agents when feedback from societal decisions is negative. As change agents, they facilitate new, more relevant operational environments, management structures, planning strategies, and design solutions. As change agents, they function at the *meta-level* to establish decision environments, laws, organizations, and processes that promote life-cycle decisions; at the *systems level* to implement life-cycle sensitive policies, processes, and frameworks; and at the *object level* to design regenerative projects.

4.12 Develop an Ethical Design Language

Ecological designers synergize design and ecological science, develop methods and solutions based on models from nature, and integrate new ecological science tools and techniques to regenerate systems. They facilitate information flow, enable communities to embrace a regenerative ethic, develop and promote an ethical planning and design language that reconnects design with life-cycle flows of dynamic systems, and document and disseminate models, tools, and techniques as a new language of design.

5 CURRENT STATE

The processes, tools, and techniques of an ecology of design are occurring in many, and often discon-nected, venues. The first step in moving to an ecology of design is to understand the state of the art. This includes understanding baselines and tools for data management, mapping, integrating, and assessing performance; understanding network resources; and understanding processes for guiding and imple-menting regenerative planning and design.

6 AN INTEGRATIVE MODEL

The *eco-balancing design model* (Fig. 4) based on the work of CMPBS, is proposed herein as an integrative decision model for an ecology of design. This model can be seen as an eco-balancing extension from mainstream planning and design models.

6.1 Eco-balancing Design Model as Extension of Mainstream Methods

The eco-balancing design model embraces main-stream overlay methods and extends the litany of overlay maps, adding maps that address solar-energy resources (slope aspect, sun angles), wind-energy resources (seasonal winds in relation to landform, wind acceleration, wind shadows), biomass resources (wood, waste-based), and water-energy resources (groundwater and surface water). This model integrates eco-balancing into assessments at the regional, intermediate (community, land use), and site scales. It includes baselining and long-term monitoring of sites as a means of informing desired changes in benchmarks.

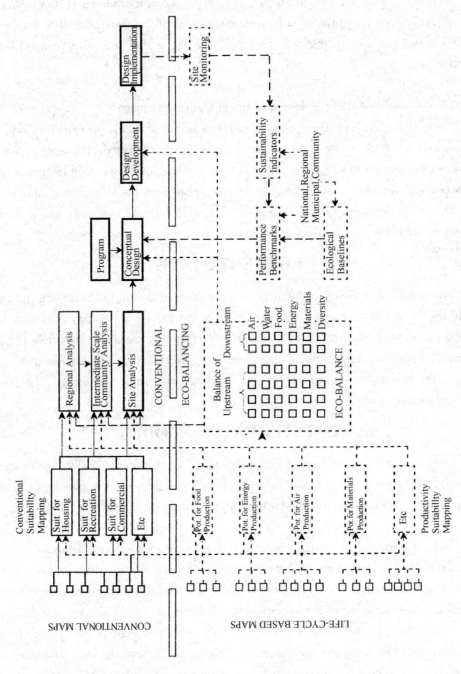

Fig. 4 Eco-balancing Design Model (Based on the work of CMPBS)

6.2 Eco-balancing Design Model as Communication and Education Tool

Cycle one could present alternatives generated by the conventional land planning application of overlay methods; cycle two could present alternatives generated by eco-balancing applications. Communication as two cycles could facilitate an understanding of the method, as well as an appreciation for differences between conventionally produced and ecobalancing solutions. As such, it could be a valuable tool in raising client and public consciousness of the pathways and benefits of ecological design.

7 PLANNING AND DESIGN FOR A JUST WORLD

Physical planners and designers also oppose peace when they address current needs with inadequate concern for future quality of life. They convert resources to waste and remain ignorant about integrating their interventions into life-cycle dynamics to regenerate the resources upon which future quality of life depends.

8 ECOLOGICAL DESIGN PROFESSION

There is a profound need for an ecological design profession. In the distant past, there was a single profession of physical design. Today, that profession is splintered into the professions of architecture, landscape architecture, and urban planning, and the designed environment is an amalgam of the activities of these and other professions. There is also a profound need to integrate the activities of the professions that plan regions and cities, design buildings, and design sites into a continuum of systems-sensitive management, planning and design of the ecological and cultural landscape integrated with life-cycle flows that regenerate system health and productivity.

The structure and locus of the ecological design profession is still emerging. Pioneers, scattered throughout and beyond the design professions, are united by their systems approach, and by their commitment to address issues beyond narrow disciplinary boundaries and integrate decisions into larger systems—ecological, economic, technological, political, and socioeconomic. Some pioneers are selfeducated in systems; others have system science degrees, interdisciplinary degrees, interdisciplinary-degree extensions, or degrees in multiple design and non-design disciplines. Time will tell whether the ecological design profession will remain as systems thinkers practicing in diverse professions, or as its own profession focused of integration and global survival.

WORDS AND EXPRESSIONS

analog ['ænələg]   n. 类似物，相似体
biome ['baiəum]   n. (生态)生物群系
disseminate [di'semineit]   v. 散布

Part V 20th Century Landscape Architecture Practice

drastically [ˈdræstikli]	adv.	激烈地，彻底地
equilibrium [ˌiːkwiˈlibriəm]	n.	平衡，平静，均衡，保持平衡的能力
lens [lenz]	n.	透镜，镜头
metamorphosis [ˌmetəˈmɔːfəsis]	n.	变形
mitigate [ˈmitigeit]	v.	减轻
Neolithic [niːəʊˈlɪθɪk]	adj.	新石器时代的
norm [nɔːm]	n.	标准，规范
notation [nəuˈteiʃən]	n.	符号
pertinent [ˈpəːtinənt]	adj.	有关的，相干的，中肯的
paradigm [ˈpærədaim, -dim]	n.	范例
solar energy		太阳能
survey [səːˈvei]	n.	测量，调查，俯瞰，概观，纵览，视察
thermodynamics [ˌθəːməudaiˈnæmiks]	n.	[物] 热力学
topographic [ˌtɔpəˈgræfik]	adj.	地志的，地形学上的
toxin [ˈtɔksin]	n.	[生化] [生] 毒素
versus [ˈvəːsəs]	prep.	与…相对

KEY CONCEPTS

Ecology of Design
System Regeneration
Life-cycle Flows
Information-flow
Nature Principles
Nature's Productive Capacity
Nature's Regenerative Capacity
Ecological Economics

NOTES

1. **Cartesian**: Of or relating to the philosophy or methods of Descartes.
   笛卡尔的，笛卡尔的哲学或方法的或与之相关的。

QUESTIONS FOR REVIEW AND DISCUSSION

1. What are the turning points of the global landscape?
2. How do you understand "global need for an ecology of design"?

LESSON 17

3. What're the triggers needed for an ecology of design?
4. How the VST cycle express the problems include individuals and cultures?
5. What are the tenets of ecology of design?

Part V 20th Century Landscape Architecture Practice

Reading Material

Forstering Living Landscape

SUSTAINABLE LANDSCAPE DESIGN-A DEFINITION

Everywhere the landscape is deteriorating-a direct result of the attitude that land is a commodity and that natural and cultural values are expendable. As awareness of global environmental problems increases, however, we are witnessing a revolution in attitudes toward the natural landscape at every level and a desire to design and plan in an environmentally responsible way.

The basic premise of sustainable landscape design is to allow the ongoing processes that sustain all life to remain intact and to continue to function along with development. While the first tenet of sustainable landscape design, and one that is actually often overlooked, is "don't destroy the site," in reality we have already destroyed too much and we can no longer measure the sustainability of a design by its minimal impact on the natural systems of a site. Today, almost every site on which landscape architects work has been abused. Sustainable design must go beyond the modest goal of minimizing site destruction to one of facilitating site recovery by reestablishing the processes necessary to sustain natural systems. This approach is not "naturalistic landscaping" or "preserving endangered species" but the preservation, restoration, and creation of self-sustaining, living environments.

Sustainable design is not a unified philosophy for which there is one accepted, rigorous method. Perhaps most important, it is a process of raising consciousness and changing basic attitudes-attitudes so ingrained we are often unaware that they shape our design and management of the land.

These changes require that we actually see the present deterioration of the landscape, that we recognize the impacts of our interventions, and that we understand each site and each piece of a site as parts of larger systems.

BASIC ATTITUDES AND PREMISES OF THE SUSTAINABLE DESIGN PROCESS

Sustainable design is not a reworking of conventional design approaches and technologies, but a fundamental revision of thinking and operation-you cannot put spots on an elephant and call it a cheetah. With sustainable design the presumptions of how a site is dealt with are different. The kind of data gathered and the way we interpret these data are

---

选自 George E. Thompson and Frederick R. Steiner, Ecological Design and Planning, John Wiley & Sons, ING. page 1~18

also different; even the methods by which we design are different. It is the sum of these changes that results in a different design.

The key to sustainable design is the systems approach-sometimes called a holistic view. Most of us are aware that nothing exists in isolation and that everything is interconnected. Many of the skills of the design professions (which include engineering), however, are geared to solving arbitrarily defined problems and providing solutions that may appear reasonable from the point of view of a single professional discipline or single client but cannot resolve the multidimensional problems of the land. With sustainable design, we are not looking at single-focus solutions to single-focus problems, such as drainage, sewage disposal, or erosion control, but rather at the management of a whole set of resources.

A second premise on which sustainable design is based is that product and process are one. Therefore, the process by which an end is achieved is often given as much, or nearly as much, weight as the product, because it is recognized that only by changing the design process is it possible to change the design result. These changes in the design process affect who participates, how they participate, and ultimately how the project is defined or redefined.

Who participates and how do they participate? The sustainable design process is inclusive and basically democratic; it is a relationship of consenting equals that builds consensus as a project proceeds. In traditional design relationships, we successfully divorce many of the obvious partners from the design process. Redefining the players and their roles, breaking down old boundaries, and empowering new parties in new partnerships are critical to a sustainable design process-which is inherently representative, interactive, and consensual. The traditional design process, even with modifications, is too exclusive, linear, and compartmentalized, with little real communication or coordination among team members and many potential team members unrepresented or participating only in subordinate roles. The sustainable design process requires inclusive partnerships that are new and unexpected, in which all concerned parties are empowered to advocate their needs and desires.

With a sustainable design process, team members interact as equally empowered partners. The client becomes a "Partner" in the design and its realization-rather than patronized as a necessary inconvenience to be told what to do by the experts or "Master builders." The design professional is also an equal participant-not a "hired gun" subservient to the client. Most importantly, the land, the people living and working on it, and those who will be using the project are full participants. And to ensure sustainability, "the unseen users, who are the other players at the table, are the future generations." With this inclusive participation in the design process, there is a recognition that all site values are important and must be respected, understood, and represented. While often there is considerable fear, on the part of both designer and client, that the inclusion of so

Part V   20th Century Landscape Architecture Practice

many people will be unwieldy and delay a tight schedule, structured participation of the stakeholders allows this process to proceed smoothly. if there is an appropriate level of involvement, there will be real consensus, as unrealized connections and unexpected allies are brought to light.

For participation to be more than window dressing, continuity is a critical factor. To ensure the truth of the vision to the end, sustainable design requires stakeholder participation from soup to nuts-from the development of the program, through the design of the building and site facilities, to construction review and beyond to a program of assessment and repair that is built into a completed project.

In addition to the type of participation, the structure of the work process is different. In contrast to traditional design methods, the sustainable design process is rarely linear. Instead, the work is characterized by a focus on the whole project and by feedback loops that create changes in the structure of the work process throughout the lifetime of a project. For example, the methods of installation and the resources of the contractor or volunteer work force may be explored at the very beginning of the design process and this knowledge used in crafting the design.

Lastly, the sustainable design process affects how the project is defined or redefined. There are few sites that are self-contained packages where planning and design simply entail designing the required building and landscape for the proposed client. Site programs and clients come and go, but the land remains. Providing long-term solutions to site problems can require looking outward to the larger context and confronting impacts to the site that occur beyond site boundaries. Solutions may include the redefinition of the project scope, a change in the physical boundaries of a site, or the recognition of larger jurisdictional boundaries and the involvement of wider groups of people, such as owners of adjacent properties or multiple agencies.

DEFINING SITE VALUES AND FRAMING APPROPRIATE SITE GOALS

To frame appropriate site goals, the designer must ask, "What values are critical to the site, and how should they be protected and even enhanced by site development?" Because we are seeing today, on almost every site, accelerating and destructive environmental trends such as erosion, compaction, excess stormwater runoff, and takeover by invasive exotic plants and animals, every project design should be considered as a part of a larger strategy to resolve these critical issues. The goal of every project should be to leave the site in a better condition than it was found.

Another critical impact of conventional development is the increasing fragmentation of natural systems. Today the natural landscape remains only as small islands surrounded by a fabric of development. These islands gradually lose their ability to support a variety of plant communities and habitats, and they are extremely vulnerable to invasions by exotic plants and animals. Sustainable design must involve serious efforts to reverse this scenario by(1)creating strategies to reconnect fragmented landscapes and establish contiguous networks with other natural systems, both within a site and beyond the site boundaries, and(2)reestablishing the widest possible range of indigenous plant and animal communities, in appropriate habitats, to restore to the site its potential diversity of species.

Clearly stating the goals and principles of a project in a mission statement guides the overall development and focuses all participants. The mission should combine both vision and realism. The result is a cumulative building of the plan even where there is a wide range of disciplines or stakeholder interests. These guiding principles evolve out of what is learned during the design process, and should be revisited and reevaluated as the project proceeds.

THE PATTERN OF A PLACE-RECOGNIZING THE INHERENT NATURAL STRUCTURE

The way you observe the landscape determines what you see. This explains why, despite the fact that site evaluation and review have been an important part of design and planning processes for a long time, conventional evaluations have not led to responsive, ecologically sound plans or designs.

The phrase "a sense of place," although deceptively simple, is a nontechnical way of summing up the totality of a place and all the processes that shape it. When we talk about an English village or the Serengeti Plains we are summing up centuries of cultural history and eons of geological and biological evolution that created the places that these names represent. Our sense of place, although sometimes experienced as a single moment or image, is actually derived from a complex living community that is continuously responding to the forces that act on it, recognized as pattern. In nature, pattern is the result of process. As Frank Lloyd Wright said: "The pebble is a diagram of the forces that have acted upon it." That diagram is a pattern, and these patterns are the end products of all the forces that have shaped a landscape to this moment. Landscapes reveal very complex patterns; they bring together and express an enormous amount of information about natural processes and the experience and influences of human culture in and on that place. When this sense of place and the natural and cultural information that it embodies is reduced to data collection-lists and descriptions of isolated phenomena, such as climatological data, soil types, and of endangered species-the picture of the living landscape, which is dynamic and interactive, is often lost.

As designers we are trained to see and work with forms and patterns. For the sustainable designer, pattern is the link between natural and social processes and design. Beyond data collection, mapping parameters, and creating overlays, sustainable design requires the designer to interpret the forms and patterns of a place and to tell its story-what the site was, how it has changed, and the directions in which it is likely to go. It is important to frame this story simply, accurately, dramatically, and without jargon. The more coherently the story portrays a place, the more deeply it uncovers connections, the more vividly it portrays site character, and the more dramatically it juxtaposes site themes-the better the finished design that will grow from it.

A useful way of summing up the knowledge revealed by an environmental analysis for a sustainable design may be expressed as a drawing of the "inherent natural structure" of a site, which is a representation of the intrinsic natural patterns of the place and includes the human modifications of these patterns. Such a drawing is shorthand for complex information and reveals the dynamic equilibrium that is the resolution of the interacting natural, social, and cultural forces of a site.

ADAPTIVE STRATEGIES FOR SUSTAINABLE DESIGN SOLUTIONS-TAKING ACCOUNT OF DIFFERENT CRITERIA

An adaptive strategy is a design solution that is tailored to a specific context and a specific problem. By definition, adaptive strategies are developed out of local contexts and local conditions; although they are not "universal solutions," they are based on universal concepts.

The sustainable designer reexamines conventional solutions in the light of environmental imperatives and asks, "Is there a better way of doing this task?" Adaptive strategies must solve more than one problem at a time, in an integrated way, using the most appropriate technology currently available. Single-focus solutions are, by definition, not strategic, because they do not account for the big picture. Only synergistic solutions can realize the efficiencies needed to resolve problems that are increasing exponentially Sustainable strategies and sustainable design use a holistic, synergistic, and interactive approach.

Working with the forms and patterns of the natural world and the processes these forms and patterns express in the landscape is the prerequisite for sustainable design and is fundamental to the preservation of the integrity of a place. Civil engineers and designers usually consider their creations "improvements on nature" and often call them just that, but most engineering solutions rarely approach the efficiency of biological systems and are often sustainable only for short periods of time. Although there is no single magic technology that can solve environmental problems, conditions can be improved when the principle of using natural models is applied.

Looking closely at the natural systems of water, soil, and vegetation, we can examine our current treatment of them, identify trends, and review the specific implications, both moral and practical, for sustainable design. Although there are many ways to describe the land and the critical natural processes that sustain it, we can begin by examining three interrelated processes and looking at how the patterns of the larger systems are reflected in design:

LESSON 17

1. Water-the hydrologic regimen
2. Soil-the cycling of mineral and organic nutrients
3. Vegetation-the structure, organization, and development of plant communities

Water-The Hydrologic Regimen

Increased runoff from development is one of the most pervasive problems in the landscape today. The engineering paradigm for drainage is to concentrate flow and velocity and carry water away from the place where it falls as quickly as possible. Conventional stormwater management relies heavily on curbs, pipes, inlets, dams, riprap, detention basins, and other "hard" engineering solutions. Where water from the uplands is collected in pipes that flow onto valley slopes, the result is gully formation. The gullies that form below outlet pipes not only prevent water from infiltrating into the ground to recharge groundwater, but also act as drains, pulling water out of the adjacent slopes. At the valley bottom, stream channels are recut in an effort to handle the increased sediment load and water volume and velocities. The result of our conventional management of stormwater is tree toppling, delta formation, and a stream in which the channel is migrating rapidly and undercutting and eroding its banks.

Most regulation today, despite some restrictions for wetlands, permits the destruction of nearly all existing upland terrain, soils, and plant communities on a site and the resulting severe disruption of hydrologic patterns. Both soil and water regulation in the United States have concentrated on "control" of problems, such as flood control, erosion control, "point" and now "nonpoint" pollution control. Conventional site design is by nature timid: It follows regulation rather than seeking to maintain whole site systems.

The sustainable design paradigm does not deal with single-focus goals, such as flood control or erosion control, but rather looks at the management of the whole resource. For example, all water, including wastewater, is treated as a resource-not as a problem-and is managed as a crucial component of the larger water system. This approach allows one to find solutions based on models that replicate the natural hydrology. Biological treatment of wastewater would not only allow it to be reabsorbed into the water system of the watershed, but also to provide the opportunity to expand and replace diminished wetland systems.

Drainage solutions should reduce runoff and maximize infiltration in the uplands, restore or maintain stream baseflow, provide groundwater recharge, and reestablish channel stability, regardless of the strength of the storm event. Vegetated swales slow water, trap sediment, and increase infiltration by using the natural system to accomplish these goals. Sustainable technologies such as "porous paving" foster infiltration and the reduction of contaminants, reinforcing natural functions.

Soil-The Cycling of Mineral and Organic Nutrients

Soil is the most hidden landscape problem of all. Soils are far more susceptible to damage than we realize. The function of soil in the biotic system is to recycle nutrients. Most of this work is done by plant roots, animal life, and microorganisms in the soil, all of which depend on a permeable soil crust, stratified soil layers, and appropriate amounts of organic matter. Much of what we do during the design and construction phase of a project destroys the life of the soil. Terrain modification, most of it unnecessary, is the greatest culprit. Grading destroys soil stratification and compacts soil, which limits root penetration, mycorrhizal growth, infiltration of water, and the exchange of atmospheric gases, chiefly oxygen and carbon dioxide.

Sustainable design must involve serious efforts to preserve soil resources, including the development of strict soil protection measures during construction, limits on the zone of disturbance, minimum-impact construction techniques, as well as innovative restoration measures such as making new soils from waste products, restoring soil tilth, and adding micronutrients and mycorrhizae to repair soil deficits.

Vegetation-The Structure, Organization, and Development of Plant Communities

Native plant communities are the most essential expression of the physical features of a place, and they support the richness of the wildlife with whom they have coevolved. What we are losing is not simply individual plant species, but the complex relationships of plants to other plants, to wildlife, and to place.

Plants, like people, live and develop as communities with characteristic companions. These communities can be described as "a distinctive group of plant species which may be expected to grow naturally together in more or less the same population proportions under similar habitat conditions. The location of these communities, such as an oak-hickory forest, is largely determined by climate. If the earth were completely uniform there could perhaps be uniform bands of vegetation. Because the earth is broken into continents, there are instead, within the continents, physiographic provinces and climatic zones; the regional variations in vegetation within these climatic zones respond to variations in the landforms, and the local variations in vegetation respond to changes in topography and soils.

Vegetation is an exquisitely sensitive indicator of these conditions, growing in an almost infinite variety of recognizable patterns. For example, where there is a distinctive gradient of any sort-from dry to wet or from cold to warm or from toxic to normal conditions-we will observe plant species forming a series of concentric bands. As we become sensitive to patterns in vegetation, the relationship between form and function is underscored. To create patterns, at any scale, that are not representative of the patterns of a place "goes against the flow" and requires an additional input of energy in direct proportion to the movement away from the patterns of the place. In the northeastern United States, weekly summer mowings are required to maintain our lawns and beat back the forest that would otherwise grow in this region. This energy input is required because a forest, and not English turf grasses, is nature's expression of the fullest and most effective use of the resources available in this landscape.

The basic building block of ecological planting design is the plant community type, assembled in the patterns on and above the ground, that express plant life in that place. Planting plans that show plants simply as idealized circles with a dot in the center, placed in geometric relationships, cannot begin to capture the complexity of ecological relationships. For example, to represent the structure of a mature forest, the design drawings should reflect both the vertical layers (canopy trees, understory trees, shrubs, and ground layer) and the horizontal mosaics, distinguishing between growth forms of every species so that the canopy trees, often the largest plants, can be shown to occur in every layer and at every size somewhere within these mosaics. Variety in the size and in the shapes used to show plants will help to express the fact that the form of each plant is partially determined by its plant companions and partially by its response to local environmental conditions, such as its place within a gap in the canopy or along a forest edge.

Succession is the name given to the process of change and development in plant and animal communities, "the gradual replacement of one community by another" in which "a succession of plant communities is always accompanied by a succession of animal associations. Plant succession leads the way because plants are the foundation of every food chain."The process of succession tends to proceed toward more complex interrelated communities of living things.

Today the impacts from development on our remaining native landscapes have inevitably meant environmental degradation. One of the most visible signs of environmental damage is the displacement of complex native ecosystems by a few invasive exotic plant species, which often form almost monospecific and nearly "static" plant communities. Takeover of a site by invasive exotic plant species disrupts the structure of the native ecosystems and interrupts the natural sequence of succession on a site, seriously diminishing both the health and diversity of native plant communities and the animals who are dependent on them.

Solving our biodiversity crisis inevitably involves the way we maintain our landscapes as well as the way we plan them. Understanding the process of succession-plant community development-is a key to long-term vegetation management and to creating and repairing native landscapes with minimal intervention. By using natural patterns we set the stage for nature to reestablish the functional relationships between plant and place. Ecological planting design offers a new vocabulary based on the language of landscapes-forest, woodland, prairie, desert, and tundra. It is a celebration of both the unique qualities of each individual place as well as the qualities that place may share with others similar to it. The attitude of the designer becomes one of continuous observation and increasing appreciation of the richness and complexity of these patterns within patterns- "worlds within worlds."

Part V 20th Century Landscape Architecture Practice

THE ECOLOGICAL AESTHETIC

Making art that is "expressive form" and that reveals and celebrates the patterns and processes of the landscape requires only that the ecological sensibility be married to an artistic one and that both sensibilities recognize the intrinsic design of the site as the highest value: "Again Lou Kahn has made clear to us the distinction between form and design. Cup is form and begins from the cupped hand. Design is the creation of the cup transmuted by the artist, but never denying its formal origins. As a profession, landscape architecture has exploited a pliant earth, tractable and docile plants to make much that was arbitrary, capricious, and inconsequential. We could not see the cupped hand as giving form to the cup, the earth, and its processes as giving form to our works. The designer attuned to sustainability accepts and respects the primacy of the natural patterns and processes of the landscape. The stream and wetland systems, the natural terrain, and the plant and animal communities are the given forms of a place. Such a designer works with them, does not violate them, and does not assume, for example, that a stream channel can be relocated or put into a pipe. With this approach, site resources are used to solve site problems. There is an economy of intervention and a minimization of destruction. In addition, there is respect for the integrity of patterns everywhere-ecological, historical, and cultural. The functional areas of a sitebuildings, roads, and parking lots-adapt to the patterns of the place rather than obliterate them. Diminishing gradients of intervention allow as much of the site as possible to succeed to more complex ecosystems. No longer locked in the repetitive conventions of "bed, bosque, border, and all," the designer discovers that natural patterns and the vocabulary of our indigenous landscapes are, like the natural world itself, infinite sources of form.

MONITORING

Sustainability is a goal that no one as yet knows how to achieve. The act of sustainable planning and design is a heuristic process; that is, one in which we learn by doing, observing, and recording the changing conditions and consequences of our actions. Observation, recording, and monitoring are crucial elements of the sustainable design process.

The function of monitoring is to tell the story of how the site has changed, is changing, and is likely to change. It continuously records and informs our actions and is the major vehicle by which "the site speaks to us," providing the information that allows the sustainable designer to work with the natural regenerative processes inherent in the patterns of each landscape.

Frequently, a major hurdle in sustainable design is our limited understanding of how landscape systems function. We often base our designs and policy decisions on landscape "myths." Examples of such myths that have influenced the design and management of forest ecosystems in the northeastern United States are that "the creation of forest edge will benefit wildlife" or "opening the canopy will stimulate forest reproduction." The creation of a site database through monitoring helps us to understand the local mechanisms that govern a site, to see long-term trends, and to determine the consequences of intervention-both past and present. Building a site database allows policy to be based on real science and helps to ensure that the most effective strategies are applied to the solution of site problems. Site monitoring feeds the continuous adaptation of the plan and management program, as information about the site is recorded and analyzed, and trends are observed. The plan, then, is not simply the initial design document, but, as Allan Savory says of his holistic resource management model, "the word plan must become a twenty-four-letter word: plan-monitor-repair-replan." Restoring, assessing the site, and modifying our actions or our nonactions are ongoing activities without which a plan or management program cannot be truly sustainable.

EVERY ACTION IS SIGNIFICANT
EVERY PLACE IS IMPORTANT

A design ethic that accepts the preeminence of the natural patterns of a place-water, soil, and vegetation-may not solve all of our problems, but it will go a long way toward changing current trends. No landscape, no matter how apparently pristine, is beyond the reach of human impact. Sustainable design must embrace the entire spectrum of landscapes at every scale and in every place and include sustainable agriculture, sustainable industry, sustainable cities, and sustainable wild lands. There are success stories: For example, fish can now be caught and eaten in the river flowing by City Hall in Stockholm, Sweden, and the water is good enough for a four-kilometer downtown swimming course.

Sustainable design provides a design framework that seeks to address all ecological values, to create an ongoing partnership with the living landscape, and to reverse the trend of needless destruction of our landscape. It is the growing realization of the interconnectedness of development and environmental processes worldwide and within our communities that drives the evolution of sustainable design. At every scale, sustainable design is fundamentally about integrating the natural structure of the site with the built environment. Where a place is understood, preserved, repaired, and celebrated as an integrated whole, it can be experienced as powerful and memorable. What follows is a gallery of projects by Andropogon that reveals the application of sustainable ecological design.

WORDS AND EXPRESSIONS

aquatic [əˈkwætik]　　　　　　adj. 水的，水上的，水生的，水栖的
arboretum [ˌɑːbəˈriːtəm]　　　n. 树园，植物园

Part V 20th Century Landscape Architecture Practice

arborist ['ɑːbɔːrist]	n.	树艺家，树木栽培家，树木研究者
asphalt ['æsfælt]	n.	沥青
biome ['baiəum]	n.	(生态)生物群系
corm [kɔːm]	n.	[植] 球茎，球根
culminate ['kʌlmineit]	v.	达到顶点
dappled ['dæpl(ə)d]	adj.	有斑点的
deteriorate [di'tiəriəreit]	v.	(使)恶化
eon ['iːən, 'iːɔn]	n.	永世，无数的年代
exotic [ig'zɔtik]	adj.	异国情调的，外来的，奇异的
herbaceous [həː'beiʃəs]	adj.	草本的
heuristic [hjuə'ristik]	adj.	启发式的
holistic [həu'lɪstɪk]	adj.	整体的，全盘的
hurdle ['həːdl]	n.	篱笆，栏，障碍，跨栏，活动篱笆
laurel ['lɔrəl]	n.	桂冠，殊荣
mosaic [mɔ'zeiik]	n.	镶嵌，镶嵌图案
intrinsic [in'trinsik]	adj.	(指价值、性质)固有的，内在的，本质的
pebble ['pebl]	n.	小圆石，小鹅卵石
porous ['pɔːrəs]	adj.	多孔渗水的
regimen ['redʒimen]	n.	摄生法
ridge [ridʒ]	n.	背脊，山脊，屋脊，山脉
scenario [si'nɑːriəu]	n.	想定
sediment ['sedimənt]	n.	沉淀物，沉积
sewage ['sjuː(ː)idʒ]	n.	下水道，污水
sewage disposal		污水处理
stratification [ˌstrætifi'keiʃən]	n.	层化，成层，阶层的形成
stymie ['staimɪ]	v.	从中作梗，完全妨碍
swamp [swɔmp]	n.	沼泽，湿地
synergistic [sinə'dʒistik]	adj.	增效的，协作的，互相作用[促进]的
trench [trentʃ]	n.	沟渠，堑壕，管沟，电缆沟
tributary ['tribjutəri]	adj.	从属的，辅助的，支流的
velocity [vi'lɔsiti]	n.	速度，速率，迅速，周转率

LESSON 18

TOWARDS A NEW LANDSCAPE PRACTICE

The rejection of the theory and practice of high-rise buildings as homes, together with an increased urge for historic conservation, are symbolic of a rebellion affecting both town and country. Society is in revolt against accepted modern values; the psychologist is beginning to take precedence over the technician.

Let us first consider *'the tranquility of geometrical proportion'*. This in essence is classicism as opposed to romanticism, the rational as opposed to the irrational. It is the creation of the intellect seeking to bring the order of the heavens to a disordered globe, of the assertion of a Virgilian sense of the nobility of man and faith in his future. As a basis of Western culture throughout the ages it has been corrupted through sentimentality and pseudo-academicism, by being represented as a gross expression of human power, or merely by being rejected as an art form. Today in its simplest shape it can be seen as an eloquent expression of a seat of learning in the master plan for Sultan Qaboos University, Oman, set appropriately in the dead landscape in which Western classicism was born.

The philosophy of classicism aimed at eradicating 'the strange ancient furniture of the unconscious mind', as Jacquetta Hawkes described it, and replace it by rational thought. That this subconscious furniture has always been with us, a restless underground assortment of inexplicables liable to explode at any time-Orphism[1] or Dionysian ecstacy, for instance-is self-evident today. Historically, Mediaevalism opened up the flood gates of the unknown, to be supressed in the Renaissance and then to re-surface through such outlets as the terrifying monsters of Bomarzo. In the Age of Enlightenment the literary genius of the English sublimated the delights and horrors of tropical forest and savannah into the English School of Landscape. In the nineteenth century the basic instincts were glossed over, only to break out frenziedly at the turn of the century through the medium of abstract art. A totally different and truly vast geography of the subconscious came to light, which Jung[2] tried to follow, explore and explain.

This history argues that modern man is aware only of the visible tangible world; that at all times except for the present man has sought to experience for his enrichment the invisible intangibles, such as that of the ubiquitous grotto; and that it is the purpose of

---

选自　Geoffrey Jellicoe, Susan Jellicoe. The Landscape of Man: Shaping the Enviroment from Prehistory to the Present Day. Thames & Hudson 1995

landscape design to retain a balance between these two worlds of the mind. Encouraged by the International Federation of Landscape Architects(IFLA)[3] with its professional membership of some fifty countries, landscape design has increased prolifically over the past eleven years. The examples chosen are intended to convey the growth of this conception of the two worlds. The story begins with the single world of the University in Oman, where the irrationals have knowingly been swept under or off the carpet, and leads on to those that encompass the abstracts, the irrationals, the biological fantasies and the unknowns that comprise the art of the biosphere.

The Public Park, which dates only from the beginning of the nineteenth century, may soon reflect society as much as the churches and public buildings of the past; together with the proliferation of art galleries and museums it could fill the metaphysical void that exists in a technocratic age. Following Germany's lead in creating permanent city parks from national exhibitions the second English National Garden Festival, Stoke-on-Trent; J. Samworth, design co-ordinator shows the traditional English conception of a park as a return to nature, and can be traced back via F. L. Olmsted to Humphry Repton and earlier; classicism, which is positive and activating, is fitted neatly into romanticism, which is negative and quiescent. In contrast, the Parc de la Villette, Paris (Tschumi and Merlini, architects), won in competition with Roberto Burle Marx as chairman of assessors, is a daring leap into the future. Based inherently upon French classical planning symbolised by Le Nôtre, the complex drawings use geometric abstract design in an attempt to carry landscape further than anything hitherto. The *Axonometric*, 1984 (Fig. 1) shows the amalgamation of no less than three abstract and independent ideas; and the *drawings of plant forms* how the biological world will fit into this whirlwind of geometry. Now in course of construction, it will only be properly comprehended in reality after some twenty years.

The Garden City movement pioneered in Britain. Its climax has been Milton Keynes, officially designated in 1967 for a population of 250,000 (later reduced). Nineteen years later, with a population of 120,000, it is possible to assess its progress. Being a city of trees (ten million have been planted to date) it is not an example of instant urban landscape, and cannot therefore be fully appreciated until the treescape becomes all embracing and effective. It was clearly designed for a prosperous two-car society and this has yet to be achieved.

The concept of the city was unique, resisting hign-rise homes long before they were discredited in favour of a treescape. The plan structure is a wavy pattern of *gridiron distributive roads* (Fig. 2) treed and embanked to give protection to the richly vivid urban villages, such as *Neath Hill* (Wayland Tunley, architect, Geoffrey Boddy, landscape designer) which lie snugly enough between the squares.

In contrast to the villages, the traffic roads are anonymous and would be without identity were it not for the occasional punctuation of the treescape such as the *passing*

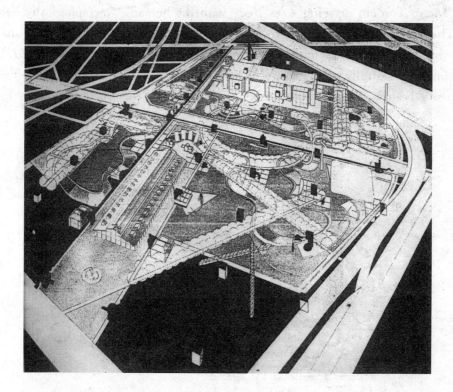

Fig. 1

glimpse of a village. The core of this green landscape-conceived city is the civic centre, oddly un-English in its monumental axial planning, its present absence of a significant silhouette, and its *shopping centre* of truly classical proportions, assuredly the grandest of its kind in England.

Just As in the Age of Enlightenment the growth of knowledge was balanced in men's minds by a feeling for romantic landscape, so in the modern world society is turning to ecology not-merely as an emotional relief but because it knows instinctively that a lack of appreciation

Fig. 2

threatens life itself. From ecology springs landscape art, with roots in the deep past. The playground in Victoria Park, London is a *fantasy of shape* (Fig. 3) that gives a child a sense of escape from the school room, responds to primeval feelings, and releases the imagination to voyage into unknown worlds of its own. Similarly animals are now seen, as at the Metro Toronto Zoo (Fig. 4) as free, with the humans. metaphorically behind the bars. The site of this Zoo is 750 acres of richly varied landscapes. The animals have been grouped in their natural habitat from the *six zoogeographic regions of the world*. Humans and animals are skilfully interwoven, the human to experience for a short while the origins of romantic beauty which lies solely in his eye, forgetting the cruelty of nature that parallels it.

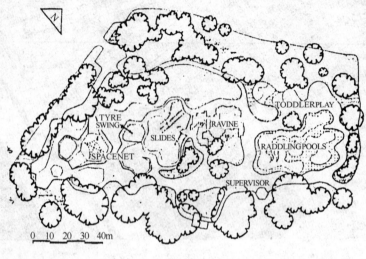

Fig. 3

The First Wave of the international style of architecture has passed, but it has left behind the experience that landscape design, with its biological basis and greater flexibility, is better able proportionately to express what is universal, what is regional, and what is individual. The International Federation of Landscape Architects was founded not only to encourage the interchange of ideas between the advanced countries but through the spread of their expertise to encourage the art anywhere in the world. The creative talent waiting to be tapped is unlimited. A pioneer to an independent way of thought is Geoffrey Bawa, educated at the Architectural Association in London and widely travelled, who returned worldly-wise to his native Sri Lanka to work within the ethos of this ancient fragment of the sub-continent of India. Among his many works, the plan of Lunuganga (Fig. 5), his own home, is the centre part of a large design set in a landscape comprising 'a low hill planted with rubber, fruit trees and coconut palm, with rice fields at the lower level, the whole surrounded by the Dedduwa Lake'. The *entrance* is through a twisted tree. The *view outwards* is a metamorphosis of the English School, which the designer had experienced, into one strange to western eyes.

Animal Domain: Undoubtedly a most dramatic feature found in no other Zoo in the world, will be the Animal Domain where nearly 600 acres of rever valley land will be set aside for Canadian animals.

The zoogeographic pavilions that accommodate species requiring controlled environments have been placed next to the core walk, to serve as gateways to their respective paddock displays. Any gateway can be reached from any other by a short walk. This is particularly important for a zoo which is to operate all year round in a north temperate climate.

Other illustrations show different ways in which, by illusion, the human is brought to the animal rather than the animal to the human. The Master Plan was commissioned by the Metropolitan Toronto Council with the following estimates:

Cost   28.4 million Canadian dollars
Annual operating costs   2.75 million Canadian dollars
Annual revenue   2.76 million Canadian dollars

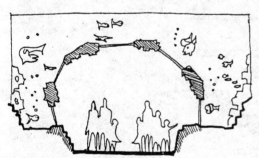

Great Barrier Reef Exhibit

In the Great Barrier Reef exhibit in the Australian pavilion people walk through a darkened underwater tunnel. The water on each side and overhead teems with vivid fish.

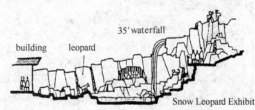

In the Asian pavilion a 35 ft. waterfall(incidentally used to aerate the zoo's pond water supply) falls over a high rock exhibit displaying snow leopards. At the entrance to the building is a Siberian tiger, the world's most northern large cat. who will be seen outdoors even in the coldest weather.

Polar Exhibit

The rock work and pools of the Polar bear exhibit allow the animals to be seen from many vantage points; from above, through underwater windows. and in particular, unusually close up views from caves inside the rocks.

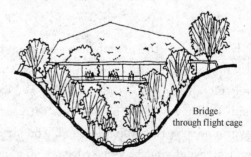

Between the World of the Oceans and the Americas pavilion there is a valley which will be covered by a giant net. The visitor crosses a high level bridge through the trees where he is surrounded by flocks of birds in flight.

Fig. 4

Part V 20th Century Landscape Architecture Practice

Fig. 5

THE Concept of the greenhouse as a magnificent garden ornament was developed in the early nineteenth century, when shape was dictated by architectural rather than horticultural rules. The great Winter Garden at Niagara Falls, designed by M. Paul Friedlung, stands in a newly-made public park with views of the Falls and with a robust children's playground as a reservoir of sound. The structure rises like an extraordinary glass mountain. Enter and you are whisked away on a magic carpet(Fig. 6)into the serene world of the tropics, civilized and elegant, where lecturers can lecture, music can play, and you yourself with your companions and the exotic vegetation, can enjoy the moment of just being.

The Four Landscapes that have been added to this History were designed by the au-

LESSON 18

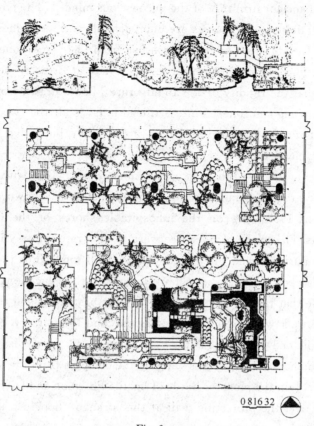

Fig. 6

thor in 1980～1985 and are intend to show different aspects of the concept of the two worlds. Sutton Place and Modena are structurally classical; Brescia and Galveston are basically romantic. The symmetrical lay-out of Sutton Place, Guildford derives from the early Renaissance plan of circa 1526, with additions in 1905. The present landscape, begun in 1980, is a grand allegory of Creation, Life, and Aspiration. The plan of the *East Walled Garden* shows the Paradise and Secret gardens, where minor changes were made in execution. While the gardens of Sutton Place today are similar to those of the Villa Gamberaia in that they express the rationals and irrationals of an individual mind, the Civic Park for Modena has a different objective. *Visibly* it is to provide recreation and relief, like any town park, for a collective urban society. *Invisibly* it is intended to reinforce the values of the old city centre by opening the windows of the subconscious upon the dignity and relevance today of the classical world. The *Leisure Centre* recalls the Roman geometry of the Via Emilia.

Compared to the assurance and intelligibility of classical landscape the romantic or biological landscape is a mystique that psychoanalysts have scarcely begun to probe. The first to do so as an exercise seems to have been Edmund Burke in his *Origins of the Sublime and the Beautiful*. All we know today is that as science discovers more and more facts of the world about us, so the art of the biosphere increases as a safety valve of the smouldering 'strange and ancient furniture of the unconscious mind.' The potential field for creative design is as infinite as its sources are unpredictable and sometimes grotesque. It was a chance supper of five different kinds of fresh fish from Lake Isoe, one after another, that inspired the 'infilling' landscape project for the estate at Brescia, beside the foothills of the Alps. To combat the rigidity of the architecture, fishes drawn from the adjoining water landscape, now metamorphosed into artificial hills, split the two parts of the estate, linking on route not only the usual pleasures of parkland, but a live farm and a cemetery to complete the cycle of life.

It is appropriate to close this saga of the *Landscape of Man* with a landscape analogy of its place in the grand scheme of things. The project to be known as The Moody Gardens, approved in 1985, lies on the inhospitable shores of the Gulf of Mexico, at Galveston, Texas. The terms of reference were to illustrate the way in which civilizations have assembled, nurtured and integrated plants of all kinds into their various forms of gardens and landscapes. The plan is self-explanatory: the educational campus and glasshouses, the route that takes you on foot or by boat past Eden and the excitement of the civilizations, the walk ways over the marshlands, and the nursery. Stand back, and you will see how fragile and precarious is the very existence of the civilizations within the cosmos. Note how the nursery has been swung by the compass from the stable classical to the unstable romantic. Join the monster heads of hostile Poseidon and friendly Demeter peering from outer space over the protecting wall at this strange, hopeful, and beautiful growth on their planet; and pause and wonder.

By Definition, a history is concerned with facts of the past. *The Landscape of Man* was conceived and begun in 1958 and in the ensuing years has endeavoured to keep abreast of modern facts. In 1986, an addenda of four original designs by the authors were included and, in 1994, a fifth design, which has introduced a new philosophy in the relation of Western man to the environment. The essence of this philosophy was contained the words of the Greek philosopher Heraclitus, 'The unconscious harmonizes the conscious'. The site of the Historical Society's grounds at Atlanta, Georgia(33 acres)is halved by a ravine or valley with a rivulet and is indigenously wooded. The northern half is occupied by Swan House, a great Italianate mansion and grounds dating from 1927, when the Society's landscape history of the city was begun. On the southern half are two very large but modest modern museums, together with car parks and a village. The brief for the landscape designer was to unite these disparate elements into a single majestic idea: that of a landscape town through history. The brief seemed insoluble. The conventional geometrical *classical* approach of a strong central feature was unsuitable both as to site and purpose. The conventional English *romantic* approach of a pretend river uniting the whole was hopeful, but again ignored the true purpose of the plan(Fig. 7)

Then, inspired by Heraclitus, came the concept of the *cosmic* design of movement through time and space, based on the power of the subconscious to write in the mind the

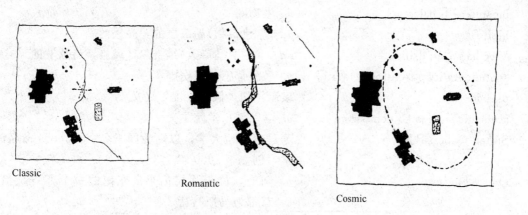

Fig. 7

objects it passes, as does a river. The precedent is the Katsura Imperial Palace[4], where the stroll garden gyrates upon itself, is known to be cosmic, and is more significant than the palace.

Even more than that of Katsura, the route is difficult to follow on the plan. It is purposely modest and is very often hidden by trees. Designed to generate its own sense of movement, it is composed of a sequence of experiences that make up a whole, as in a symphony. It must elude discords, such as the crossroads. In principle a circle, it returns to base and begins again.

Let us follow the path, immersed though it may be in trees. The origins of life are in the quarry before the stairway of the great terrace. From here we pass up woods past an Indian settlement to a white village of 1830. We descend, cross over the rivulet on a timber-roofed bridge and climb the way to the grotto (beneath the crossroads) that symbolizes the destruction of the city in 1863. We emerge into a new Atlanta. First we pass through one, two, three prettily trellised flower gardens with a Victorian playhouse and then into the garden of Swan House and the ethos of Atlanta Triumphant. After visiting this splendid tribute to the Italian Renaissance, we continue along the existing pathway enriched with pools, fountains, green arches and a spectacular view of Swan House itself. Abruptly we enter and walk thorugh a sweet domestic garden of the mid century. We continue through a valley of doubts and fears to rise to the great terrace and the grove of Heraclitus, the author of the saying, 'All things are in flux.'

WORDS AND EXPRESSIONS

tranquility [-'kwiliti]   n. 宁静
geometrical [dʒiə'metrikəl]   adj. 几何学的，几何的
proportion [prə'pɔːʃən]   n. 比例，均衡，面积，部分
    v. 使成比例，使均衡，分摊

biosphere [ˈbaiəsfiə]	n. 生物圈
high-rise	adj. （建筑物）超高层的，高楼的
Virgilian [vəːˈdʒiliən]	adj. （古罗马诗人）维吉尔［风格，诗歌］的
sentimentality [ˌsentimenˈtæliti]	n. 多愁善感，感伤癖
pseudo-	表示"伪，假拟，虚"之义
academicism [ˌækəˈdemisizəm]	n. 学院派；学院主义
Sultan Qaboos University	苏丹卡布斯大学，以阿曼国王名字 Qaboos 命名的大学，创立于 1980 年
Oman [ouˈmɑːn]	n. 阿曼，位于阿拉伯半岛东南的一个苏丹统治国，首都为马斯喀特
assortment [əˈsɔːtmənt]	n. 什锦；各色俱全
mediaevalism [ˌmiːdiːˈiːvəˌlizəm]	n. 中世纪精神［特征、信仰、风俗］
monster [ˈmɔnstə]	n. 怪物，妖怪
enlightenment [inˈlaitnmənt]	n. 启迪，启蒙，启发；（18 世纪欧洲的）启蒙运动
tropical [ˈtrɔpikl]	adj. 热带的，热情的
savannah [səˈvænə]	n. 热带草原；南美稀树草原（亦作：savanna）
gloss over	辩解；掩饰
frenziedly [ˈfrenzidliː]	adv. 狂热，激怒，狂乱
adstract art	抽象派，抽象主义
ubiquitous [juːˈbikwitəs]	adj. 无所不在的，普遍存在的
grotto [ˈgrɔtəu]	n. 洞穴，岩穴，人工洞室
gallery [ˈgæləri]	n. 美术陈列室［馆］；画廊
metaphysical [ˌmetəˈfizikəl]	adj. 形而上学的，纯粹哲学的，超自然的
void [vɔid]	n. 空间，空旷，空虚，怅惘
permanent [ˈpəːmənənt]	adj. 永久的，持久的
Stoke-on-trent	斯托克/特伦特河畔，英国城市
via [ˈvaiə, ˈviːə]	prep. 经，通过，经由
Humphry Repton	汉弗莱·雷普顿(1752～1818)，英国景观园艺家，Landscape gardening 一词的发明者
Parc de la Villette	拉维莱特公园，建于 1987 年，坐落在法国巴黎市中心东北部，占地 55 公顷，为巴黎最大的公共绿地
Roberto Burle Marx	布雷·马克斯(1909～1994)，巴西著名景观设计师
amalgamation [əˌmælgəˈmeiʃən]	n. 融合，合并
whirlwind [ˈ(h)wəːlwind]	n. 旋风
Milton Keynes	米尔顿·凯恩斯，英国在 20 世纪 60 年代建造的卫星城，是卫星城镇规划理论的实践代表之一
treescape [ˈtriːskeip]	n. 多树的风景，树景
gridiron [ˈgridˌaiən]	adj. 方格形的，棋盘式的
distributive [disˈtribjutiv]	adj. 分发的，分配的，分布的

LESSON 18

civic [ˈsivik]	adj. 城市的，市镇的，公民的
monumental [ˌmɔnjuˈmentl]	adj. 纪念碑的，纪念物的，不朽的，非常的
silhouette [ˌsilu(:)ˈet]	n. 外形，轮廓，侧影
Metro Toronto Zoo	蒙特罗多伦多动物园，位于加拿大多伦多，是世界上最大的动物园之一
metaphorical [ˌmetəˈfɔrikəl]	adj. 隐喻性的，比喻性的
Geoffrey Bawa	杰弗里·巴瓦，斯里兰卡最有名的建筑师
interweave [ˌintə(:)ˈwi:v]	v. (使)交织，织进，(使)混杂
Sri Lanka [sriˈlæŋkə]	n. 斯里兰卡(南亚岛国)
ethos [ˈi:θɔs]	n. 民族精神，思潮，风气
rubber [ˈrʌbə]	n. 橡胶
coconut palm	椰子树，椰树
magnificent [mægˈnifisnt]	adj. 华丽的，高尚的，宏伟的
ornament [ˈɔ:nəmənt]	n. 装饰，修饰
horticultural [ˌhɔ:tiˈkʌltʃərəl]	adj. 园艺的
Niagara Falls	尼亚加拉瀑布，位于加拿大安大略省渥太华
vegetation [ˌvedʒiˈteiʃən]	n. 植被，(总称)植物、草木
Modena [ˈmɔ:dnə]	n. 摩德纳，意大利北部一座城市
Brescia [ˈbreʃə]	n. 布雷西亚，意大利北部一城市
Galveston [ˈgælvistən]	n. 加尔维斯顿，美国得克萨斯州东南部的一座城市
symmetrical [siˈmetrikəl]	adj. 对称的，均匀的
Guildford [ˈgilfəd]	n. 吉尔福德，英格兰东南的自治城市
Villa Gamberaia	著名的文艺复兴花园
Virgil [ˈvə:dʒəl]	n. 维吉尔，罗马诗人
Augustan [ɔːˈgʌstən]	adj. 奥古斯都的，奥古斯都时期的。奥古斯都(公元前63~公元14)，是罗马帝国第一任皇帝
Ovid [ˈɔvid]	奥维德(公元前43~公元17)，罗马诗人，代表作为《变形记》
metamorphose [ˌmetəˈmɔ:fəuz]	v. 变形，变质，使变成
Lucretius [lu:ˈkri:ʃəs, -ʃi:əs]	n. 卢克莱修，罗马的哲学家和诗人。他的 De Rerum Natura (论量物的本性)，是一首为了把人们从迷信和对不可知的恐惧中解放出来并试图用科学词汇解释宇宙的长诗
psychoanalyst [ˌpsaɪkəʊˈænəlɪst]	n. 心理分析学者
Edmund Burke	埃德蒙·柏克(1729~1797)，英国政治家，保守主义鼻祖
grotesque [grəuˈtesk]	adj. 奇形怪状的，奇异
parkland [ˈpɑ:kˌlænd]	n. 温带疏林，稀树草原
marshland [ˈmɑ:ʃˌlænd]	n. 沼泽地

Part V 20th Century Landscape Architecture Practice

Poseidon [pouˈsaidn, pə-]	n.	波塞顿，掌管海洋、地震及马匹的神，是宙斯的兄弟
Demeter [diˈmiːtə]	n.	得墨忒耳，主管收获的女神
Heraclitus [ˌherəˈklaitəs]	n.	赫拉克利特，希腊哲学家，他坚持斗争和变化是宇宙的自然状态的观点
ravine [rəˈviːn]	n.	沟壑，峡谷，溪谷
rivulet [ˈrivjulit]	n.	小河，小溪，溪流
indigenous [inˈdidʒinəs]	adj.	本地产的，土生土长的
mansion [ˈmænʃən]	n.	大厦，官邸
cosmic [ˈkɔzmik]	adj.	有秩序的，和谐的
Victorian [vikˈtɔːriːən]	adj.	维多利亚时代的，与此相关或属于这一时代的
triumphant [traiˈʌmfənt]	adj.	胜利的，成功的，狂欢的，洋洋得意的
flux [flʌks]	n.	不断的变动，变迁

KEY CONCEPTS

the Garden City movement
instant urban landscape
romantic landscape
biological landscape

NOTES

1. **Orphism** [ˈɔːriˌfizəm] An ancient Greek mystery religion arising in the sixth century **b. c.** from a synthesis of pre-Hellenic beliefs with the Thracian cult of Zagreus and soon becoming mingled with the Eleusinian mysteries and the doctrines of Pythagoras.

奥菲士教起源于公元前6世纪的古希腊神秘宗教，它综合了前希腊信仰和扎格列欧斯的色雷斯教并且很快与衣洛西斯奥义和毕达哥拉斯教义相混合。

2. **Jung** [juŋ] Swiss psychiatrist who founded analytical psychology. Among his contributions to the understanding of the human mind are the concepts of extraversion and introversion and the notion of the collective unconscious. Jung's works include The Psvchology of the Unconscious(1912)and Psychological Types(1921).

荣格，卡尔·古斯塔夫 1875～1961 瑞士精神病学家，创建了分析心理学。在了解人类心智方面做出的贡献是提出了外倾型和内倾型的概念以及集体无意识的概念。其著作包括无意识心理学（1912年）和心理类型（1921年）。

3. **International Federation of Landscape Architects**(IFLA)

1948年IFLA在英国正式成立，总部设于法国巴黎。IFLA成立的宗旨乃是在促进有关专业造园景观与其他相关艺术和学科领域的关系，共同努力创造人类更舒适的生活环境及永续发展。

4. Katsura Imperial Palace
   桂离宫

QUESTIONS FOR REVIEW AND DISCUSSION

1. Which inheritance would you prefect to, classical or romantic? Give your reasons.
2. Tell what you know about the IFLA.
3. Do your think that the public park in China reflect society as much as in some developed countries? What about your solution about that?
4. If your are to plan a zoo, will your follow the method used in Metro Toronto Zoo? Why?
5. After reading the article, what is the *cosmic* design in your opinion?

Part V 20th Century Landscape Architecture Practice

Reading Material A
Parks, Botanical gardens, Festival gardens: Germany

  Munich's Westpark, with its display of plantsmanship in discrete areas, was made in an old gravel quarry for a Federal Garden Exhibition in 1983. It achieves the remarkable feat of binding together a site cut by two motorways by means of a 'green bridge'. Tall earth banks moulded around the approach to the bridge and its edges soak up the sound of traffic, whose impact is minimized. The park was designed by Peter Kluska and some of the planting was by Rosemary Weisse(d. 2002), the Kassel-based landscape architect who specialized in the use of perennials. She was influenced by Professor Richard Hansen (1912~2001)at the Technical University of Bavaria, who extended the work on perennial planting and grasses which Karl Foerster began and applied it to public parks as well as gardens. [14] Weisse used a mix of perennials which were adapted to the hot and dry conditions at Westpark, with its stony soil, not adding too much fertilizer to encourage strong growth. Planting has been in loose drifts with little space between, and gravel is used as a mulch. Weeds are removed before they set seed, but some wild grasses and flowers are left alone. Maintenance is from paths which meander in and out, and edged with plants which are resilient to walkers'feet such as *Geranium sanguineum* 'album'. The aim is to create an all-year-round naturalistic garden with the minimum of maintenance, similar to the meadow or prairie, but more controlled. Different plants are encouraged which will give colour and shape in their leaves, flowers and seed-heads, and cover levels of other plants which are dying off. Contrasting colours such as red *Lychnis chalcedonica* and white *Campanula lactiflora* grow amongst wild grasses. *Stipa gigantea* and *Verbascum bombaciferum* divert attention from bearded iris that have finished flowering. Hypericum and helianthemum, muscari and allium, aster and euphorbia, emerge from the background of thyme and nepeta.

  The Emscher park north of the Ruhr district is really a series of parks in a regional development which is still unfolding. The end of coal mining and steel production in the Ruhr valley created the prospect of a ribbon of some seventy kilometres of bleak wasteland. But instead, the area surrounding seventeen cities along the River Emscher, a tributary of the Rhine, is being transformed into an imaginative park, where nature and art have been united to celebrate past landscapes. Redundant gasometers, steel works, railway lines, coking ovens, and waste tips have been joined in a series of 'incidents' which extend from Duisburg in the west to Bergkamen in the east.

选自　Janet Waymark Modern Garden Design: Innovation Since 1990 Thames&Hvdson 2003

Seven wedges of green have been drawn at right angles along the line marked by the River Emscher-described as a long green backbone with green ribs sticking out. [15] Connecting former coal mining towns, each wedge has developed a quality of its own, based around the industrial architecture still standing. Garden festivals have been held to promote each region as it has emerged.

The green pattern is connected by a cycle path and walking routes, the River Emscher's polluted and noxious stream has been channelled into an underground sewer and the new bed filled with clean rain water. Many tons of contaminated soil have been dispatched to the bottom of pits where they are covered with fresh earth and fast-growing vegetation. Where possible the natural colonization of plants and trees has been left undisturbed-echium and sedum, willow, birch, poplar, beech, buddleja and robinia-but some management is necessary to control more rampant species. New woodlands are explored by school groups and walkers, and children make dens and treehouses under the supervision of foresters.

Potsdam Federal Garden Show, Germany, 2000

An old Russian military site has been transformed by a garden festival, providing a permanent exhibition hall, and land for new housing nearby. Different zones, each with their own character, are linked by paths and bridges.

Had there been previous recognition of the potential for industrial skeletons to be re-clothed and rejuvenated, as in the Duisburg-Nord Landscape Park? In 1967 the American Robert Smithson had recorded photographically New Jersey's territory of oil derricks, smoking chimneys, and deserted construction with attendant waste. His essay, entitled *A Tour of the Monuments of Passaic*, was a lament for man's devouring of the earth's resources, and his blindness to the scars he would leave behind. The Duisburg-Nord Landscape Park was made on land partly bought from the Thyssen company. A competition for its development rejected an historical and philosophical design from the Frenchman Bernard Lassus in favour of Peter Latz's industrial land art, which proposed the minimum intervention with natural regeneration, and the maximum celebration of the strong architectural elements formed by the Meiderich smelting works. Steel plates which lined the foundry pits have been made into a collage which is also a stage for theatre and concert performance in the Piazza Metallica. Chimneys, gantries, girders, metal tunnels and chutes are now lit up at night, the pink, green, blue and red-strip lighting outlining the bones

Part V *20th Century Landscape Architecture Practice*

of the works and reflecting in water-filled pits below. The emphasis has been on the celebration, not demolition, of old industrial contructs. Lighting also outlines a metal tetrahedron, built on an old spoil heap now stabilized as a lookout over the Ruhr, and the top of the winding mechanism at the Zollverein Shaft Xll, where a centre for design, culture and industrial history has been built. Small gardens have been made wherever the ground plan of old works allowed; there are muscari growing in industrial container bases, and waterlilies flower in tanks.

Near Gelsenkirchen, land artists have produced some striking displays, some temporary, some permanent. Richard Serra has placed a metal slab 14.5 metres high on a black spoil base on the top of the Schurenbach Tip. Another manmade hill, the Mechtenberg tip, became the theatre for more transitory works in the Mechtenberg Landscape Park between Bochum, Essen and Gelsenkirchen. In 1995 artist Peter F. Strauss, landscape architect Harmut Solmsdorf and an accommodating farmer, Bernhard Stricker, traced the course of the underground mines, and fields of energy made by overhead cables, in broad bands of oilseed rape and clover round the contours of the hill, leaving red soil paths cutting diagonally across. In 1999 artist and architect Martha Schwartz was commissioned to transform the Mechtenberg hill with bales of hay into lines and trapezoidal shapes. At the same time, the Bulgarian Christo and his wife Jeanne-Claude(both b. 1935), more usually concerned with wrapping buildings, were constructing a great wall of oil drums in the theatre which was once the Oberhausen gasometer.

A recent venture into urban regeneration in Germany has taken place in Potsdam, west of Berlin, which hosted the 2001 Bundesgartenschau on an old Russian military site. The developing infrastructure, such as a new tram route, should stimulate further growth. The triangular site exploits geometry, with avenue axes defining the boundaries and rectangular embankments enclosing sunken arenas, one of which contains cubes full of gardens. Like a game of dice, the garden cubes contain smaller cubes tipped on edge on a grass carpet, each one full of flowering plants. Corten steel bridges join the embankments and make viewpoints; beds of red roses divide the great hall for horticultural shows from the slopes of the arena beyond.

WORDS AND EXPRESSIONS

Munich [ˈmjuːnik]　　　　　　　　　　n. 慕尼黑(德国巴伐利亚州首府)
plantsman [ˈplɔːntsmən;ˈplænts-]　　　n. 苗圃工作者，花卉栽培者
discrete [disˈkriːt]　　　　　　　　　adj. 分离的，不连续的
quarry [ˈkwɔri]　　　　　　　　　　　n. 采石场
perennial [pəˈreniəl]　　　　　　　　n. 多年生植物
Bavaria　　　　　　　　　　　　　　n. 巴伐利亚州(位于德国南部，昔时为一独立王国)
stony [ˈstəuni]　　　　　　　　　　　adj. 多石的

LESSON 18

mulch [mʌltʃ]	n. 覆盖(物)；[林] 林地覆盖物, 护根物, 地面覆盖料
drift [drift]	n. 吹积物
weed [wi:d]	n. 野草, 杂草
resilient [riˈziliənt]	adj. 有复原力的, 能复原的
Geranium	老鹳草属
Lychnis chalcedonica	皱叶剪秋罗, 又名鲜红剪秋罗
Campanula laciflora	宽叶风铃草
Verbascum	毛蕊花属
prairie [ˈprɛəri]	n. 大草原, 牧场
bearded [biədid]	adj. 有芒刺的
iris [ˈaiəris]	n. (pl. irises, irides [ˈaiəridi:z]) [植] 鸢尾属植物, 鸢尾, 蝴蝶花
hypericum [haɪˈperikəm]	n. 金丝桃属植物
helianthemum	半日花属
muscari	百合科, 蓝壶花属
allium [ˈæliəm]	n. 葱属植物
aster [ˈæstə]	n. [植] 紫菀属植物, 紫菀
euphorbia [juˈfɔ:biə]	n. 大戟属植物
thyme [taim]	n. 麝香草属的植物, [植] 百里香
Ruhr [ruə]	n. 鲁尔(德国一地区)
bleak [bli:k]	adj. 荒凉的
tributary [ˈtribjutəri]	n. 支流
Rhine [rain]	n. 莱茵河(源出瑞士境内的阿尔卑斯山, 贯穿西欧多国)
redundant [riˈdʌndənt]	adj. 多余的, 过剩的
gasometer [gæˈsɔmɪtə(r)]	n. 大型储煤气柜, 贮气罐, 煤气罐
coking [ˈkəukiŋ]	n. 炼焦, 焦化
	adj. 炼焦的
Duisburg [ˈdju:sbʊrk]	n. 杜伊斯堡[德国西部城市]
wedge [wedʒ]	n. 楔形物
rib [rib]	n. 肋骨
noxious [ˈnɔkʃəs]	adj. 有毒的, 有害的
sewer [ˈsjuə]	n. 排水沟, 下水道
contaminate [kənˈtæmineit]	v. 污染, 弄脏
dispatch [disˈpætʃ]	v. 发送, 派遣
colonization [ˌkɔlənaiˈzeiʃən]	n. 拓殖
sedum [ˈsi:dəm]	n. 景天属的植物
birch [bə:tʃ]	n. 桦树, 白桦

283

Part V 20th Century Landscape Architecture Practice

beech [biːtʃ]	n.	山毛榉树
poplar	n.	白杨，白杨木
robinia [rəˈbɪnɪə]	n.	［植］洋槐，刺槐
rampant [ˈræmpənt]	adj.	蔓生的
den [den]	n.	（舒适的）私室（作学习或办公用）
forester [ˈfɔrɪstə(r)]	n.	护林人，林务官，森林学者
skeleton [ˈskelitən]	n.	骨骼，基干，构架
reclothe [ˈriːˈkləuð]	vt.	使再穿衣服，使更衣
rejuvenate [riˈdʒuːvineit]	v.	更新，使改观
derrick [ˈderik]	n.	井架，钻塔
Passaic [pəˈseiik]	n.	巴塞克（美国新泽西州东北部的一座城市）；巴塞克河
lament [ləˈment]	n.	悲叹，哀悼，挽歌
devour [diˈvauə]	v.	毁灭，破坏，贪婪地掠夺
regeneration [riˌdʒenəˈreiʃən]	n.	重生，新生
smelting [ˈsmeltiŋ]	n.	熔炼
foundry [ˈfaundri]	n.	铸工厂，铸造厂
collage [kəˈlɑːʒ]	n.	拼贴，美术拼贴，拼贴的作品
gantry [ˈɡæntri]	n.	桶架，高架移动起重机及铁路轨道之装置
girder [ˈɡɜːdə(r)]	n.	（桥梁和大建筑物的）主梁，钢桁的支架
chute [ʃuːt]	n.	（物件可以滑下或落下的）斜道，滑道，斜槽，立槽
demolition [ˌдеməˈliʃən]	n.	破坏，毁坏
tetrahedron [ˈtetrəˈhedrən]	n.	［数］［晶］四面体
heap [hiːp]	n.	堆，大量，许多
lookout [ˈlukaut]	n.	瞭望台，监视哨
Zollverein [ˈtsɔlfərain]	n.	［德］关税同盟
waterlily	n.	睡莲

LESSON 18

Reading Material B

Barcelona and the Resurgence of Spain

Spain's emergence as an innovator in landscape design is relatively recent. Although there was much innovation in art and architecture, albeit intermittently, Spain's turbulent political history in the twentieth century kept it looking inwards. Spain remained neutral during the First World War, and many creative people were drawn to cities such as Barcelona. Tensions between the Republican left and the Nationalist right led to the Civil War(1936~1939), and victory for the Nationalists under Franco(1892~1975) who was effectively Spain's dictator until his death. Franco's conservatism, repression, and refusal to modernize had a stultifying effect on Spanish culture, and provoked unrest amongst Basques, Catalans and Andalucians. After Franco's death, there was a resurgence in the arts; Spain's membership of the European community in 1985, and its hosting of the Olympic Games in 1992, were two steps towards prosperity and a new outward approach to the world.

Catalonia has been a cradle for creativity throughout the twentieth century. Barcelona, its capital, likes to think of itself as more forward-looking than Madrid. In 1929, it played host to an International Exhibition, and the site now holds the re-created pavilion of Mies van der Rohe, which has had immense influence amongst architects and landscape architects worldwide. Repressed after it fell to Franco in 1939, twenty years were to pass before Spain was opened to foreign investment and tourism, and Barcelona developed in a mindless, unplanned scramble of property speculation and immigration. There was no concern for parks and green spaces.

Population grew fast. In 1900 it was about 500,000. By 1990 the Barcelona region had expanded to four million people, and the city proposed a green belt, limiting urban development and linking open spaces in the mountain ranges running parallel with the coast. Green corridors including woodland and nature parks were planned to link up around Barcelona-the Parque de Collserola and Montjuïc on the west, the Parque de la Serralada de Marina on the east.

But within the city, changes had already begun. The Parque Juan Miró, approved in 1983 and built on the site of an old slaughterhouse, was planned by Solana, Galí, Arriola and Quintana as four large, sandy squares, shaped by the planting of *Washingtonia robusta* palms. This is a hard surface park for people to play petanque or laze on shaded benches. Behind the squares is a large pool, in which is reflected the red, yellow, blue and green *Dona I Ocell*, a tall tubular sculpture made by Miró. Redundant textile works, lorry works and railway land have also been turned into parks.

选自 Janet Waymark Modern Garden Design: Innovation Since 1900 Thames & Hudson 2003

Part V 20th Century Landscape Architecture Practice

Above, left
Parque Joan Miró, Barcelona, 1983
The *Dona I Ocell*, Miró's tubular sculpture in bright colours, admires itself in a pool, or surprises the visitor by its appearance between trees in the park below.

Above right
Parque I'Espanya Industriel, Barcelona
Luis Peña Ganchegui's park draws in the towers of a railway to make them a part of this city park, relating them to the lake below like so many warships.

Right
Barcelona Pier, 1997
This park has enlivened a dreary part of the waterfront, with its grid planting of *Gleditsia* and palms vying for attention with the inanimate arms of the lighting elements.

In 1992, the Olympic Games brought new investment to the site of the 1929 Exhibition on Montjuïc. More recently, attention has focused on the coastline. The Parque de I'Espanya Industriel has been designed by the Basque architect Luis Peña Ganchegui with towers seemingly belonging to warships circling menacingly around a lake; there are sculptures by British sculptor Anthony Caro and Andrés Nagel. One of the most jaunty parks is Barcelona Pier, where architects Jordi Henrich and Olga Tarrasó have worked with Barcelona City Urban Projects Service from 1997. Instead of a bleak stretch pointing to the sea, there is now a display of *Gleditsia triacanthos*, *Phoenix aactilifera* and *Washingtonia robusta* palms, and *Casuarina equisetifolia* planted in a grid. Beside them, and masquerading as trees planted in their own grid, are brushed steel lighting elements with three arms capable of throwing light in different directions, and looking remarkably like a forest of mobiles which could have been made by American George Rickey(b. 1907).

Barcelona's Botanical Gardens, commissioned by the City Council to transform a waste dump on Montjuïc facing the Olympic site, opened in 1999. Most of the funding was provided by the European Union, with the remaining twenty per cent coming from the City.

The landscape architect Bet Figueras and the architect Carlos Ferrater designed a network of large, triangular beds in the amphitheatre left by the tip set in the red hillside, separated by wide, white, angular paths made in horizontals. The beds are broken by flights of steps or paths which join lower horizontal paths. There are long views across Barcelona. The purpose of the Botanic Garden is to conserve the Mediterranean vegetation of the Levant, the Iberian Peninsula, North Africa, Chile, Australia, California and the Canary Islands, grouping some two thousand species by ecological principles in their geographical settings. Plants are therefore placed in communities as they would be in their own habitats, and are not displayed as museums of taxonomic groups. Water plants have not been forgotten in this dry landscape; a pool greets the visitor moving from the entrance buildings. Rainwater is stored underground, and the irrigation system works on solar power. Waste is recycled as compost; no pesticides are used.

The initial rawness has receded, with vegetation acclimatizing on the red triangular beds and green slopes behind their equally red triangular corten steel supports. This is a remarkable landscape, a mix of land art, regeneration and sustainable botany, which engages all the senses.

Above
Barcelona Botanical Gardens, 1999
Created to conserve Mediterranean plants around the world, Barcelona's Botanical Garden's designers Carlos Ferrater and Bet Figueras revelled in the triangle and the zigzag. White, angular paths rise in tiers above the central water garden, separating groups of plants on the hillside.

Part V 20th Century Landscape Architecture Practice

WORDS AND EXPRESSIONS

intermittent [ˌintə(ː)'mitənt]	adj. 间歇的，断断续续的
turbulent ['təːbjulənt]	adj. 动荡的，骚乱的，暴乱的
Franco	佛朗哥(1892～1975)，西班牙独裁者，长枪党首领，第二次世界大战中支持德、意法西斯侵略战争
conservatism [kən'səːvətizəm]	n. 保守主义，守旧性
stultify ['stʌltifai]	vt. 使显得愚笨，使变无效，使成为徒劳
unrest ['ʌn'rest]	n. 不安的状态，动荡的局面
Basque [bæsk]	n. 巴斯克人/语
	adj. 巴斯克人的
Catalan ['kætələn]	n. 加泰罗尼亚人/语
	adj. (西班牙)加泰罗尼亚(Catalonia)的，加泰罗尼亚人的，加泰罗尼亚语的
Andalusia [ˌændə'luːzjən]	n. 安达鲁西亚人/语
	adj. 安达鲁西亚的
Madrid [mə'drid]	n. 马德里(西班牙首都)
Mies van der Rohe	密斯·凡·德·罗，世界著名建筑大师
speculation [ˌspekju'leiʃən]	n. 思索
Joan Miró	米罗(1893～1983)，西班牙画家，作品受超现实主义和表达主义影响，主要作品有《梦之画》、《狂犬吠月》等
laze [leiz]	n. 懒散，闲散
Dona ['dəunə]	n. 〈西〉小姐，太太，夫人
tubular ['tjuːbjulə]	adj. 管状的
lorry ['lɔri]	n. 卡车；载重汽车；〈古〉铁路货车
warship ['wɔːʃip]	n. 军舰，战船
menacingly ['menəsiŋli]	adv. 胁迫地，险恶地
jaunty ['dʒɔːnti]	adj. 轻松愉快的，亮丽的
Washingtonia robusta palm	光叶加州蒲葵
phoenix dactilifera	海枣
Gleditsia triacanthos	美国皂角
Casuarina equisetifolia	木麻黄
masquerade [ˌmæskə'reid, maːs-]	v. 伪装，乔装
mobile ['məubail]	n. 动态雕塑
dump [dʌmp]	n. 垃圾堆
Levant [li'vænt]	n. 累范特，地中海东部地区
Iberian	adj. 伊比利亚的，伊比利亚人的

LESSON 18

	n. 伊比利亚人，古代伊比利亚人，伊比利亚岛
taxonomic [tæksə'nɒmik]	*adj.* 分类学的，分类的
compost ['kɒmpɒst]	*n.* 混合肥料，堆肥
acclimatize [ə'klaimətaiz]	*vt.* 使适应(或习惯)新环境(或气候等)，使服水土

APPENDIX A

PROFESSIONAL ORGANIZATIONS AND INTERNET SITES

American Society of Landscape Architects(ASLA)Includes job huntting information and links to other landscape sites.
http://www.asla.org/

Association of Professional Landscape Designers
http://www.apld.com/

Canadian Society of Landscape Architects Canadian national organization for landscape professionals.
http://www.csla.ca/

Council of Botanical and Horticultural Libraries
http://huntbot.andrew.cmu.edu/CBHL/CBHL.html
Council of Educators in Landscape Architecture(CELA)Site includes links to schools with programs in landscape architecture.
http://www.ssc.msu.edu/~la/cela/

Council of Landscape Architecture Registration Boards
http://www.CLARB.org/

European Foundation for Landscape Architecture EFLA represents the national professional associations of landscape architects of the member countries of the European Union. Includes a directory of European schools of landscape architecture.
http://www.efla.org/
International Federation of Landscape Architects-Central Region(Hungarian Assoc. of Landscape Architects)
http://www.ifla.net/
Landscape Institute U.K. national organization for landscape professionals.
http://www.l-i.org.uk/

APPENDIX B

PROFESSIONAL INTERNET SITES

Frederick L. Olmsted, by Christopher Glynn Parker. A beautifully designed site with comprehensive biographical information and well-organized project information. Includes thumbnail images and list of links to other Olmsted sites.
http://www.fredericklawolmsted.com

Frederick Law Olmsted National historic site, U.S. National Park Service.
http://www.nps.gov/frla/
National association for Olmsted parks. Includes links and other resources.
http://www.olmsted.org/
Landscape Information Hub(LIH) (*Univ. of Greenwich*) Intended for landscape architecture teachers, learners, and practitioners. Includes descriptions of landscape design and planning projects as well as web links and print sources organized in topical subject guides. UK emphasis.
http://www.lih.gre.ac.uk
Sapling: architecture, planning & Landscape information gateway Web sites are individually reviewed and rated. UK-based.
http://www.soult.com/sapling/
Subject Guide for Landscape Architecture(*Leeds Metropolitan Univ.*) An online bibliography of print sources and web links, organized by broad topic.
http://www.lmu.ac.uk/lis/lss/subjinfo/landarch.htm

Landscapeonline.com(*Landscape Communications*) Site includes directories by U.S. state of landscape professionals and supplies.
http://www.landscapeonline.com/

Protecting cultural landscapes: planning, treatment and management of historic landscapes, by Charles A. Birnbaum, National Park Service, 1994. (Preservation brief: 36)
http://www2.cr.nps.gov/TPS/briefs/brief36.htm

Sunset magazine: a century of Western living 1898~1998, historical portraits and bibliography
http://sunset-magazine.stanford.edu/

JGarden: the Japanese garden database. Substantial database of historical and contemporary Japanese gardens in Japan and elsewhere. Includes garden descriptions, links to garden web sites, an extensive bibliography, and more.

http://www.jgarden.org/

Museum of garden history, London, U. K. British emphasis.

http://www.cix.co.uk/~museumgh/

The Daily Aesthetic(*Univ. of Kentucky*)Focusses on the parks and recreational spaces of African-American communities prior to the legal integration of public facilities in 1956. Includes narratives, images, and oral histories.

http://www.uky.edu/Projects/TDA/

History of landscape architecture(*Univ. of Oregon*, *Dept. of Landscape Architecture*)A selection of digitized color photographs of gardens, agriculture, classical Western landscapes, paradise gardens, Islamic, Spanish, Moghul, medieval gardens, 18th & 19th century America. Not searchable.

http://darkwing.uoregon.edu/~helphand/homepage.html